New Perspectives on Consumer Culture Theory and Research

Edited by

Pavel Zahrádka and Renáta Sedláková

CAMBRIDGE
SCHOLARS
PUBLISHING

New Perspectives on Consumer Culture Theory and Research,
Edited by Pavel Zahrádka and Renáta Sedláková

This book first published 2012

Cambridge Scholars Publishing

12 Back Chapman Street, Newcastle upon Tyne, NE6 2XX, UK

British Library Cataloguing in Publication Data
A catalogue record for this book is available from the British Library

ISBN (10): 1-4438-4157-9, ISBN (13): 978-1-4438-4157-3

TABLE OF CONTENTS

List of Illustrations

LIST OF TABLES

ACKNOWLEDGEMENTS

We thank everyone who helped with the organization of the conference *Consumer Culture: Between Aesthetics, Social Distinction and Ecological Activism*, from which this volume mostly drew its essays, especially Veronika Kubová, Zuzana Chytková, but also Jaroslav Cír, and the conference volunteers, undergraduates from the Palacký University, Olomouc. We are also grateful to Steven Schwartzhoff, Karleigh Koster, Tomáš Karger and Josef Šebek, who helped in preparing this volume for publication. We wish to express our gratitude to the The Ministry of Education, Youth and Sports of the Czech Republic which made possible the preparation of this volume through its financial support in the year 2012 through its Institutional Development Plan, Program V. Excellence, Philosophical Faculty of Palacký University: Support for Young Academics at Palacký University.

—Olomouc, September 2012

INTRODUCTION

CONSUMER CULTURE: BETWEEN AESTHETICS, SOCIAL DISTINCTION AND ECOLOGICAL ACTIVISM

PAVEL ZAHRÁDKA AND RENÁTA SEDLÁKOVÁ

In the Czech Republic the subject of consumption has not received sufficient attention from the perspective of Consumer Culture Theory (CCT).[1] The opinion has long prevailed among the majority of Czech social scientists that consumer culture and consumptive behaviour is a socially destructive phenomenon and one of the main causes of problems in contemporary society. This impression has prevented them from scrutinizing the symbolic dimension of consumption and led them to a critical analysis of the social causes and results of excessive consumption and to an emphasis on alternative and sustainable ways of life.[2] The examination of symbolic and aesthetic aspects of consumer culture or the mutual interaction of culture and marketing communication, for example, have remained outside the realm of academic interest. As a result of the critical attitude towards consumer culture in the Czech Republic the political and ethical dimensions of consumption, such as those pointed to by Tanja Busse in her book *Die Einkaufsrevolution* (2006), have also been ignored. However contemporary consumer

---

[1] Analyses of post-communist transformation, an issue addressed by a number of authors from the Academy of Sciences at the turn of the century, do include the analysis of a broad spectrum of economic and social changes affecting the quality of life in a transforming Czech Republic, do also address the issue of consumption. The approach of theses scholars, however, reflects rather a macro approach viewing Czech society from the perspective of modernization theory (Mlčoch – Machonin – Sojka 2000).

[2] An exception is the work of the sociologist Jiří Šafr (2006, 2008), whose research is devoted to consumer culture in the Czech Republic as a factor in social stratification.

behaviour cannot be reduced solely to the satisfaction of the subjective needs and desires of consumers (as liberal economists or staunch critics of consumer culture claim).[3] Numerous studies from the USA (Arnould 2007) and Europe (Sassatelli 2006) show that contemporary consumers look beyond the private sphere of consumption and often also consider the environmental, social and political results of their actions before making a purchase.

The absence of comprehensive academic interest in the topic and problems of consumer culture does not mean that consumer culture is not a subject of research. Such research, however, takes place outside of the sphere of the university in the commercial sector and is primarily focused on issues of how to successfully sell products and services. Due to competitive concerns, the results of commercial research have not been widely distributed and therefore have not been subjected to detailed public or professional examination. Commercial research into consumer culture within the Czech Republic has thus unavoidably led to the privatization of results, which runs contrary to the ideal of science as an open and critical project (Popper 1959).

The goal of the conference *Consumer Culture: Between Aesthetics, Social Distinction and Ecological Activism* was to create a counterbalance to this "science in the shadows" (Ullrich 2006, 119–124), overcome the mutual distrust between the academic and commercial spheres and make possible the transfer of recent discoveries between the two parties. That is why the conference organizers invited not only leading European academic researchers from diverse disciplines, but also representatives from the commercial sector who deal with research, production and innovation in consumer culture. This allowed for the confrontation of two previously separate and distinct discourses and perspectives.

The conference also grew out of a reaction to the fact that over the last decade the humanities and social sciences in the Czech Republic have been facing increasing government pressure to establish more effective cooperation with the commercial sector. We believe that the study of

[3] This fact is recognized much more clearly by the authors of marketing campaigns promoting the products of brands such as Benetton or Dove. A distinctive feature of these campaigns is social involvement and responsibility. While the creators of the Benetton campaign focused on breaking down stereotypical prejudices concerning race or sexual orientation, the campaign for Dove cosmetics entitled "Dove Campaign for Real Beauty" challenged the "narrow", and for many women unattainable, ideal of feminine beauty. See further Karin Lövgren, "Grey Is Gorgeous: On Dove's Campaign for Real Beauty Targeting Older Consumers", 146–163.

consumer culture represents a suitable focal point for useful collaboration between the university and commercial sphere. For example, the question often asked in the commercial sphere of what effect advertising has on consumers (or rather, under what circumstances is an advertisement effective) is in fact the same question as the one asked in the humanities and social sciences about what effect culture and symbols have on the individual and society, or on another level what influence media have on the recipient. Asking the question whether advertisements for cigarettes lead teenagers to start smoking is analogous to examining whether playing violent computer games leads players to commit violent acts in the real world. Put simply, while the commercial sphere knows a lot about consumption, the humanities and social sciences know a lot about culture and the ways it functions. However, these fields of knowledge have remained separate up to now.

Another reason for organizing the conference was the establishment of an interdisciplinary platform for research on consumer culture in the Czech Republic. This platform should make possible not only cooperation between the university and commercial spheres, but should also focus attention on a critical analysis of consumer culture and its social, moral and ecological aspects and thus maintain the autonomy of longitudinal university research with respect to sometimes short-term commercial goals.

The theoretical background of the conference proceeds from two basic assumptions. First, we believe that consumption is a cultural process. By consuming things we not only maintain our physical existence, but also our culture in the broadest meaning of the term. Consuming goods allows individuals to form and express their identity. Consumption and culture are mutually dependent. For example, advertisements are not only a commercial phenomenon, but also a rhetorical form which affect the way we communicate (even in traditional non-commercial domains such as education and politics). Also marketing principles influence our interaction with others and our self-presentation, in both our professional and personal lives. In general, the mechanisms of economic competition increasingly permeate our social lives and to a significant extent contribute to shaping them (Wernick 1991, vii–viii).

Second, we believe that consumer culture is a dominant element of social life which helps define the values, identity, behaviour and institutions of contemporary Western Civilization. Research into consumer culture therefore represents a means of understanding ourselves and our contemporary society. Due to the complex nature of the subject of this investigation an interdisciplinary approach is necessary. Consumer culture can be studied from multiple methodological and theoretical perspectives, because consumer goods are not only carriers of symbolic meaning but also commodities. Attention can then be focused on the rules determining allocation of consumer goods and services within the society. Being a consumer also implicitly means that the individual is aware of her needs and strives to satisfy them, i.e. we demand a particular way of life which carries with it certain material costs (Slater 1997, 3). This fact raises ethical questions about the legitimacy of our needs and their scope, as well as the principles of the social distribution of consumer goods. The aim of the conference was to thematically cover the stated perspectives, themes and problems of the study of consumption. The thematic framework of the conference included not only an exploration of the symbolic dimensions of consumer culture, its aesthetic aspects and impact on individual lifestyles, but also the broader social context of production and reception of consumer culture and its social, economic and ethical consequences.

The conference *Consumer Culture: Between Aesthetics, Social Distinction and Ecological Activism* was held on 7–9 October 2010 on the premises of the Arts Center of the Philosophical Faculty of Palacký University Olomouc. The Ministry of Labor and Social Affairs of the Czech Republic took on patronage of the whole event and the conference was an official part of the European Year for Combating Poverty and Social Exclusion (EY2010). Its main organizers were Pavel Zahrádka, Veronika Kubová (The Department of Sociology, Palacký University Olomouc) and Renáta Sedláková (Department of Journalism, Palacký University Olomouc).

The conference was divided into seven thematic sections: (i) Aesthetics of Consumer Culture, (ii) Consumption Patterns, (iii) Market Research and Making of Markets, (iv) Consumption and Media, (v) Consumption and Social Distinction, (vi) Marketing Communication and Culture, and (vii) Critique of Consumer Society. It was attended by fifty European and overseas experts from academia and the commercial sphere. Among the invited speakers were Kate Soper (London Metropolitan University), Kai-Uwe Hellmann (IKM Berlin), Moritz Gekeler (HPI School of Design Thinking Potsdam), Wolfgang Ullrich (Karlsruhe University of Arts and Design), Søren Askegaard (University of Southern Denmark Odensee), Franz Liebl (Berlin University of the Arts), Rainer Gries (University of Vienna) and Jaroslav Cír (Perfect Crowd Prague).

For this collective monograph contributions were selected covering three thematic areas: (i) Consumer Culture in Post-socialist Countries, (ii) New Prospects on Consumer Culture Research, (iii) Consumer Culture Critique. The first section on *Consumer Culture in Post-Socialist*

Countries is introduced by the overview study "Theory and Research on Consumer Culture in the Czech Republic before and after 1989" by Pavel Zahrádka and Renáta Sedláková. The article deals with consumer culture before and after 1989 in the former socialist Czechoslovakia and the contemporary Czech Republic. It captures the socio-cultural conditions of consumption as well as theoretical reflections (Erazim Kohák, Jan Keller) and the results of research (Hana Librová, Jiří Šafr) on consumption in the Czech Republic in the past twenty years in the social sciences and humanities which can be relevant to the development of Consumer Culture Theory. While in the analysis of consumer culture before 1989 attention is paid to the phenomenon of the shortage economy and its implications for the consumer behaviour of the population, the analysis of consumer culture after 1989 reports primarily on the results of critical inquiry focused on the social and environmental consequences of consumption and a description of an alternative sustainable lifestyles.

In the following contribution "Understanding the Meaning of Consumption in Everyday Lives of 'Mainstream' Youth in the Czech Republic" Czech sociologist Michaela Hráčková Pyšňáková presents her qualitative research on how mainstream Czech youth think about their everyday consumption after the year 1989. This approach represents an important and informative contribution to the existing youth research in the Czech Republic as although many of the key characteristics of late modernity identified by Beck and Giddens are centred on consumption and lifestyles, young people's experience with consumption in the Czech Republic as a response to social transformation has not been given sufficient attention. The results, based on the qualitative findings of research conducted with 95 young people indicate that belonging to the mainstream does not imply straightforward compliance with dominant power structures. Instead, it reflects a degree of reflexivity in which these young people challenge stereotypes of passive conformism in complex, yet often paradoxical ways that are not yet well accounted for by current youth research in the Czech Republic. The article concludes by suggesting that the notion of "mainstream" youth offers a potential way of understanding young people's relationship to social change in what appears to be an increasingly individualised society.

The third article, written by environmentalists Petr Jehlička and Joe Smith, overturns accounts of food self-provisioning in post-socialist Central and Eastern Europe that are rooted in myths of the "urban peasant". After reviewing and rejecting those accounts the authors introduce very different explanations for high rates of growing and sharing food outside the market system based in social anthropological research in the region. The authors have extended that work with their own qualitative and quantitative research over a period of six years in the Czech Republic, and here present findings that confirm the contribution that food self-provisioning is making to both the social and ecological sustainability.

In the last study "Multiplexes as the Limes of 'Global Hollywood'" Marcin Adamczak deals with multiplexization presented in broader perspective of economic, political and cultural processes related to globalization, which transformed the consumer culture and film culture after 1980. Among them, the most prominent seems to be creation of powerful media conglomerates, significant increase in film budgets, especially P&A budgets, and growing dominance of "Global Hollywood" at international film market. Multiplexization was an important part of those changes. It brought a redefinition and transformation of social cinema going practice and experiences of viewer participating in a film show. It could be called after Toby Miller "the reprise of vaudeville bill", when watching movies is connected with a set of other social practices, like shopping and resting after whole week of work in realities of late capitalist societies. This is clearly seen by fluid embodiment of cinemas into the architecture of shopping centres, where cinemas are creating the common consumer-cultural space with shops and restaurants. It also seems like a shift in the map of cultural space from high culture zone achieved in the 1960s to low culture (folk culture) in Pierre Bourdieu's terms from *Distinction*. It contributed to the emergence of two separate cinematographic systems (art-houses and traditional cinemas along with multiplexes) situated in separate institutional and discourse contexts and related with separate types of reception expectations and gratification. In this way multiplexes are seen as the material and symbolic signs of the reign of "Global Hollywood", beyond the borders of which lies a fragmented world of small and individual national cinematographies and the increasingly disappearing auteur model.

The second part of the volume *New Prospects on Consumer Culture Research* opens with the article "A Strategic Approach to Costumer Orientation" by Franz Liebl who is concerned with innovative approaches to reaching the customer in the field of strategic marketing. Customer orientation has been one of the most important concepts in strategic marketing during the last 50 years. However, the interpretation of customer orientation as a mere customer centricity has lost its power since then. From an entrepreneurial view of strategy, which focuses on the creation of new markets and new rules of competition, customer orientation has to be reconceptualized. Several case studies are used in order to rethink and reformulate the concept of customer orientation and to extend and radicalize the concept in various directions. The results show that more complex conceptualizations are needed in order to satisfy the unmanageable consumer.

Ivana Uspenski in her text "Mass Intelligence and the Commoditized Reader" addresses the influence of new media on the changing concept of reading and reception. She suggests that reading strategies are no longer products of a reader's own intentions, or the author's. Dominant producers and readers of the new media texts become computers as cybertext machines. Not only do cybertext machines get involved in the reading process, through this process they also produce mass intelligence, which is one of the manifestations of new media reader. The reader oneself becomes a commodified construct, a merchandise which can be bought and sold in the online advertising industry. This new media reader is understood as commoditized due to the fact that the basic purpose of mechanical reading in new media surroundings, especially on the Internet, is for the data read to be converted into clicks, exposures, and demographic data, transformed into merchandise. This phenomenon is marked as mass intelligence—the non-critical and arbitrary global gathering and accumulation of human knowledge, by offering readers mass-interests texts which they can read, and to which they can react, comment on or hyperlink to with the sole purpose of making these readers quantifiable goods. Uspenski concludes that, as opposed to collective intelligence, mass intelligence is not a productive force but a commodity.

In the next paper "Grey Is Gorgeous: On Dove's Campaign for Real Beauty Targeting Older Consumers", Karin Lövgren presents the results of her textual and visual analysis of the Dove advertising Campaign for Real Beauty with focus on the representation of age and gender and the results of her qualitative research on how the older models used in the advertising campaign are perceived by women in the age range 45–63 years. The Unilever company Dove launched in 2006 a hybrid advertising campaign claiming to question beauty ideals, advocating for more diverse norms on what is considered beautiful. Through use of Internet and in print advertising a special product line targeting older consumers have been introduced. In adverts for these products older models have been used. Generally models in adverts are young, even when addressing older consumers. This is claimed to be because also older consumers identify with younger role models. In this article the campaign is analyzed against the background of the formulaic advert genre and age and gender are analysed as marketing tools.

In the last text "Life Satisfaction: Impulsive Buying Behaviour and Gender" Samuel Lins presents the results of his quantitative research focused on verifying the relationship between impulse buying, life satisfaction and gender. A standardized questionnaire was distributed via web to 214 Brazilian students from the Federal University of Paraíba (103 male and 111 female), with a mean age of 22 years (min = 16 and max = 36). Two scales were used as evaluation instruments: (i) Consumer Buying Impulsivity Scale (CBIS) and (ii) Satisfaction With Life Scale (SWLS). Correlations and comparisons of means were performed to examine how the five factors of the CBIS associate with life satisfaction and gender. The results indicate that only the cognitive deliberation factor is negatively associated with life satisfaction, that women are more satisfied with life and more impulsive buyers, and that, when buying they also are more cognitive and affective than men.

The last part of the volume *Critique of Consumer Culture* is introduced by the contribution "Beyond Consumerism: The Critique of Consumption, Democracy, and the Politics of Prosperity" by British philosopher Kate Soper. Here she presents her conception of alternative hedonism, which represents a new type of criticism of consumer culture emerging not from externally postulated ethical or environmental measures, but rather from the perspective of the quality of life of the social actors who are dissatisfied with the negative effects of the consumerist lifestyle. The market driven consumerist lifestyle has long been defended and promoted as an agent of freedom and democracy. But it is also widely condemned for its social exploitation, and now increasingly for its environmental destruction and unsustainability. Affluent societies are thus entering upon a cultural moment of unprecedented disquiet about unchecked consumption. The upshot is the emergence of consumer culture as a site of new forms of democratic concern, political engagement, and cultural representation. The paper argues that in addition to the environmental and ethical reasons for this new concern, there is the evidence of growing disaffection over the negative legacy of the consumerist lifestyle for consumers themselves. The alternative hedonism implicit in these forms of consumer ambivalence is analysed with a view to disentangling its outlook on human needs and fulfilment from both earlier leftwing critiques of commodification and from postmodernist celebrations of consumer culture as a resource of identity politics and self-styling. Alternative hedonism is presented in this context as the impulse behind a new political imaginary that could help us to move towards a fairer, environmentally sustainable and more enjoyable future. The paper asks how can this new outlook on the politics of prosperity be best promoted and represented and how might consumption now come to function as a pressure point for the relay of political changes needed to secure a sustainable economy.

In his paper "The Historicity of Brands: Inter-generational Production of Structural Sustainability", Rainer Gries argues that successful products and brands have become media of modern societies and act as platforms of social exchange. Since the 19th century brands have been operating as economical and cultural "real estates" in the market and in the collective mind. These continuities over centuries and over generations show brand products as generators of social confidence and cohesion. Hence, such long-term product communications have become essential mediators of structural sustainability in our modern society and according to the author we should be aware of this in order to actively and intelligently participate in these negotiation processes via products and brands. Gries argues that our future societies will benefit from adopting a greater awareness of both the positive potential, as well as the subversive power that these kinds of media carry, so that contributions to the sustainability of our consumer society can continue to develop with a greater sense of ethical responsibility.

In his paper "Critical Marketing, Consumption Studies and Political Economic Analysis", Alan Bradshaw explores the relationship between studies of consumption and critical political economy perspectives. Rather than review different disciplinary fields that address consumption, he focuses on a particular tradition of scholarship—critical marketing. Critical marketing is mostly associated with UK scholars and can be regarded as a sub-area of research within marketing that seeks to subject marketing to critical analysis. The paper explores the absence of a political analysis from such research. The issues that rose relate to broader issues of how the question of political economy is often evaded within studies of consumption and hence conclusions broader are pursued that may be relevant to various subject areas.

In the last paper "Subversive Use of Things: Craftsman Creativity as Criticism of Consumer Culture?", Agata Skórzyńska deals with the commodification of culture as one of the best commented processes occurring across the division between economy and culture. The innovative idea first diagnosed by the philosophers of the Frankfurt School is, however, also a widely criticized view on the relation between consumption and culture. According to the postmodern and poststructuralist theory we are now confronted by the opposite process: a specific cultural turn in consumer society in the second half of 20th century. The core of postmodern criticism was the recognition that a commodity turns into a symbolic rather than a material object and the base of the new economy of the developed societies is the exchange of symbols, establishing semiotics as the necessary background to analyze economic processes or to participate in markets of meaning. Skórzyńska claims that the autonomy of art and culture, postulated by Adorno as a mode of resistance against the commodification, is no longer adequate. Instead of isolation, she observes an emergence of the new subversive practices of everyday life including critical use of things, spaces or images of consumer culture. Paradoxically, these practices require a specific return to the materiality of the thing because the subversive use of the object consists in reconfiguration of the appearance and function, which is similar to the craftsman's performance rather than creativity of an autonomous artist.

References

Arnould, Eric. 2007. "Should Consumer Citizens Escape the Market?" *Annals AAPSS* 611: 96–111.

Busse, Tanja. 2006. *Die Einkaufsrevolution. Konsumenten entdecken ihre Macht.* München: Karl Blessing Verlag.

Mlčoch, Lubomír, Pavel Machonin, and Milan Sojka. 2000. *Ekonomické a společenské změny v české společnosti po roce 1989.* Praha: Karolinum.

Popper, Karl. 1959. *The Logic of Scientific Discovery.* London: Hutchinson.

Šafr, Jiří. 2006. *Social Standing and Lifestyle in Czech Society.* Praha: Sociologický ústav AV ČR.

—. 2008. *Životní styl a sociální třídy: vytváření symbolické kulturní hranice diferenciací vkusu a spotřeby.* Praha: Sociologický ústav AV ČR.

Sassatelli, Roberta. 2006. "Virtue, Responsibility and Consumer Choice. Framing Critical Consumerism." In *Consuming Cultures, Global Perspectives: Historical Trajectories, Transnational Exchanges*, edited by John Brewer and Frank Trentmann, 219–250. Oxford: Berg.

Slater, Don. 1997. *Consumer Culture and Modernity*. Cambridge: Polity.

Ullrich, Wolfgang. 2006. *Habenwollen. Wie funktioniert die Konsumkultur?* Frankfurt am Main: Fischer.

Wernick, Andrew. 1991. *Promotional Culture.* London: Sage.

PART I:

CONSUMER CULTURE IN THE POST-SOCIALIST COUNTRIES

THEORY AND RESEARCH ON CONSUMER CULTURE IN THE CZECH REPUBLIC BEFORE AND AFTER 1989

PAVEL ZAHRÁDKA AND RENÁTA SEDLÁKOVÁ

This study outlines the basic features of consumer culture in the Czech Republic before and after 1989, and offers an overview of its theoretical reflections and research. Its aim is to outline the prevailing conditions and trends in Czech society which have shaped the consumer behaviour of Czech people and to summarize the knowledge and theoretical basis of which contemporary Consumer Culture Theory (CCT) can build on. Our intention is not to recapitulate social, economic or demographic developments in the Czech Republic during the transition from a socialist to a democratic regime. Therefore, we do not cover studies undertaken in the fields of economics or socialist economic prognostics, and the list of concepts, theories and research findings presented here is necessarily selective. We open the text with the conceptual definition of consumer culture, and then we deal with the social and economic conditions of consumption in the former Czechoslovakia (and in the countries of the former Eastern Bloc) and subsequent changes in the consumer behaviour of Czechs under the conditions of the emerging capitalist society, as well as theoretical reflections and research thereon.

Within social theory the terms “consumption” and “culture” are sometimes presented as opposites (Habermas 1990, 248–266). While culture is understood as an autonomous sphere defying the process of commodification and the promotion of utilitarian and material interests, consumption is conceptualized as a manifestation of a market economy which devalues and commercializes the lived world. In this paper, we understand consumer culture as the relationship of individuals to material objects and services and the ways in which they are used, or respectively the meanings which social actors ascribe to objects of their consumption and according to which they dispose of them. We do not use the term “culture” in an evaluative sense but rather in its descriptive semiotic interpretation as a system of meanings expressed in symbolic forms through which people communicate and share experiences, meanings and beliefs (cf. Thompson 1990, 132). In this sense the controversy over the joining of the terms "consumer" and "culture" loses its meaning, and on the contrary the way in which they are complementary is revealed. On one hand, consumption is directly dependent on culture because only culture gives meaning to things. On the other hand, culture is reproduced by consumer goods, through which the expression and communication of meaning takes place (McCracken 1988, xi).

Furthermore, we believe that consumer culture is mutually shaped not only by the meanings and uses consumers associate with a given consumer product, but also by the socio-economic environment and dominant system of thought. Our goal is to show that the relationship to consumer goods in former Czechoslovakia (and after 1993 in the Czech Republic) before and after 1989 was influenced both by the socio-political situation and dominant economic system and the theoretical reflections of consumption.

Consumer Culture before 1989

Consumer culture in communist Czechoslovakia was conditioned by the socialist political-economic system which was built on both the principles of the Marxist critique of capitalism and the vision of "real socialism", which was to overcome the internal contradictions of the capitalist social order. The socialist system was also shaped by other intellectual or ideological influences, such as the intellectual tradition of the workers' revolutionary movement, the ideology of the ruling Communist Party and the leaders of the Communist parties in the individual Eastern Bloc countries. Namely, social theory describing social reality and the behaviour of social actors is created through so-called "interactive kinds" (Hacking 1999, 103–104), that is kinds which classify social actors and at the same time can, if they are aware of their classification, cause a change in the behaviour of these social actors. For the purpose of this study, we limit ourselves to a brief explanation of two fundamental features of the socialist system which have their origins in Marxist doctrine: the elimination of the market economy and of private ownership.

Marxist critique adopted some basic ideas (often in a simplified form) from Karl Marx (1992) who assumed that technological development can guarantee sufficient goods to satisfy the needs of all people. The dynamic development of productive forces is, however, according to Marx, in conflict with the static nature of productive relationships, which in capitalist systems are derived from ownership. Technological development makes material progress possible only for a minority of the population (at the expense of exploiting the majority), which seeks by any means to maintain the existing social order. The asymmetry in the ownership of the means of production, according to Marx, leads to the fact that low-income workers are forced to sell their productive faculties on the market for wages which do not correspond to the real work invested in the production of the product. On the contrary, the owner strives for the accumulation of profits, which is, however, only possible if the worker is not paid for the full value of his or her work and the so-called "surplus value" is taken by the owner. According to Marx, the commodification of the labour of the worker subordinated to the demands of the impersonal labour market, and the resulting division of labour, makes impossible the objectification of the subjective needs of the workers in material creations. It thus makes human self-realization through creative work impossible. This leads not only to the alienation of the worker from the fruits of his own labour, but also to the alienation of the worker from other people and from himself.

For the governments of the former Eastern Bloc overcoming the ills of the capitalist system meant eliminating their systematic causes: private ownership and market conditions. The declared goal was the creation of a society without significant differences in income and wealth among its members, where collective ownership would prevail and production would not be determined by market mechanisms, but rather by centralized and reasoned decisions about the production of public goods. Production in a socialist society was supposed to be, from an ideological perspective, oriented towards the demands of masses of consumers, but not towards the interests of privileged groups. The elimination of the market and private property, however, leads to the absence of a reliable mechanism which would determine through the principle of supply and demand what needed to be produced and at what price the goods manufactured should be sold. The socialist system replaced this mechanism with centralized planning and its necessary organizational compliment—a centralized bureaucratic apparatus. In addition to deciding on the allocation of resources and setting the structure and scale of production and distribution, the planning centre also set the standard price of products.[1]

[1] In setting the price of products, in addition to ideology (a significant portion of all prices had a social character, for example, basic food items, medicines and children's clothes were assigned low prices), a major factor was the Marxist theory of value, whereby the value of manufactured objects was equal to the amount of socially necessary work (labour time) needed for their production (Nove 1991, 20–30). The price of products usually included the fixed costs of materials, labour costs, the costs of materials and energy and a profit margin (Mlčoch 1990).

Detailed analysis of the basic characteristics of the socialist economic systems of the Communist countries of Eastern Europe and their impact on consumers was studied in the 1980s by the Hungarian economist János Kornai (1992) and we will proceed from his analysis. Kornai notes that central planning of economic activity and *ex-ante* price control lead to several major problems in the system for which he coined the term "shortage economy". If the price of a product is set centrally not by its exchange value but by the amount of labour invested in its production, then it fails to capture the difference between high quality products and low quality goods if their production requires the same amount of work. In a situation where there is no market economy there is no mechanism to provide feedback on the quality or lack of quality of a given product. In addition to this, the system of central planning leads to the emergence of a monopoly in the given industries, because, from the perspective of central planning, the offering of varied types of a particular product greatly complicates the ability to forecast its sales. In the eyes of central planners, narrowing the offer of goods manufactured also prevents the undesired phenomenon of waste, which is a necessary consequence of economic competition (for example, in the form of expenditures on marketing or the production of goods that no one wants).[2] The establishment of a state monopoly of production was motivated also by ideological reasons: according to the supporters of a socialist system, economic competition is in conflict with the communist vision of a conflict-free and mutually cooperative society.[3] The absence of feedback through market mechanisms and the existence of an economic monopoly in the end lead to a lack of interest in the needs of the consumer and a decrease in the quality of manufactures goods (Nove 1991, 71). Within the context of the centrally planned economy, manufacturers were dependent not on consumers, but to a greater or lesser extent on the superior state apparatus.[4] As a result of this dependence, state enterprises were not sufficiently motivated to

---

[2] The aversion to diversifying the offer of consumer goods is illustrated by an anecdotal story about Nikita Khrushchev's visit to an exhibition of American consumer goods in Moscow in 1959, where he declared with amazement: "Why would you want so many washing machines when one works perfectly well?" (Marling 1994, 278).

[3] In this context, Alex Nove (1991, 41) draws attention to the false dichotomy between economic competition and cooperation. The real opposite of economic competition is economic monopoly.

[4] This dependence, however, was not one-way. Enterprises also had a certain space for negotiation with the state planning apparatus. Various negotiation strategies (such as ways to maximize inputs [stocks] and minimize outputs [goods produced]) were described by Mlčoch (1990).

achieve economic performance, because any earnings were remanded to the state and potential loss was covered by a modification of the economic plan, respectively by a softening of the budget constraints of the particular company. Manufacturers were thus freed from responsibility for product quality, and the consumer was faced with the choice of "take it or leave it". The lack of needed goods, the absence of choice and the low quality of goods were, moreover, amplified by excess value given to central planning, which was unable to capture the complexity and flexibility of the market on the microeconomic level. The reason for this is both the cumbersome communication and coordination between central administrative units, and, secondly, the transfer of decision-making power from the local context to the remote centre.

The political commitment of the socialist system to ensure society-wide increase in material well-being, to satisfy the basic needs (food, education, health care, housing, work) and to supply an abundance of consumer goods, therefore, stumbled on the dysfunctional economic system of central planning. The paternalistic effort at a society-wide, dominance of manufacturing industry over the customer industry and centrally controlled redistribution of resources—a strategy designed to strengthen citizens' dependence on the political-economic centre—foundered on the shortage economy. The failure to fulfil proclaimed social commitments and insufficient supply of products in both their variety and quantity influenced consumer culture in socialist Czechoslovakia significantly.

In the socialist system the consumer was exposed, repeatedly and in an extensive way, to the phenomenon of shortage.[5] Under the pressure of shortages, customers were often forced to alter their purchasing strategy. These forced changes took many forms which were often accompanied by feelings of frustration and represented a certain kind of loss for the consumer: waiting in lines for the desired product, finding an alternative product, waiting for the desired product to become available or abandoning the intention of obtaining the particular product. The pressure on the consumer to adapt to the availability of products (the transition from what I want to what I can actually want) leads in the shortage economy to the creation of a paradoxical balance between supply and demand at the expense of the dissatisfaction and frustration of consumers. The socialist system, unlike the capitalist system, created in fact a market oriented primarily on the seller (Kornai 1992, 245). The seller thus takes

---

[5] Here we are limiting our examination to the horizontal relationship between buyers and sellers, not to the vertical relationship between enterprises and superior administrative units in the socialist system.

on such dominance over the buyer that in the asymmetrical power relationship the buyer is forced to (1) actively seek information about where the desired product is or will be available;[6] (2) adapt their expectations and wishes to the limited supply; (3) gain the favour of the seller (the privileged position of the seller often leads to their elevated and bland behaviour towards consumers, to under-the-counter sales or even to bribery of the sellers by the customer); (4) buying in bulk as a result of the unstable availability of goods in short supply, and thus creating personal reserves; (5) resorting to semi-legal or illegal social practices, thus creating a "second economy" next to the official economy (providing small plots of land for personal use to members of agricultural cooperatives, unofficial work by craftsmen, stealing from state cooperatives, smuggling goods from Western countries, etc.). The economy of shortage, of course, also had its positive effects, including first of all (6) the Czech do-it-yourself (DIY) tradition, that is individual creativity and self-supply, particularly in agricultural products grown in private gardens. As a rule, individuals and families dealt with the problem of insufficient supply with self-help and "learned through their own activity to make up for what was missing in terms of trades and crafts" (Večerník 1991, 48; trans. R. S.).

The failure to fulfil the social obligation to increase the relatively low level of material well-being of the population of socialist Czechoslovakia (caused by the insufficient quality, variety, and availability of products for the general public) and overtake Western capitalist states in consumption per capita threatened the social stability and legitimacy of the existing system. In reaction to this the political elite allowed the establishment of the Tuzex (domestic export) chain of shops, in which foreign currency and Tuzex vouchers could be used to buy foreign, especially Western goods, which were not available in normal shops. Despite the proclaimed ideology of a classless society, a gradual process of social stratification thereby took place through the ownership of products in short supply or of better quality. This was true not only between the political elite and the allegedly "homogenous" majority of the population (workers, the working farmers, and working intelligentsia), but primarily within the mainstream

---

[6] In addition to traditional forms of promotion by means of the shop window, media advertisements did exist to a limited extent, but these were by no means advertisements for particular brands but propaganda ("propaganda" was then the official term for advertisement) for a particular type of product. Advertisements were often of an educational character (propaganda for vegetables, eggs, or the communist system itself) or promoted products for which there was no demand, but due to the central planning of the economy could not be offered at a lower price. See also Kohout 1982.

of society. Having access to products which were in short supply or to Western goods (jeans, cosmetics, gums etc.) was evidence of the higher social and economic capital of the owner and a mark of social status (Sredl 2007). At the same time, in the socialist system these types of goods acquired a new symbolic and political importance, as they were also evidence of the better quality of life in the Western capitalist countries.

According to the Czech sociologist Ivo Možný (1991), the shortage economy was one of the main causes of the rapid fall of the communist regime in the former Czechoslovakia. Using examples of the end of real socialism in the 1980s, he shows that consumers colonized the communist state because they were forced, as a result of the shortage economy, to violate the established rules and norms in order to meet their needs. Although according to the rhetoric of the official ideology, the society should move towards a classless society, in the social reality of everyday life it was clear that the society was hierarchically divided and property and privileges were distributed selectively in accordance with the decisions of the Communist Party of Czechoslovakia and the nomenclature core groups. For an ordinary citizen to obtain the desired products in short supply, it was necessary to have not only sufficient financial resources, which had a tendency to lose their value, but also significant social capital. In other words, it was necessary to know someone who worked in a suitable position, such as store managers, who would "save" a portion of the goods when they were delivered for their friends and exchange them for other goods or services in short supply. Through these semi-legal or illegal methods, which Možný calls "colonization of the state", it was gradually possible to obtain what people needed or wanted. Due to the hypocritical egalitarian rhetoric of the regime it was however not possible to make further profit from the resources obtained in this way because this would reveal the corruption under the surface. According to Možný (1991, 61–65), it is this fact which contributed significantly to the fall of the communist regime in the former Czechoslovak Socialist Republic as possessions and profits could not be publicly used or kept even by the holders of leading positions in the communist hierarchy which, in turn, progressively increased doubts about the system even within the ruling class.

For completeness, we should add that basic information (such as stratification of Czechoslovak society and its occupational composition, preferred leisure activities, car use, tourism preferences and housing quality), from which it would be possible to infer consumer behaviour in the former Czechoslovakia, can be found in the investigation of class structure (Charvát, Linhart and Večerník 1978; Tuček 1992; Machonin 1992), in the national census during the socialist period and also in a systematic long-term format in the annual statistics published by the Czech Statistical Office.[7] Moreover, surveys of consumption and micro-censuses were carried out. A micro-census was a representative survey of household incomes which took place in the Czechoslovak Socialist Republic from 1956 at 3–5 year intervals. From the end of the 1950s, systematic research was also carried out on family expenses based on daily diaries of income and expenses, these served to calculate the living standard of households (Večerník 1991, 2001). The results of these surveys were intended primarily for use in long-term planning of production in the centrally planned economy, but they were also intended as evidence for declarations about the improving living standards of the citizens of the socialist state.

Research on Consumer Behaviour in the Czech Republic after 1989

The collapse of the state-controlled economic system in the former Czechoslovak Socialist Republic took place in the course of the Velvet Revolution in November of 1989. The political and economic transition to a democratic form of governance, a restored market equilibrium (which found expression in the elimination of shortages of goods), liberalization of market entries, decentralization of the economy and demonopolization of the market, privatization and commercialization of state-owned enterprises, as well as membership in multinational organizations, including NATO and the EU, by and large took place much faster than the social and cultural change of Czech society.[8] As interest in the day-to-day political scene and the resulting steps in macroeconomic transformation gradually declined among the general Czech population, a general retreat into the sphere of satisfying one's own needs though consumption in the broadest sense of the word took place on the background of the individualized society. Although the disposable income of Czech households rose from

---

[7] For example in 1967, 13.5% of households owned an automobile, in 1984 the number was 59%; in 1967, 70% had black and white televisions; in 1984, 88% had a refrigerator, while in 1984 the number was almost 100% (Tuček 1992). Compare with ČSÚ: Sčítání lidu 1921–1991.

[8] This showed itself for example in the increase in the number of people with so-called "status inconsistencies", that is individuals whose levels of social, cultural and economic capital are greatly out of balance (Večerník 1998). An example of this is the quick career growth of owners or managers of businesses associated with illegal or immoral activities.

the year 1990, this occurred only gradually, and according to some indicators the purchasing power of households reached the level it had been in 1989 only after ten years (Mlčoch, Machonin and Sojka 2000) or even later (Večerník 2010, 102); however, this income allowed a considerable portion of the population to cover not only their basic needs, but also their individual requirements. New trends in consumption thus began to reflect the psychological aspirations of consumers influenced by a desire to move with the times and be modern and fashionable. In response to this, shopping with credit cards[9] and consumer and long-term loans have increased in the Czech Republic, as is illustrated by statistical development of the consumer market and the indebtedness of Czech households.[10] The debt curve began to rise in the mid 2000s in response to the decline in interest rates (Dubská 2010). At the end of the 1990s, a period often spoken of as a period of "belt tightening", Czechs were ready and willing to spend, especially for designer clothes and luxury merchandise, which became a symbol of social success; and at the same time reduced their savings.

Over the past twenty-two years Czech towns have become closer to Western towns, thus when visiting Prague one can buy many of the same brands in stores as one would find in London, Munich or LA. Consumerist lifestyle has become an integral part of life for the majority of adults and children in the Czech population, who often spend their free time in a constantly growing number of shopping centres. These became a phenomenon in the Czech Republic at the beginning of the 21st century. In 2010 there were 76 mid-sized and large shopping malls and retail parks operating in the Czech Republic with rentable sales space of more than 10,000 square meters (the largest of these is Prague's Letňany with more than 80,000 square meters). This number is unmatched in other post-communist countries. These are not limited to hypermarkets, but include also hobby-markets which successfully appeal to the Czech tradition of DIY and gardening, and a large number of them dedicate space to gastronomy, so there are not only shops but also restaurants and other services. A unique project showing the enthusiasm of a portion of the Czech population for this type of shopping and leisure activity was the

---

[9] According to statistics from the Association of Bank Credit Cards, in the middle of 2011 more than 9.2 million cards had been issued in the Czech Republic and of these approximately one fifth of these were credit cards (the population of the Czech Republic is 10.2 million). Compare Sdružení pro bankovní karty 2011.

[10] At the end of 2009 Czech households owed 973.5 billion CZK to banks and 104.1 billion CZK to other leasing and non-bank lending institutions. Since the year 2000 their total debt has increased by eight times (Dubská 2010).

documentary film *Český sen* [*Czech Dream*] by Vít Klusák and Filip Remunda about an advertising campaign for a fictional shopping centre. The marketing campaign for the hypermarket Czech Dream, promising unheard-of low prices through a creative marketing campaign using elements of negative advertisement (advertising slogans such as "Don't Go", "Don't Spend", "Don't Rush") drew thousands of visitors waiting for the opening to Letňany in Prague on May 31, 2003. All that was there, however, was a canvas mock-up of the front wall of a hypermarket. In documenting the entire campaign for Czech Dream in a film by the same name, the authors demonstrated not only how successful advertisements are produced, but also the reactions of the deceived visitors which alternated between amusement and angry verbal attacks. The fact that Czechs love to shop is also demonstrated by economic statistics about the growing volume of sales of shopping centres especially in the autumn pre-Christmas season.[11] At the same time, Czechs are strongly focused on the price of products, so in addition to monitoring leaflets for sales, they also buy online heavily. The boom in consumerism among the Czech population was accompanied not only by a growing offering of products, but also by an increase in advertising, including long-term brand-building strategies (see further Gries, "The Historicity of Brands: Inter-generational Production of Structural Sustainability", 200–213), and campaigns which try to stand out or stand for other than purely commercial issues (such as advertisements for Dove brand cosmetics or Benetton clothing).

What values, then, have Czechs adhered to over the past twenty years? Or rather, what values are they inclined to declare in research surveys representative of the adult population of the Czech Republic, carried out mainly by the Centre for Public Opinion Research (CVVM) of the Institute of Sociology of the Academy of Sciences? Over the long term, on the highest rungs of an imaginary ladder of values remain those associated with a functioning family, good friends, health, as well as good work and living in a good environment. To these are progressively added other values linked to religious or political beliefs, but also an emphasis on self-realization at work. Over the years observed since 1990, the emphasis placed on the character of work done gradually decreased while, by contrast, increased emphasis was placed on having a well-paid job. Also, since 2006, the rating category of a good life, which is made up of indicators that take into account an attractive and healthy environment, health care, a happy family, helping family and friends, and good relations with friends, increased notably. Increased importance was also attributed to items which indicate hedonism and a hedonistic approach to life, such

[11] This trend stopped in 2008 with the onset of the world economic crisis.

as the good life, enjoying oneself, an exciting life, orientation towards one's own interests and undisturbed privacy, but also in a second direction more associated with career advancement, a desire for individual accomplishment, social status and luxury. On the lowest rungs of our imaginary ladder we find values associated with the need to be informed about events in the country or around the world, even though on the other hand factors do emerge associated with the protection of the environment or helping the needy (Prudký et al. 2009, 199–198).

Since the 1990s, the Sociological Institute of the Academy of Sciences of the Czech Republic has conducted many research projects capturing the material and cultural life of the inhabitants of the Czech Republic. First of all, at the beginning of the 1990s, considerable attention was paid to the analysis of transformation and changes in the social structures of Czech society (see for example Machonin and Tuček 1996). The perspective of CCT, however, is not emphasized in these research projects. The concluding reports lack a data assessment approach which would complement an economic-psychological perspective, looking at consumption as a more or less rational process of satisfying needs, with the perspective of a sociological and cultural orientation on the symbolic and status dimensions of consumption as an instrument of reproduction, dissemination, sharing, or by contrast, changing of cultural meaning, as well as considering the results of consumption for the broader ecosystem and its sustainability.

Jiří Šafr and Research on Cultural Consumption

Looking through the lens of CCT, we present the study of Jiří Šafr (2008), which starts from a cultural perspective of examining social inequalities with a focus on analysis of the symbolic meaning of cultural practices, such as leisure activities, media consumption, or sports activities. Although Šafr's analysis of cultural consumption is relevant to CCT, the author focuses primarily on measuring the social stratification of Czech society from a relational perspective, i.e. he examines how social strata in society are shaped on the level of everyday life through inequality in individual's access to resources and their lifestyles. Like Bourdieu, Šafr (2008) observes on the one hand regularities in various forms of consumer behaviour and by using data from a number of studies, shows that the ways individuals spend their leisure time are not, even in a modern individualized society, expressions of purely personal choices, but grow from a wider social context and are shaped by it.[12] On the other hand, his results indicate that neither membership in a certain social class nor level of income is today a reliable indicator of an individual's tastes or consumer preferences. In particular, in Czech society we often meet with "conspicuous consumption", that is, situations in which individuals deliberately consume goods which they objectively cannot afford and for which they have to borrow money or severely limit themselves in another way. Additionally, the mere ownership of luxury goods often is not sufficient, and it is necessary to know the rules and rituals associated with their consumption. According to Šafr, the lifestyle of Czechs at the beginning of the 21st century is influenced by the social settings, which is shown by the connections between the cultural taste of individuals (attending cultural events, dressing, appearance, eating habits, health care and preferred themes in media), the way they spend their leisure time and their position within the social strata.

Furthermore, Šafr (2008) tests the hypothesis of cultural omnivore[13] of members of higher social strata, that is, their ability to move through the widest possible range of cultural life, an ability which those in lower social classes do not possess. As for the number of preferred genres and themes followed in the media, he shows that while members of lower social classes choose programs from low culture and choose only one or two favourite themes, those from higher social classes consume cultural products from the genres of low culture as well as more demanding programs from high culture and on average are interested in nine thematic areas. Women are greater "omnivores" than men. While men more often prefer media presentations of sports, cars and politics, women, by contrast, prefer media presentations of cooking, fashion, interpersonal relationships, housing, health and news about celebrities.

In a study published along with Špaček in 2010 based on data from 2007 onwards, Šafr shows that while people moving among the higher rungs of an imaginary ladder of Czech society devote themselves to activities which can be described as culturally more demanding, such as visiting museums, exhibitions and other cultural events, working on

---

[12] A key source of data was research on lifestyle, culture and consumption Market & Media & Lifestyle TGI which surveyed 15,000 respondents from the Czech population between the ages 12–79 and was conducted by the firm Median (Šafr 2008).

[13] Richard Peterson (1992) makes a distinction between the concept of cultural omnivores and univores. While higher social classes become omnivores, consuming a broad spectrum of cultural goods and services from all levels of culture, members of lower social classes remain marked and limited to low culture.

computers or the Internet, listening to classical music, and reading books while in the case of sports they participate in downhill skiing, swimming, cycling, hiking or aerobics, while individuals with a lower social status more often prefer watching television, meeting friends, going to pubs, playing the slots, and reading tabloids. It is therefore apparent that their lifestyles are different. These findings suggest that in the Czech context inequalities in cultural practices based on symbolic differences are gradually setting and justify using the cultural perspective in researching social stratification (Šafr and Špaček 2010). In studying social stratification it is, therefore, not possible to take into account only economic factors, but we must also consider the symbolic significance of the whole lifestyle, which corresponds to the perspective of CCT.

Hana Librová and Research on Voluntary Modesty

Hana Librová has researched consumption from different environmentally friendly perspectives since the beginning of the 1990s. After the Velvet Revolution Librová started to pursue her research interest in families which, in comparison to the majority of the Czech population, were less consumption oriented and more interested in being environmentally friendly. She studied the changes within community lifestyles due to ecological threats against the background of the Western society of late modernity and sought to identify forms of environmentally responsible consumption. The first of her books, we will summarize, entitled *Pestří a zelení* [*Bright and Green*] was published in 1994, the second one *Vlažní a váhaví* [*The Half-hearted and the Hesitant*] in 2003. A good example of the shifts, which took place in the lifestyle of the families, researched during the ten years between two waves of the research is possible to see in the subtitles of both books. The first one is called *Chapters on Voluntary Modesty* and the second one *Chapters of Ecological Luxury*: both reflect mostly on the ways of thinking about appropriate contemporary options which would spread environmentally friendly ways of life.

From the very beginning, the key point of Librová's interest was the environmentally friendly way of living compatible with sustainable development and the question why and how some people in the Czech and Slovak republics (at the beginning of the 1990s still connected in one state) were willing to live ecologically without using all available opportunities for consumption and wasting resources and how they were coping with every-day tasks. It is necessary to mention that the families researched were not typical representatives of the Czech population, quite the opposite; they were rather unique as were their lifestyles and opinions. That is why from the perspective of the majority of the Czech population such a way of life was not quite comprehensible, especially at the time just after the fall of the communist regime when new shopping centres started to be opened and presented opportunities to buy irresistible amounts of diverse goods, which were not available till that time.

Librová's research started in the beginning of the 1990s and was led by a desire to investigate the values and approaches of ecologically active people. She interviewed forty seven families living in so-called "voluntary modesty" and she divided them into two groups. The first of them she called "Green". Their attitudes were environmentally friendly and a portion of them were active members of ecological groups. The reasons for the environmentally friendly and more sustainable living of the second group were different from the "Greens", and members of these families were devoted to different ideas and activities. In addition to varied spectra of civic-conscious attitudes, there were also references to Christianity and religious thoughts and she called this group "Bright".

The Bright had more specific features than just an environmentally friendly way of living. Most of them lived in smaller towns or villages and were emotionally connected to this local place, and they were usually active participants in the community life of their town. There were lots of religious people among them, mostly catholic, and they usually had bigger families with three or more children. Another very common feature was the effort to use all goods until they had completely worn out. These families also had a tendency to use very low amounts of running water, especially for flushing toilets. Thus, their way of living was also very frugal in terms of electricity consumption. They were also willing to share items of long-term consumption (car, automatic machines), to lend them to friends or neighbours, to help them with different tasks or to practice co-housing. Almost all of these families did not have a car, and they usually did not need one. They were public transport users and keen bicyclers. They never flew by airplane and spent holidays at home, at their cottages or in a tent under typical circumstances. More fancy ways of spending holidays were not common for them. The key values of these people were family and community life as well as a knowledge of and relationship to a particular place and its environment.

The reason for their way of living was not primarily economic. It was not possible to categorize them, or at least not to categorize all of them, as poor from an economic point of view. That is why Librová identified their way of living as "voluntarily modest". This was precisely the group in which she placed hope that they could become the core of the more nature-friendly and low-consuming part of society.

However, the second wave of the research (Librová 2003) with just the fifteen most typical families living in a state of voluntary modesty approximately ten years later brought different findings. In the context of economic transformation and under the pressure of societal changes in the 1990s, most of these families changed their way of life to one which was more consuming and mainstream oriented, but a number of them still remained different, and in some way modest, and almost all of them still lived at the same place as before. In many cases the members of these families were publicly active and the women were emancipated and studying or holding a job. While in 1992 all of them were in the home, now they were trying to combine work and family life and the division between typical women's and men's roles was not present as it had been before. All the women were fulfilled and satisfied with living in their environment, even with its difficulties, and none thought about moving to a bigger town as some of the men did in the first wave of the research. While at the beginning of the 1990s most of these families were almost poor, their financial situation was much better now. Usually they did jobs which they were satisfied with, had meaning for them and they were successful at; some of them became artists, some organic farmers. They were still growing their own fruits and vegetables, cooking at home and devoted to old things and repairing them. They had updated their living places, especially their kitchens, and all but one had bought a car, cell phone and personal computer. From that point of view the consumption of those families had grown, but they rejected consumerism at the same time. Many of them were disappointed by the development of civil and religious life in the Czech Republic, but they were still active organizers of civic life.

In the revolutionary thought of her second book Librová suggested that the modesty of the Bright is a luxury in spite of the fact that the Greens understand luxury as a negative example of an environmentally harmful approach, and "ecological luxury" may sound suspicious. However, our society has entered a time when nature is not the basic physical predisposition of human existence, but it is slowly becoming a privilege. She shows that luxury means not just expensive material goods but every ordinary moment in everyday life which stands outside of the repetitive process of social reproduction and has its aesthetic or spiritual dimension.

Librová's definition of luxury is inspired by Norbert Elias book *The Civilizing Process* (1994) according to which luxury is a sign and means of cultural evolution and the key element of the process of mankind's civilization. She was inspired by Veblen and Bourdieu as well and defines luxury as "a way of existence which exceeds the physical reproduction by spiritual and aesthetic dimension" (Librová 2003, 58; trans. R. S.). She creates links with values which are nonmaterial or unrelated to usefulness, as well as with the possibility of free choices and the key position of aesthetic and spiritual aspects of life.

Librová then specified ecological luxury as "environment friendly behaviour which consciously reduces footprints in the environment; it is available to diverse self-restrictions and is related to nonmaterial culturally estimated values." (ibid., 58; trans. R. S.). The provocative thought which allows us to understand an ascetic and modest lifestyle as luxurious is based in the nature and function of consumer goods on the postmodern market. Consumption does not symbolize social status under these conditions, because most industrially fabricated commodities are available to all in a sufficient quantity. Thus, the upper classes are pushed to base and express their position in the social hierarchy by new attributes. The role of material commodities as status making attributes was replaced by well-considered choice of consumed commodities, and by the ability to focus on the intrinsic value of experiences. Unlimited consumption began to be considered as vulgar, tasteless and unreasonable. Careful selection and the switch to purposeful modesty and ecological luxury is a new way of expression of high status and has become a quality which is imitated by people from lower classes. Luxury is losing its status-making function by spreading luxury items throughout the general public at the same time. This new luxury Librová quoted from dimensions specified by Hans Magnus Enzensberger (1997; quoted in Librová 2003, 54–56) who specified six attributes which have become luxury, however, they also rank among the key and basic conditions of sustainable life at the same time: (1) the luxury to dispose of one's own private time; (2) the possibility to pay attention to only the topics, events, people or media which/whom you personally consider important or worthy; (3) space for living and spending time in a place where you want not to be disturbed or accompanied by unwelcomed others; (4) quiet or silence, i.e. the possibility not to be disturbed by noise; (5) free access to nature; (6) security without security services which excludes others and constrain one's freedom.

A person who is able to avoid these constraints is living in luxury. To remain away from a noisy workplace, crowded public places, fabricated fast food and polluted air demands some kind of modesty which avoids having a lack of time for ourselves and relatives or a feeling of loneliness in the crowd of strangers. To avoid all of the dangers of the society of late modernity is getting to be more and more difficult. Even more so that not all of them are easily recognizable as explained by Beck in *Risk Society* (1992). The main luxury of living at the beginning of the 21st century thus becomes living in a secure quiet environment close to loved ones away from deadlines and rush. Luxury does not mean unlimited consumption or a flood of goods but items that would not be available to everyone and would not be possible to buy at all. From this point of view Librová's second book is not about criticism but a deep reflection on the contemporary society where there has been a progressive change in how people allocate and understand their time and also provides an analysis of changes in social stratification when environmental luxury becomes a sign of high social status.

The research showed that motives for voluntary modesty are connected with the shift from material to post-material values as defined by Inglehard (1997). From this point of view ecological luxury can follow after the material or consumed saturation, not earlier. However, the experience from Central Europe evidenced by Librová's research shows that there is a group of people, no matter how small or exceptional, who attained these values not on the basis of material oversaturation but as a result of their own reflexive approach to nature as a key value or through the imitation of status-marking activities.

Theoretical Reflection on the Consumption in the Czech Republic after 1989

We have recapitulated basic research findings concerning consumption in the Czech Republic in last twenty years. For now let us move to its more theoretical conceptualization. Examinations of consumer culture in the humanities and social sciences in the Czech Republic tend to be dominated by a critical approach which is often inspired by the findings and arguments of internationally recognized scholars of the latter half of the 20th century. Within the critical approach to consumer culture, however, there has been a shift in the focus of the criticism. Marxist criticism focused on the phenomena of exploitation and alienation has lost its critical vigour, especially in association with the rise of the social state and the rise in the living standards of the lower and middle classes. In the second half of the 20th century, consumer culture began to take on an association with waste and manipulation in academic circles. This trend in social theory was also followed later by theoretical reflections on consumption and consumer culture in the 1990s in the Czech Republic. The dominant current within the examination of consumer culture in the

Czech Republic after 1989 became environmental criticism in the form of moral or technical ecology or analysis of alternative ways of sustainable living. The anthropocentric critique of consumer culture in the Czech Republic adopts the arguments that were developed during the second half of the 20th century by Western critics of consumer culture (see Packard 1957; Marcuse 1991; Ritzer 1993). Among the most influential schools of thought are: (1) the ideology critique (excessive consumerism is a result of manipulation of consumers needs); (2) the critique of consumer culture as mass culture (consumer culture leads to the commercialization of culture, i.e. to its qualitative decline as a result of adaptation to the average tastes of a mass audience); (3) the liberal critique (competitive consumption leads to the problem of collective behaviour); (4) the hedonistic criticism (even assuming that the increase in levels of consumption were sustainable, changing consumer lifestyles in terms of quality of life and hedonistic enjoyment is in the interest of consumers themselves). From among the authors who have dealt with the theory of consumption, we have chosen as representatives of the environmental and anthropocentric criticism on consumerism the philosopher Erazim Kohák and the sociologist Jan Keller and will present their work in the following paragraphs.[14]

Jan Keller and the Social Causes of Ecological Crisis

In his book *Až na dno blahobytu* [*To the Bottom of Affluence*] (1993), Jan Keller examines the social causes of ecological crisis (depletion of natural resources and pollution which has crossed the threshold of the environment's absorptive capacity), which he considers an unquestionable fact. He identifies its social cause to be the idea of well-being, which lies in the notion of continuous economic growth and a rising average standard of living. Keller points out that the expansion of economic growth does not in fact lead to an increase in the quality of life of the population, but is required by the market system itself, if it is not to be led to stagnation and collapse, and thus to a threat to political elites. He rejects arguments that legitimize continuous economic growth on the basis of (a) the promise of an increase in the general standard of living, (b) a solution to poverty in the developing countries of the Third World and (c) prevention of further environmental devastation. In doing so he uses an eclectic argumentative strategy (using arguments borrowed from almost every kind of criticism of consumer culture) and supports his opinions with the findings of academic

---

[14] Other authors who concern themselves with critical analysis of the environmental impacts of consumer behaviour from the philosophical or environmental perspective include Josef Šmajs (1995) and Bedřich Moldan (2009).

writing. In general, Keller criticizes all three justifications as containing internal inconsistencies: the harmful effects of economic growth are to be solved by maximizing their cause, namely economic growth.

According to Keller, the concept of prosperity and increasing levels of consumption is, in view of the ecological crisis, unsustainable and no longer leads to an increase in the quality of human life. Economic growth is in fact exhausted by the elimination of damages incurred in by industrial production[15] and increasing the level of consumption is in fact limited to "forced consumption", i.e. to consumption which offsets past losses (such as the construction of an artificial swimming pool as a result of the pollution of rivers and ponds), consumption caused by the need to redress the damage done (e.g. purchase of double windows to prevent noise from the recently built highway near the home of the consumer) and the consumption caused by past development (the increasing need for transportation due to the expansion of trade and separation of activities that were previously performed in the same place). Economic indicators are therefore not a reliable indicator of growth in living standards, they capture only the movement of goods sold and purchased, not the overall quality of life, which, according to Keller, is stagnating or even decreasing despite economic growth (1993, 18). Another counterargument that Keller offers in contrast to the vision of continuous economic growth is the fact that even if the potential economic growth were projected into the income of the population, it would not lead to comparable growth in the standard of living of the whole population. Increased purchasing power namely leads to higher prices for positional or scarce goods. For certain sections of the population, according to Keller, "becoming richer" thus means further social descent.

Keller further rejects the argument that economic growth in the prosperous countries helps poor countries through loans or increased demand for their goods to gradually eliminate their poverty. From the literature (Dobson 1991) he cites the conclusion that global economic growth of 3% over 25 years would lead to a doubling of production and consumption. Such consumer pressure would, however, present an ecological disaster and the depletion of raw materials. Second, Keller criticizes the strategy of loans to third world countries because they are repaid gradually by means of disappearing natural resources. In light of these findings, indebtedness and poverty in the countries of the southern

---

[15] As an example, Keller (1993, 18) cites the money invested in cleaning up the shore of Alaska after the wreck of the tanker Exxon Valdez, which appeared in the statistics of American economists as a growth in GNP.

hemisphere seems to be a prerequisite for the economic growth and prosperity of northern countries (Keller 1993, 22).

Keller considers not only systemic, but also the psychological reasons for economic growth. Increasing consumption is not for Keller emanation of our basic biological needs, but the result of (1) the need to compensate for damages incurred in connection with economic growth, (2) manipulation of consumers through the advertising industry, which raises in them new and artificial needs, (3) the psychological frustration of consumers due to the inability to intervene in the political and economic events and disorientation and uncertainty in a complex and constantly changing modern world (the world of consumer goods, by contrast, offers a sphere which is transparent and completely controllable by the consumer).

The social conditionality of our needs for Keller is evidence that the setting of the consumer trend can be changed successfully. But how can be this change achieved? Keller first argues against advocates of the market who assert that threats to the environment can be dealt with through market mechanisms, namely by including ecological damages, which up to now have had the status of negative externalities, into production costs and thereby penalizing polluters while promoting environmentally friendly modes of production. Keller rejects such "ecological accounting" because it allows only the rich to pollute (i.e. those who can afford to subsidize the costs of environmental damage) and in addition, these market measures do not prevent an ecological disaster (there are sufficient raw materials and alternative resources on the Earth to destroy the ecosystem). Finally, he presents a third, ethical-philosophical, reason: the autonomous status of nature needs to be acknowledged and it should never be approached in a purely instrumental way. The Czech philosopher Erazim Kohák develops this theme further in his work and we will return to it later.

According to Keller, positive changes can be achieved by adhering to three fundamental principles of a zero-growth economy, which he takes from the work of Richard Douthwaite (1992). It is necessary to (1) attach the same value to the future as to the present, (2) take into account the interests of others as well as one's own, (3) acknowledge nature's autonomous status (instead of green accounting he postulate categorical requirement that nature must not be polluted). The result of these principles would, according to Keller, be a decentralized society that respects the diversity of ecosystems; reduces traffic, spatial migration and international trade; supports local business based on local resources, a modest way of life based on meeting basic human needs and the return of a large part of the population to the agricultural sector, which would be transformed from today's industrial character to a kind of physically demanding gardening which, while it would lead to an decrease in productivity, would eliminate the problem of unemployment.

Erazim Kohák and Ecological Ethics

Philosopher Erazim Kohák also anticipates an ecological catastrophe in his books, one which, in his opinion, will be caused by the effort of the state to achieve the vision of unlimited growth in a world of finite raw materials and resources. It has three main causes: overpopulation, the power of technology and consumerism. (1) Overpopulation is manifested in three symptoms. First, people live off the core nature's substance, not its annual increase, i.e. people consume so much food that they threaten its further growth. Second, people stop sharing their habitat with other species and push them out (in the worst cases causing their extinction). Third, the humans are reproducing at such a rate that they are not able to take sufficient care for their offspring. (2) The dominance of technology manifests itself through the disruption of the ability of the biosphere to react to human intervention and through the threat to the very existence of the environment. (3) Consumerism, according to Kohák, is the conviction that the purpose of life is the continued increase in the level of material consumption, which will solve social problems and guarantee happiness to people, and that the achievement of this is one of the primary tasks of the state.

The ecological crisis, in his view, cannot be averted by mere technical ecology, that is by the dampening of the impact of production on the non-human world through improved technology, because it does not solve the contradiction between endless growth in consumption in the context of limited quantities of raw materials. Solving environmental problems requires a normative consideration of the role of man in relation to non-human world and a review of his value orientation. The author documents the need for normative principles of human action by citing the example of the "tragedy of the commons" (Hardin 1968). Let us imagine a pasture which is used by a hundred sheep, and all the farmers from a village have equal access to it. If each of the farmers tries to maximize their profits from the pasture, i.e. they graze more sheep on it than the others, and if by doing so the maximum sustainable limit is exceed, the pasture will be destroyed. The tragedy of the commons presents a situation in which different individuals acting rationally in their own interests destroy a common resource, even though they are aware that, in the long run, such behaviour is undesirable. In a situation in which there are excessive demands it is necessary, according to Kohák, to place normative limits on the availability of resources and the best way of doing this is through moral ecology.

In his book, *The Green Halo: A Bird's Eye View of Ecological Ethics* (2000), Kohák interprets the different types of ecological ethics, without entirely inclining to one of them. (1) "Ethics of the Fear of the Lord" is a theocentric doctrine based on the assumption that nature is God's creation, and thus should be approached with respect and care, rather than instrumentally. (2) "The Ethics of Noble Humanity" is an anthropocentric doctrine based on the assumption that man is, unlike other animals, capable of using reason to overcome a natural interest in satisfying their own needs and act in the long-term interests of humanity, such as, for the good of nature. (3) "The Ethics of Reverence for Life" is a biocentric doctrine based on the intuitive view that life is valuable in itself. This conclusion can be achieved either by direct experience or through formal-logical reasoning along the lines of Paul Taylor (1986). The reasoning is based on a formal definition of good for a living creature (for each animal good means the opportunity to fully live its life in a way which is appropriate to its species) and the assumption that all living creatures are valuable because they are, and therefore deserve respectful treatment. A biocentric attitude towards the world can be, according to Kohák, summarized through the following propositions: (a) All living beings have the same right to life; (b) Earth is a system of interdependencies; (c) Each member of the biotic community has value simply because of its existence; (d) The concept of human superiority is unjustified and is an expression of human racism. (4) "The Land Ethic" is a holistic doctrine based on the teachings of Aldo Leopold (1949). According to this concept, the life of the individual depends on the integrity and stability of the whole (ecosystem), and therefore the whole contains intrinsic value. Good is that which supports the stability and integrity of the biotic system.

The author concludes that a necessary condition for solving the ecological crisis is a change in value orientation of man which replaces the ideal of the continuously increasing level of consumption with a vision of a more modest and sustainable way of life on Earth and will lead to an acceptance of responsibility for the consequences of our actions, not only in relation to other people, but also to the non-human world. For Kohák which type of environmental ethics will lead to this goal is a secondary issue. What is important, he claims, is knowledge that the crisis cannot be solved simply by the invention of more productive and efficient technology. This technological solution to environmental threats is inadequate, because it does not affect the basic value orientation towards economic growth and material living standards. An unlimited growth in demands on a limited Earth is, according to Kohák, contradiction and as a consequences leads to an inevitable catastrophe.

Conclusion

Although critical reflection on consumerism in the Czech Republic is not completely unknown, as illustrated by the works of Librová, Keller and Kohák, a lens emphasizing Consumer Culture Theory in the Czech academic environment is still missing. Although many studies have been carried out investigating the consumer behaviour of the Czechs and their value system, these results have not been looked at through the lens of CCT, and it remains a marginal line of thinking about social life in the Czech Republic.

We believe that the perspective of CCT can contribute to a significant degree to answering questions relating to consumer culture and consumer behaviour in the Czech Republic. Among the new directions in researching consumption and consumer culture in the Czech Republic through the tools and insights of CCT we list primarily (a) analysis of consumption as a means of shaping collective and individual identity, (b) analysis of the influence of the market environment and market mechanisms on culture, (c) analysis of institutional and social structures (class, race, gender, ethnicity) affecting consumption, (d) analysis of the spread of ideology by means of consumer goods and the interpretive strategies of consumers (see also Arnould and Thompson 2005, 871– 875).

What, for example, are consumer preferences and trends in the Czech population of the 21st century? The Czech commercial television station, Nova, bet on the popularity of fashion brands and the personal stories from behind the scenes of the fashion and media industries in preparing the series *Perfect World* for its 2010 season. This series, which falls into the genre of so-called "dramedy" (a mix of drama and comedy) along with elements of soap operas, was inspired by successful films like *The Devil Wears Prada* inserted into the editorial environment the fashion magazine *Grace* in the centre of Prague, offering viewers the illusion that at least some people can live in the fashionable world of unlimited consumption, but perhaps it is for exactly this reason that it was not particularly successful with Czech TV viewers. Does this suggest that they are not ready for the formally and aesthetically perfect lines of modern design and surgically or digitally modified beauty, yet or is it exactly the opposite? What changes in consumer behaviour will new information technology bring which provides not only new options for consumers, but also space for creative marketers? Can consumer culture in the Czech Republic become an effective tool to promote certain social or ethical values? How do culture and marketing communication interact in the Czech Republic? What values and stories are promoted through the aesthetics of contemporary consumer culture? And what untapped symbolic potential does consumer culture have at its disposal? Is it possible that through the one-sided focus of the aesthetics of the consumer world and marketing on the images and stories of successful and happy people, fulfilled dreams and beautiful illusions leads to the resignation and frustration of sick, unsuccessful and unhappy people? Does consumer culture contribute to their social exclusion? These are only a fraction of the questions that the lens of Consumer Culture Theory being developed in the Czech Republic might help to answer.

References

Arnould, Eric, and Craig Thompson. 2005. "Consumer Culture Theory (CCT): Twenty Years of Research" *The Journal of Consumer Research* 31 (4): 868–882.

Beck, Ulrich. 1992. *Risk Society: Towards a New Modernity*. New Delhi: Sage.

Charvát, František, Jiří Linhart, and Jiří Večerník. 1978. *Sociálně třídní struktura Československa: vývoj, data, srovnání*. Praha: Horizont.

ČSÚ. 2012. "Sčítání lidu 1921–1991." Accessed January 6. http://notes3.czso.cz/sldb/sldb.nsf/i/scitani_lidu_1921_1991.

Dobson, Andrew. 1991. *Green Political Thought*. London: HarperCollins.

Douthwaithe, Richard. 1992. *The Growth Illusion: How Economic Growth Has Enriched the Few, Impoverished the Many, and Endangered the Planet*. London: Resurgence Book.

Dubská, Drahomíra. 2010. "České domácnosti dluží bilion." Accessed January 6. http://www.czso.cz/csu/csu.nsf/1e01747a199f30f4c1256bd50038ab23/242b7e3f33b86868c12576e3004e51a1/$FILE/ckta120310.doc.

Elias, Norbert. 1994. *The Civilizing Process: Sociogenetic and Psychogenetic Investigations*. Oxford: Blackwell.

Enzensberger, Hans Magnus. 1997. "Luxus – odkud a kam s ním?" *Literární noviny* 36: 1–9.

Habermas, Jürgen. 1990. *Strukturwandel der Öffentlichkeit: Untersuchungen zu einer Kategorie der bürgerlichen Gesellschaft*. Frankfurt am Main: Suhrkamp.

Hacking, Ian. 1999. *The Social Construction of What?* Cambridge, MA: Harvard University Press.

Hardin, Garrett. 1968. "The Tragedy of the Commons." *Science* 162: 1243–1248.

Inglehart, Ronald. 1997. "Postmateralist Values and the Erosion of Institutional Authority." In *Why People Don't Trust Government*, edited by Joseph S. Nye, Philip D. Zelikow, and David King, 217–236. Cambridge, MA: Harvard University Press.

Keller, Jan. 1993. *Až na dno blahobytu.* Brno: Hnutí Duha.

Kohák, Erazim. 2000. *The Green Halo: A Bird's Eye View of Ecological Ethics.* Chicago: Open Court.

Kohout, Jaroslav. 1982. "Sociologické výzkumy spotřebitelů." *Sociologický časopis* 20 (4): 417–430.

Kornai, János. 1992. *The Socialist System: The Political Economy of Communism.* Oxford: Oxford University Press.

Leopold, Aldo. 1949. *A Sand County Almanach.* New York: Oxford University Press.

Librová, Hana. 1994. *Pestří a zelení. Kapitoly o dobrovolné skromnosti.* Brno: Veronica, Hnutí Duha.

—. 2003. *Vlažní a váhaví. Kapitoly o ekologickém luxusu.* Brno: Doplněk.

Machonin, Pavel. 1992. "Změnil se typ společenského uspořádání v letech 1967–1984?" *Sociologický časopis* 28 (1): 73–83.

Machonin, Pavel, and Milan Tuček, eds. 1996. *Česká společnost v transformaci: K proměnám sociální struktury.* Praha: Sociologické nakladatelství.

Marcuse, Herbert. 1991. *One-dimensional Man: Studies in Ideology of Advanced Industrial Society.* London: Routledge.

Marx, Karl. 1992. *Capital: Critique of Political Economy.* London: Penguin.

Marling, Karal Ann. 1994. "Nixon in Moscow. Appliences, Affluence and Americanism." In *As Seen on TV: The Visual Culture of Everyday Life in the 1950s*, edited by Karal Ann Marling, 242–283. Cambridge, MA: Harvard University Press.

McCracken, Grant. 1988. *Culture and Consumption.* Bloomington: Indiana University Press.

Mlčoch, Lubomír. 1990. *Chování československé podnikové sféry.* Praha: EÚ ČSAV.

Mlčoch, Lubomír, Pavel Machonin, and Milan Sojka. 2000. *Ekonomické a společenské změny v české společnosti po roce 1989.* Praha: Karolinum.

Moldan, Bedřich. 2009. *Podmaněná planeta.* Praha: Karolinum.

Možný, Ivo. 1991. *Proč tak snadno?* Praha: Sociologické nakladatelství.

Nove, Alec. 1991. *The Economics of Feasible Socialism.* London: HarperCollins.

Packard, Vance. 1957. *The Hidden Persuaders.* New York: David McKay.

Peterson, Richard. 1990. "Understanding Audience Segmentation: From Elite and Mass to Omnivore and Univore." *Poetics* 21 (4): 243–258.

Prudký, Libor et al. 2009. *Inventura hodnot. Výsledky sociologických výzkumů hodnot ve společnosti České republiky.* Praha: Academia.

Ritzer, George. 1993. *The McDonaldization of Society.* Newbury Park: Pine Forge Press.

Šafr, Jiří. 2008. *Životní styl a sociální třídy: vytváření symbolické kulturní hranice diferenciací vkusu a spotřeby.* Praha: Sociologický ústav AV ČR.

Sdružení pro bankovní karty. 2011. "Statistiky čipových karet ke stažení." Accessed January 6. http://www.bankovnikarty.cz/pages/czech/profil_statistiky.html.

Šmajs, Josef. 1995. *Ohrožená kultura.* Brno: Zvláštní vydání.

Špaček, Ondřej, and Jiří Šafr. 2010. "Volný čas, sport a kulturní vkus: rozdíly podle společenského postavení." In *Jaká je naše společnost? Otázky, které si často klademe*, edited by Hana Maříková, Jiří Kostelecký, Tomáš Lebeda, and Markéta Škodová, 81–99. Praha: Sociologické nakladatelství.

Sredl, Katherine. 2007. "Consumption and Class during and after State Socialism." In *Research in Consumer Behavior*, edited by Russel Belk, and John Sherry, 187–205. Oxford: Elsevier.

Taylor, Paul. 1986. *Respect for Nature. A Theory of Environmental Ethics.* Princeton: Princeton University Press.

Thompson, John. 1990. *Ideology and Modern Culture.* Stanford: Stanford University Press.

Tuček, Milan. 1992. "Komparace výsledků šetření sociální struktury z roku 1967 a 1984." *Sociologický časopis* 28 (1): 60–72.

Veblen, Thorstein. 1994. *The Theory of the Leisure Class.* New York: Penguin.

Večerník, Jiří. 1991. "Distribuční systém v Československu: empirická fakta, výkladové hypotézy." *Sociologický časopis* 27 (1): 39–56.

—. 2001. "Sociální zprávy v České republice po roce 1989." *Sociologický časopis* 37 (3): 329–341.

—. 2010. "Konzumní společnost – vstup do ráje hojnosti a manipulace." In *Jaká je naše společnost? Otázky, které si často klademe*, edited by Hana Maříková, Jiří Kostelecký, Tomáš Lebeda, and Markéta Škodová, 100–113. Praha: Sociologické nakladatelství.

Večerník, Jiří, and Petr Matějů, eds. 1998. *Zpráva o vývoji české společnosti 1989–1998*. Praha: Academia.

UNDERSTANDING THE MEANING OF CONSUMPTION IN EVERYDAY LIVES OF "MAINSTREAM" YOUTH IN THE CZECH REPUBLIC

MICHAELA HRÁČKOVÁ PYŠŇÁKOVÁ

Introduction: What Is "Mainstream" Youth?[1]

"Mainstream" is a term frequently used by laypeople, sociologists, marketing researchers, journalists and youth policy makers. In general, it refers to what is common or popular, what is widely accepted, commercial or dominant. The notion of mainstream is sometimes associated with passive conformity, absence of reflexivity, crowd or mass-like behaviour and uniformity. Such taken-for-granted assumptions about the mainstream are a vital part not only of a lay language, but they also appear to be widely accepted in contemporary Czech sociology of youth. Drawing on qualitative research concerned with the meaning of consumer lifestyles in daily lives of "mainstream" young people in the Czech Republic this article has three aims:

(a) to challenge the current representation of "mainstream" youth in youth research in the Czech Republic which portrays these young people as passive conformists;

(b) to examine how young people use their consumer lifestyles as a means of dealing with the structural constraints and new possibilities typical of late modernity in order to maintain, construct, display, interpret and negotiate their sense of belonging to society; and

(c) to ascertain the extent to which the concept of "mainstream" youth offers a valuable lens for understanding young people's relationship to

---

[1] This article partly draws on my dissertation project; partly it is based on a paper "We're Not Sheeple! The Meaning of Consumption in Everyday Lives of Mainstream Youth" presented at the conference *Consumer Culture: Between Aesthetics, Social Distinction and Ecological Activism*, Palacký University Olomouc, October 7–9, 2010.

social change and how it might be relevant for further youth research in the Czech Republic.

Although my study draws upon qualitative research concerned with young people's relationship with consumption, this article aims to do more than equate "mainstream" youth with young consumers of popular culture or brands. The concept of "mainstream" youth presented in this study attempts to capture the active ways in which young people themselves negotiate the structural, cultural and social changes in what has been described as an increasingly individualised or risk society (Macháček 2004; Roberts 2009). This article aims to explore how these changes are experienced by these young people via their daily engagement with consumption. The next aim is to explore how these changes are reflected in these young people's interpretations of what it means to be "normal" and "ordinary" in the contemporary Czech Republic, and how, under the circumstances of late modernity, these young people construct and maintain their sense of ordinariness (or as I prefer, the term "mainstreamness").

Specifying the Concept of "Mainstream" Youth

As "mainstream" youth is a part of both lay and academic discourses, it is necessarily to specify my own usage of this concept. In this article, I draw on a debate which frames "mainstream" young people as *a largely neglected element in youth research*. In this body of research the notion of "mainstream" youth refers to *more ordinary* in terms of *not spectacular nor problematic or disadvantaged youth*. What lies at the heart of this debate is a criticism of a long-established tendency in youth research to neglect ordinariness and normality in favour of overemphasising more extreme and melodramatic experiences of youth (e.g. Willis 1990; Miles 2000; Schildrick 2006; Roberts 2011). Such criticism has been raised for example in the early 1990s by MacDonald and Coffield (1991):

> our work […] emphasizes the importance of studying "ordinary" young people rather than exotic, unusual or unrepresentative youth groups […]. So although studies of youth during the 1970s made valuable contributions to our understanding of the sub-cultural aspects of various youth groups, research developed in essentially élitist directions, paying little attention to the realities of the everyday lives of the majority of young adults (MacDonald and Coffield, 2–3).

MacDonald and Coffield (ibid.) use the notion of the "invisible majority" as a criticism of the British youth studies at that time, pointing at its tendency to focus on disadvantaged and problematic youth groups and youth at/as risk whilst neglecting those who do not fit into these categories. However, even two decades later it appears that the "mainstream" youth still continues to represent the "missing middle" (Roberts 2011) in youth research. France argues that the metaphor of a missing-middle sits easily with reference to youth studies, because there is still relatively little known about "ordinary" youth (France 2007, 57). Roberts (2011) takes this argument further and points out:

> Recently, youth sociology has perhaps been equally blinkered, with studies of those more obviously at risk of social exclusion overshadowing the seemingly "ordinary" and unproblematic. […] "Ordinariness", then, has taken a back seat in the youth research agenda, seemingly deemed uninteresting (Roberts 2011, 23–25).

There are two main points about the "mainstream" youth in this debate which are particularly appealing in regard to the sociology of youth in general. The first point is that the ordinary youth (or as I prefer, "mainstream" youth) can be understood not only as a particular category or a group of young people, but also as a conceptual challenge to the orthodoxies, stories and dichotomies which dominated in youth research at a particular time. Brown's (1987), Jenkins' (1983), Willis' (1990) and Miles' (2000) studies of "ordinary" youth challenge the notion of mainstream in the British subcultural studies and the dichotomy of what is passive and active in arguing that only a minority of young people are actually involved in youth subcultures. Based on empirical evidence, these authors demonstrate that belonging to the mainstream does not imply passive conformity, but rather negotiation with structural conditions. Similarly, Pilkington (2004) and Shildrick (2006) challenge club cultural and post-subcultural studies in arguing that this approach tends to neglect cultural diversity and expressions of the majority of young people (they use the terms "ordinary youth" and "normal youth") who do not fit into post-subcultural frames. In his more structurally framed study of club cultures, Hollands (2002) criticises research on youth transitions which tends to focus on those young people who are excluded from the society, whilst neglecting more "ordinary" youth in terms of service workers, further and higher education students, professional workers and middle-class youth. In other words, the notion of "mainstream" youth reflects a disappointment within a group of youth researchers, who properly argue that although the sociology of youth as a discipline aspires to describe, understand and interpret what it means to be a young person, it continues to do so through an examination of those groups of young people which are rather unrepresentative in regard to the "everydayness" experienced by the majority of young people (MacDonald and Coffield 1991; Miles 2000; Roberts 2011).

The second point is that the above studies challenge a common sense notion about mainstream youth which tends to frame them as a relatively monolithic group, passively conforming to the dominant society. Instead of slipping into what Brubaker (2002) calls "groupism", the focus in the above debate is (although not exclusively) on the active ways through which young people negotiate structural constraints and on how, under such circumstances, they actively construct what it means to be "ordinary" in the context of late modernity.[2]

Challenging Orthodoxies about "Mainstream" Youth in Contemporary Youth Research in the Czech Republic

Although the works quoted above were written mostly in the context of the British sociology of youth, they tackle problems which are in many ways particularly relevant to a representation of "mainstream" youth in contemporary Czech youth research. What dominates the current youth question in the Czech Republic is a concern with how the post-revolution young generation deals with the changed conditions given by the late modernity (e.g. Macháček 2004). Most research of this kind draws upon Beck's individualisation thesis (1992) and Giddens' theory of reflexivity (1991) according to which the structural deterioration of traditional institutions liberates people from conventional roles and constraints (class, gender and family relationships), but at the same time engenders new forms of dependency (Beck and Beck-Gernsheim 2002). People become the agents of their own identity making, but this is not a choice. It is an indispensable condition of social integration in late modernity. Empirically oriented research on youth transitions[3] has thus focused on how processes

---

[2] Brubaker (2002) defines groupism as "the tendency to take discrete, sharply differentiated, internally homogenous and externally bounded groups as basic constituents of social life […], and fundamental units of social analysis" (ibid., 164). In line with Brubaker, this article does not perceive the mainstream youth in terms of a "substantial group or entity, but in terms of practical categories, discursive frames, cognitive schemas and cultural representations" (ibid., 167). In other words, an interpretive approach allows framing "mainstream" youth as a concept which is socially constructed and negotiated.

[3] The study of youth transitions focuses on the way in which institutions structure the process of how young people grow up. The transitional approach conceptualises youth as the process of "becoming adult" (Wyn and White 1997, 95).

of individualisation are reflected in the transformation from socialism to capitalism, and the extent to which such a transition has redefined the way in which young people grow up in the Czech Republic. Macháček (2004) points out that in comparison to their parents, young people in the Czech Republic now live in a society where individual performance, as well as the diversification and individualisation of lifestyles have increasing importance. This means that for contemporary Czech youth there is a much greater range of options to choose from, in the context of education, work or lifestyles, for example. This in turn creates a situation in which the risks associated with such choice falls upon their shoulders. New choices and freedoms are compromised by new pressures and uncertainties for young people.

However, the problem with contemporary youth research in the Czech Republic is a tendency to focus almost exclusively on marginal or spectacular youth. This creates a problem as prioritising visible or disadvantaged groups of young people has led not only to the neglect of the experiences of "mainstream" youth who cannot be easily pigeonholed into the above categories, but also to a very limited understanding of "mainstream" youth. What the notion of "mainstream" youth appears to reflect are the "silenced voices" (Griffin 1993) or the "invisible majority" (Roberts 2011). The metaphor of the "missing middle" (ibid.) appears to be entirely apposite in the context of Czech sociology of youth. To complicate this situation further, the irony is that although the "mainstream" youth is generally absent in contemporary Czech youth research, it does not mean that notions of mainstream youth and mainstream as a general concept are absent. On the contrary, both terms constitute a vital element in contemporary structurally oriented youth research (e.g. MŠMT 2007; NIDM MŠMT 2000) as well as in emerging cultural and sub/post-subcultural studies (e.g. Smolík 2010). However, in this article, I argue that the academic representations and interpretations of mainstream youth in these texts are problematic. "Mainstream" youth is represented either purely through statistics or it is constructed via interpretations of research concerned with spectacular and subcultural youth.

An extract taken from the *State Youth Policy Conception for the Years 2007–2013* (MŠMT 2007) is a good example. *The Conception* is a strategic plan approved by the Ministry of Education, Youth and Sports in the Czech Republic in 2007 and it covers the most relevant domains of contemporary Czech youth policy. Based on several empirical sociological studies and long-term series comparisons, *The Conception* portrays contemporary mainstream youth in the Czech Republic as young people whose value-orientation points to:

> hedonism and pragmatism, accompanied by the diminishing importance of global and social values. The mainstream within the young generation is adapted to society and identifies with it. Mainstream media are an important instrument of social conformity [...]. The mainstream of the young generation is to a large extent manipulated by the media and accepts the opinions and positions generated by them. The hedonistic and pragmatic orientation of the young generation, coupled with the absence of social vision, contribute to the increased consumption of alcohol, nicotine and drugs. [...] A large part of children and young people adapt to society in contact with media manipulation and become consumers dependent on designer goods. Drugs are also a part of this "designer lifestyle". Being "in" means at least smoking marihuana. Another section of this population retreats to drugs trying to escape an aggressive market economy (MŠMT 2007, 5–6, 11).

Although in this context mainstream youth represents a point of reference for what is considered "normal" youth, the notion of normality is rarely connected to agency, but rather it is usually interpreted in terms of passivity, conformity and manipulation, especially when it comes to the issue of consumption. Given the fact that the content of *The Conception* draws on several sociological studies, it can be argued that what this document encapsulates is not as much a reflection of contemporary "mainstream" youth as a reflection of an academic "common sense" about mainstream youth. Indeed as Griffin (1993) puts it:

> The relationship between young people's experiences and academic "common sense" about "youth" is not straightforward. Youth research does not simply reflect aspects of young people's lives, nor does it merely misrepresent their experiences, as though the latter were sitting around the truth waiting to be discovered—or misunderstood. Youth research is more complex than this, given the ideological role it plays in constructing the very categories of "youth" and "adolescence", and in presenting stories about the origins of specific forms of youthful deviance and resistance (Griffin 1993, 2).

Griffin's point is particularly pertinent when considering how mainstream youth has been explored, conceptualised, constructed and theorised through academic youth research. My argument is that youth researchers simply do not observe and describe the social reality, but they also actively construct the concept of youth. And they do it not only through what they focus on, but also through what they neglect. This article seeks to identify the gaps and contradictions which exist in sociological constructions, and more importantly, in academic common sense about the "mainstream" youth. The quotation taken from the *State Youth Policy Conception* (MŠMT 2007) that portrays mainstream youth as a relatively homogeneous group characterised by conformity, passivity and manipulation, is a good illustration of this prevailing academic common sense. This article aims to challenge prevailing construction of "mainstream" youth's adaptation to society as passive conformism. Instead of taking this construction as a given, it questions why the notion of "mainstream" youth in the above quotation carries with it notions of passivity and sheep-like behaviour.

Young People's Consumer Lifestyles in Late Modernity

To understand my criticism, it is necessary to look at current youth research in the Czech Republic from a broader perspective. What characterises current youth research in the Czech Republic is a tendency to construct contemporary youth through youth-at-risk and youth-as-risk discourses. Such tendency is very strong in current youth research in the Czech Republic on youth consumption.[4] If there is any notion of consumerism, then it is framed either as a risk-taking activity involving young people's leisure time, such as binge drinking, smoking, or drug abuse (Sak 2000; Vanžurová 2006; Truhlářová and Smutek 2006; Šťastná and Šucha 2010) or as an indicator of young people's moral decline in terms of hedonism, mostly related to their supposed loss of interest in public issues (MŠMT 2007; NIDM MŠMT 2000; Sak and Saková 2004; Potůček et al. 2002). In other words, what defines most of the conceptions of "young consumers" based upon the interpretations of youth researchers in the Czech Republic is the dread that the increasing interest of young people in consumption will possibly cause their moral corruption. Such a possibility has been mentioned by Potůček's et al. (2002) collection of scenarios of further development of the Czech society. In a chapter devoted to the generational question, Potůček proposes a scenario according to which the increasing value orientation towards materialism and hedonism on the part of young people born after 1975 might lead to the formation of a "generation according to the rules of money" (ibid., 224). The comment made by Sak and Saková (2004) further illustrates this anxiety:

---

[4] My aim is not to condemn the whole of contemporary youth research in the Czech Republic. My criticism refers to what Griffin (1993, 2001) terms as a "mainstream" perspective–a dominant set of debates which justify, produce, reproduce and construct hegemonic discourses around youth at a particular time.

> This generation of youth more than any other previous generation passes through many crossroads. It makes a choice between drugs and normal life. [...] It decides between hedonism and parenthood, between an authentic life and the consumer life of mass society (Sak and Saková 2004, 7–8).

What appears to characterise the above discourses is a tendency to treat young people as troubled victims of economic and social structures that fails to consider the possibility that consumer lifestyles might provide them with the means of dealing with these constraints (for this criticism see Pyšňáková and Miles 2010). In other words, young people's active engagement with consumption is interpreted as both a cause and a source of their pathological behaviour (Vanžurová 2006; MŠMT 2007; NIDM MŠMT 2000).

> The causes of the current situation should be sought in a social environment where a loss of barriers typical of totalitarian regimes is more likely to promote aggression and consumer lifestyle rather than the creation of co-oriented and quality relationships. The influence of an aggressive consumer culture is also significant, including the impacts on values of the young generation and an insufficient supply of attractive leisure activities (NIDM MŠMT 2000, 38).[5]

A vital part of the above discourses includes an implicit assumption that unless young people learn how to manage their free time properly, they are at risk of becoming vulnerable dupes, manipulated by consumer culture (e.g. MŠMT 2007; NIDM MŠMT 2000). Being a consumer in late modernity is, however, much more complex than the above interpretation implies. In order to adequately develop a concept of mainstream youth in the context of late modernity via an examination of youth consumer lifestyles, it is necessarily to go on to discuss the broader social and cultural changes which have influenced the norms and values of contemporary mainstream society. Young people in the Czech Republic are active consumers, but they do not consume in isolation. People are not born as consumers; their identities as consumers are formed through their experiences of living in a consumer society. This article aims to explore what exactly this means. In this respect, Sassatelli's (2007) recent work, in which the author offers an insight into how we might reconceptualise our understanding of contemporary mainstream youth via the concept of the consumer, appears to be especially instructive:

---

[5] NIDM MŠMT: National Institute of Children and Youth, Ministry of Education, Youth and Sports.

> It is extremely difficult to describe consumers, all consumers, as a homogenous "mass" enthralled by the strategies of publicity. It may be true that in contemporary Western societies we are all consumers, but it is also true that we all consume in different ways. When we operate as consumers we deploy cognitive and normative frameworks which we have developed throughout our lives, starting from the particular position we occupy in the social structure, negotiating with a variety of roles which are not reducible to our experiences as consumers. Our identity as consumer interacts, as it were, with other social identities and relations (Sassatelli 2007, 84).

This explanation is useful for conceptualising the "mainstream" youth as active members of a consumer society, for it situates consumer culture as a space for negotiation and as a potentially complex set of relations. This is particularly important with regard to empirical research which indicates that the shift towards the processes of individualisation, along with an increasing reflexive attitude towards one's choices and decisions, are clearly evident through the life experiences, trajectories and the values of young people in the Czech Republic (Macháček 2004). In this sense, Giddens' (1991) conception of lifestyle appears to be particularly useful. According to Giddens, the relationship between individuals and society is dynamic and fluid and involves constant negotiation, development and change. The processes of increasing individualisation and de-standardisation go hand in hand with a weakening of collectivist traditions, an increase of expert knowledge and an intensification of individualist values and norms (Giddens 1991; Beck and Beck-Gernsheim 2002). In other words, individuals are forced to negotiate lifestyle choices on a daily basis, and this process has become increasingly important in the constitution of self-identity and activity, despite the standardising influence of commodification on consumer culture. Thus:

> Lifestyles are routinised practices, the routines incorporated into habits of dress, eating, modes of acting and favoured milieus for encountering others; but the routines followed are reflexively open to change in the light of the mobile nature of self-identity. Each of the small decisions a person makes every day. [...] contributes to such routines. All such choices (as well as larger and more consequential ones) are decisions not only about how to act but who to be. The more post-traditional settings in which an individual moves, the more lifestyles concern the very core of self-identity, its making and remaking (Giddens 1991, 81).

In terms of consumer lifestyles, there is high anxiety because every (consumer) choice seems to implicate the self, as everything that an individual chooses to eat, to dress, to read or to buy, expresses who he or she is. In this concept, people are involved in new types of personal risks, as they might possibly make wrong choices (Beck 1992; Slater 1997). As such, what constitutes normality in late modernity is the reflexive project of the self (Slater 1997). In this context, consumer lifestyles appear to represent more than a form of escapism or hedonism as some youth research attempt to propose. As regards Czech youth studies, such a conceptualisation of consumer lifestyles appears to be under-researched. But it is precisely in this blurred area that I am seeking to explore the relationships between the structures of consumerism and the agency of young consumers. My focus, then, is to explore how "mainstream" youth construct their sense of "ordinariness" and to explore how they draw a balance between seeing themselves as relating to societal forces and seeing themselves as independent actors in their own right. The suggestion here is that an empirically informed understanding of "mainstream" young people's relationship to consumption might provide material for understanding what it means to be a young person these days. And simultaneously, conceptualising consumer lifestyles as a means of dealing with the normative demands of individualisation can help us to understand young people's broader relationship with contemporary society.

Methodology

The research followed an interpretive/structuration approach and used diverse qualitative research methods, such as essays written by participants, focus groups and semi-structured interviews in very small groups. The ontology of interpretativism is that the social world is constructed through the shared meanings of actors. The epistemological foundation for knowing such a world is that the researcher is a part of this world of meanings and actions, and therefore has access to it through interpretation and understanding (Silverman 1993; Denzin and Lincoln 1998). My epistemological position was also influenced by a constructivist grounded theory approach to data collection and analysis, which I adopted early on in my research project. This constructivist position questions the theorist's traditional role of an objective observer (Mills et al. 2006) and a co-construction of meanings between my participants and me as a researcher is emphasised throughout the research process. This position made me reflect upon my own underlying assumptions and my intellectual background, and it increased my sensitivity to listen carefully to and to analyse participants' "voices" as openly as possible (Charmaz 2006; Mills et al. 2006). This allowed me to explore and hopefully, to better understand the subjective meanings and interpretations of the lived experiences related to the consumption of young people involved in the research project (Huberman and Miles 2002). Giddens' (1984) structuration approach allows for attention to actions and patterns of action that have the qualities of structure (even if they are not properly external to actors). In the context of my own research, I use an interpretive/structural approach as a bridging perspective that allows me to develop a fuller insight into the meanings young people attached to their consumer practices. Furthermore, I was able to place these meanings within the broader cultural and structural context within which these subjective meanings were framed and shaped.

The initial aim of the research was to build an understanding of the meaning of consumer lifestyles in young people's lives. Special attention was paid to the meanings of brands. I was looking for young people who were active consumers and who were interested in a discussion concerned with consumerism and brands. I was primarily interested in ordinary youth. It can be argued that it is impossible to define what it means to be ordinary in an increasingly de-traditionalised and individualised late-modern society, where traditional structures appear to lose their significance and youth culture itself is characterised by a plurality of lifestyle choices. For the purposes of my project, I framed ordinary youth (or as I prefer, "mainstream" youth) as those young people who were generally missing in Czech youth studies and who were at the same time in these studies labelled as the "mainstream". I was searching for participants who did not declare a strong affiliation to any specific youth subculture on purpose; nor could they be described in terms of totally economically disadvantaged youth groups. One of the criteria of the theoretical sampling was that these young people perceived themselves as ordinary and were also recognised as such by their peers. However, as I realised during the discussions and interviews, their interpretation of normality did not appear to be in contradiction with a variety in their consumer lifestyles in terms of fashion, music, places and leisure activities etc., nor did it mean that they did not have to deal with financial insecurity. Many of them went out clubbing, skated and visited a variety of alternative music festivals. At the same time, they enjoyed shopping at the mall. But such circumstances appeared to be a normal part of their lives.

Table 2-1 Research design

Phase	Method	Participants	Aims
1.	collection of participants' essays	35 young people: 20–24 years	– exploring the meaning of consumption, "exploratory" essays: "When and where did I feel excluded or included based on my image?" and "What does the expression 'cool' mean in contemporary society?" – emergence of the first themes and concepts
2.	6 focus groups	54 young people: 15–27 years	– further exploration of young people's relationships with consumption; discussions on young people's experiences with exclusion and inclusion based on their consumer choices; exploring the meaning of brands – emergence of new themes, saturation of old concepts, discovering paradoxes
3.	2 semi-structured interviews in small groups	6 young people: 19–21 years	– further exploration, exploring the meaning of consumption in the context of young people's lifestyles

The empirical element of the research was conducted in the city of Brno, from 2006 to 2008, with a total of 95 young people, 59 women and 36 men, aged between 15–27 years. The sample included metropolitan youth who were studying, working, or studying and had part time jobs. All of them were active consumers, and their consumer lifestyles in terms of fashion, music, places and leisure activities were diverse.

Findings

The empirical findings indicate that consumption plays a very important role in these young people's lives. However, the role of consumption should not be understood in terms of being the single most important element of their existence, but rather as being a ubiquitous part of their everyday lives. It also appears the young people engaged in this research understood consumption as a means rather than as a source for facilitating who it is they are. These young people did not rebel against consumerism nor did they fulfil the role of the passive victim of a consumer society. Rather, they actively used consumption as a means of negotiating and establishing their place in the social world, as a means of maintaining their relationships to their peers and as a means of locating their own identities. My participants emphasised their need to stand out from the monolithic mass, which they described in terms of "sheep-like" behaviour, and yet they did not consider themselves rebels or radicals. In general, these young people considered themselves normal and ordinary. They constructed their identities around a notion of normality and ordinariness which was not interpreted in terms of being average, but which in practice was linked to notions of one's individuality and uniqueness. And yet, it was again within and through their consumer lifestyles where they felt connected to each other.

The focus on an empirical understanding of the complexities of young people's relationships with consumer culture questions the victim/dupe model which is widely accepted in current Czech youth research on youth consumption, which positions "mainstream" young people as passive consumers (e.g. MŠMT 2007). It also problematises an orthodoxical assumption of the negative impact of consumer culture on young people's values in terms of being one of the key causes of their social-pathological behaviour (e.g. NIDM MŠMT 2000).

My empirical findings suggest that being "mainstream" does not imply straightforward compliance with dominant power structures, but rather it reflects a degree of reflexivity in which young people challenge stereotypes of passive conformism in complex yet often *paradoxical* ways. The paradoxes I found are discussed in more detail in the following sections, in which I examine the reoccurring theme of how the young people in my project used their consumer lifestyles in order to deal with the tensions and normative demands of what appears to be an increasingly individualised society (Beck and Beck-Gernsheim 2002). However, my focus is not only on tensions, insecurities and risks (Macháček 2004; Roberts 2009), but also on new opportunities and choices (Pyšňáková and Miles 2010).

In order to illustrate this point, and in order to establish an empirically based flavour of what constitutes young people's consumer lifestyles in the contemporary Czech Republic, the following sections present an extended analysis of a piece of my qualitative research that looks directly at these issues. In order to discuss the above notions in more depth, I shall now turn to the set of data collated around the "paradox of conforming non-conformity". The paradox of conforming non-conformity focuses on the tensions between the normative demands of what appears to be an increasingly individualised society, as proposed by Roberts (2009) and Macháček (2004), for example, and the ways in which "mainstream" young people endeavour to sustain a sense of their own autonomy and normality whilst dealing with the new constraints arising from the obligation of individually made decisions and choices (Pyšňáková and Miles 2010; Pyšňáková and Hohnová 2010). The paradox of conforming non-conformity started to emerge during the focus group discussions, in relation to a question concerned with the meaning and the role of brands in young people's lives.

Consumerism and Conformism

One of the points I want to highlight at the beginning of this analysis is that many of the young people participating in this project were aware of explicit social pressure, especially when discussing the notion of consumption. It is also essential to note that many of my participants displayed some degree of reflexivity, through which they characterised a particular phenomenon at a particular time. The following discussion of a brand-devotee[6] demonstrates the ability of my participants to link the notion of consumption to a broader context of social and cultural change in the post-revolutionary Czech Republic.

> Zdena:[7] Yeah, I think that these people [brand devotees] are sufficient evidence in themselves of the materialistic values in contemporary Western society. So the emphasis is, for example, on individualism, performance, fame, power and prestige. And there is increasing pressure to be one's self. Sometimes, I think that these kinds of people are not very

---

[6] The expression "brand-devotee" captures the nuanced ways in which young people interpreted the meaning of their own and others' relationships towards the consumption of designer goods. A brand-devoted person was characterised by participants as an individual whose self-identity was constituted through the brand. On the contrary, another expression that my participants brought up during discussions—a "brand-reflexive" person—was defined as an individual who simply does not care. This carelessness does not mean that he or she is a "brand-ignorant" in a sense of lacking the appropriate cultural capital or material resources necessary to purchase designer goods. Neither does it mean that a "brand-reflexive" person would necessarily adopt antagonistic and anti-brand attitudes. Brand-reflexive individuals use consumption as means of displaying their social status based on their ability to make clear that what they decide to consume is a matter of personal choice rather than the product of external pressures.

[7] All names of participants have been changed.

> self-confident. And some of them use brands as a sort of compensation. Well, not everybody who wears designer togs must necessarily use them as compensation to strengthen his [or her] personality. But I believe that for those who are togged out from head to toes in brands it is a means of strengthening their egos. It is a kind of narcissism. And I think that their core values are position, power, prestige, money, performance and success.

Zdena's (27 years) definition of a "brand-devotee" can also be read as a personal disagreement with conformity to a set of prevailing social expectations and social values based on her everyday experience. Zdena's critical perspective on contemporary values such as materialism, power, prestige, performance and success can at the same time be interpreted as a sophisticated critique of ideological aspects of consumption. However, her categorisation is not unproblematic in the sense that, like many other respondents in the project, she is herself an active consumer insofar as she is actively involved in everyday forms of consumption that constitute an important part of her everyday life.

> Zdena: I would say I am more a brand-non-devotee type of a person. It is not important to me. Well, on the other hand, I do not like totally refrain from having some designer togs, and I actually have one or two which I favour. So I am willing to spend some money for it, and I like it, kind of... Yeah, but I would not talk about it a lot, especially not in front of my parents. They think that it is a total waste of money.

In order to justify this fact, Zdena based her argument on the assumption that consumerist values are shallow and devoid of deeper meaning. It does not mean, however, that the meanings and strategies she and other participants deploy in their own consumer activities are superficial. The following discussion from another series of focus groups reinforces this logic.

> Magda: My friend buys clothes only in second-hand shops. It is a matter of principle. She is talented, creative and colourful. She invented her own style this way. You can't see any logos on her clothes, but she is a trendsetter anyway. For example, recently she came up with the idea of wearing beads in her hair. The fact is that she can't afford to buy expensive brands, but she makes no effort to do so anyway. It is just, you know, she is different, her look is so different. But still, she is not the kind of person who would find it difficult to fit into our class at school.
>
> Interviewer: What is important in her life?

> Magda: Freedom. Freedom is extremely important to her. And not being on a leash. And school, I mean education, so she can make something of her life.

Magda's (16 years) emphasis on "freedom" can be interpreted as a key insight into what it means to be a young person at this point in the Czech Republic's history. At first glance, Magda's comment might seem to be contradictory to Zdena's previous critique of the values of the consumer society. Yet a careful reading indicates otherwise and points to similar rather than to divergent opinions. Both of these extracts appear to demonstrate not only an awareness of the norms and dominant values in contemporary society, which are centred on individual freedoms and rights, but also their relative acceptance through having and making individual decisions and choices. In order to understand the paradoxical nature of conforming non-conformity which I propose in this section, the above examples must be read as demonstrations of negotiation between structural conditions and the individual (Giddens 1984).

While analysing my data, the category of *passively conforming "mainstream" youth* presented in several studies on Czech youth (e.g. MŠMT 2007) became problematic, and it appeared to be insufficient and contradictory to my own findings. Focusing on participants' interpretations of their relationships with consumption as a negotiation between structure and their agency, a new interpretation of "mainstream" youth, drawing on a paradox of conforming non-conformity, started to emerge. In order to buttress this argument, it is necessary to embed the research participants' views on consumption in the broader context of late, high modernity (Bauman 2001; Beck 1992; Beck and Beck-Gernsheim 2002; Giddens 1991). Bauman (2001, 2007) suggests that consumer choice represents the basis of a new concept of freedom in contemporary society and that freedom of the individual is constituted in the individual's role as a consumer. From this perspective, identity has become increasingly reflexive and is now actively constructed through privatised patterns of consumption (Giddens 1991). Hence, in reflexive modernity, identity is perceived as to be achieved and worked at individually in the context of relatively freely chosen possibilities.

In this respect, my participants' emphases on individualised consumption can indeed be interpreted as conformity. But we always have to ask—conformity to what? My suggestion is that the above extracts do not demonstrate as much a blind acceptance of the values of consumer society. Rather they point to young people's conformity to the conditions of late modernity in which individually made decisions and choices are not an option but a norm. From this perspective, consumer lifestyles might be an important means of young people's social integration. Indeed, it can be argued that in this context, conformity does not necessarily equate to passivity, but rather it represents a calculative attitude toward one's life (ibid., 1991). From this perspective, the above data demonstrates that an understanding of ordinary young people's daily experience with consumption might be useful for conceptualising the "mainstream" youth as active members of a consumer society.

Reflexive Consumers

The following extract demonstrates that my participants certainly think about self-chosen consumer identities as an important aspect of their personal projects. Adam's reflection on his consumer choices provides an invaluable insight into his experience of what he perceives as being an active agent.

> Adam: My sister is a brand-devotee, in the sense that she has got a little kid and she wants the best for her baby. So she goes only for high-quality brands—not because she is posh, but because she is a caring mum. And I think it is the same with me. I am also, you know, a brand-devotee. For example, I started to buy only bio products, especially food, like free trade coffee at Starbucks, and I also have some T-shirts from eco-cotton. It is like I have the feeling that I can make some difference, like, being ecologically active, you know, like having influence and impact without being a hard-core activist. I think this makes me a brand-devotee. It does not mean that I need designer clothes. Actually If I had some extra money, which I do not have, because all that eco-bio-nature stuff is quite expensive, I might go to Armani and buy something there [laugh].

Adam's (21 years) notion of being a brand-devotee that chooses brands intentionally to reflect his own values appears to demonstrate that consumption plays an important role in his and his sister's lives not because they can "buy" ideal prefabricated identities, but because they feel they are able to construct their own identities as active consumers. Neither of them condemns consumerism, but they use it as a means of constructing their identities as a "good mother" or "an environmentally conscious consumer". This interpretation raises many questions regarding the notion of "mainstream" youth. An examination of how young people interpret their consumer choices as a form of active agency, which at the same time provides them with a feeling of being included in contemporary (and increasingly individualistic) consumer society, provides a lens through which this study seeks to reconceptualise the notion of "mainstream" youth. For example, Adam does not interpret his environmentally conscious consumer choices as a form of radical rebelliousness. On the contrary, during our discussion he himself tries to make clear that behind his consumer lifestyle is no "hard-core activist". It appears that an ability to negotiate his preferences and to make sense of his biographical narrative determines the options he exercises. However, his interpretation also seems to reflect his own internalisation and acceptance of the norms typical of late modern society. For example, he perceives his need to change something and to be influential as something that he does on an individual rather than on a collective level (Beck and Beck-Gernsheim 2009). In other words, Adam feels the need to be responsible for his choices. As our discussion continued, it became obvious that radicalism is not the only extreme which Adam used as a point of reference to distinguish himself.

> Interviewer: So, how come you decided to become an eco-friendly consumer; did your parents raise you that way?
>
> Adam: Actually, no, quite the opposite. My parents buy food in Penny Market. They prefer quantity over quality and basically anything that is on sale, shoes, clothes, everything. Like mum, she does not care what chemicals are in the food she eats. A low price is all that matters. But she is very family-oriented, and so is my dad. I like them very much, but at the same time, they just, hmm, you know, they provoke me. They are ignorant consumers par-excellence. In everything.
>
> Interviewer: What do you mean by that?
>
> Adam: Because her ignorance does not bother her, because she just does not care. I mean, she cares about us, but when it comes to other things, she does not think about her decisions. I think it is because she was raised in a regime where nobody cared and people were passive. And it is not only about not being eco-friendly. It is about her whole lifestyle. And this is what provokes me, like she reads gutter press, like Blesk, and watches commercial Nova [TV channel]. And she could do something about that, but she does not. I think it is a matter of being too lazy to change her easy life.

Adam's reflection demonstrates his awareness that in comparison to circumstances in the former Czechoslovakia, contemporary young people in the Czech Republic experience far more choices than the previous generation. This idea has been articulated in Roberts' (2009) research on contemporary youth transitions in post-socialistic countries. Roberts argues that when it comes to choices, we are not witnessing what is simply a quantitative change, but also a transformation of values, norms and beliefs (ibid., 2009). This appears to be reflected in Adam's interpretation of the generational differences between him and his parents. Their attitude towards consumption appears to correspond with Šafr's (2006; 2008) notion of contemporary generational distinctions caused by an unwillingness of the middle and older generations to cast aside or change their "socialist" habitus. In other words, it is not consumption per se that causes these differences, but different understandings and interpretations of the meaning of consumption. The point I want to make is that Adam's interpretations of his consumer practices point to what Threadgold and Nilan (2009), in their own research on contemporary youth in late modernity, have identified as a "reflexive habitus". In other words, for many young people living under the conditions of late modernity, being reflexive about one's choices becomes habitual (ibid., 54). For example, Adam interprets his mother's consumer choices (such as watching a commercial TV channel and reading gutter press) as unreflexive and passive. As such, his mum represents for him what many of my participants labelled "sheep-like behaviour". In contrast, he perceives his own consumption in terms of permanent (almost habitual) reflexive choices that provide him with a means for active expression of his values and life perspective. He thus perceives himself as a relatively free individual. More importantly, it appears that it is not consumption itself but individualised patterns of consumption which allow him to label other consumers as passive. Adam's case represents what I traced elsewhere during my research. Many of the young participants I interviewed equated freedom with the possibility of making an individual choice. Nika's (20 years) reflection comes from a semi-structured interview in a small group in which I aimed to further explore the meaning of consumption in the context of my participants' consumer lifestyles.

> Nika: It seems to me that today people are wasteful with everything. Terribly. With food, with clothes, with everything. Contemporary society, especially people who have money, consume too much. Our society is, I do not know, it is indeed a consumer society. Yes, this is the right word. People have everything and they appreciate nothing. They take everything for granted, and they have high demands. Our society is more and more demanding.
>
> Interviewer: And how about you?
>
> Nika: Me? I think I fit into this society. Definitely as a consumer. But I am older now, so I think more about what I am doing. Well yes, I love to be dressed according to latest trends, and I am more indolent. But if I tell myself that this is unnecessary—I do not drive a car, for example, and

> instead use public transportation, or I do not buy water in a plastic bottle every day, but I use it and fill it with water from a tap.

The possibilities of personal freedom, based on the fact that they could choose between different options, were fundamental to my participants' beliefs in their own non-conformity, despite the fact that they were active consumers. Accordingly, Adam, like Nika, exhibits a paradoxical form of conforming non-conformity. Their personal investments in notions of freedom are expressed through their active critiques of the very behaviour in which they themselves are engaged. Although my participants were active consumers, this did not mean that they were uncritical, indifferent, ignorant or passive to the conditions that surround them. Like Adam, Nika's ability to be reflexive and critical with regard to her own consumer behaviour allows her to make a difference, through the choices she makes *as a consumer*. She didn't engage in rebellious protest against the consumer society, but rather committed the less visible, but in her eyes, more effective "ordinary" actions as a consumer, such as making the right choice in using public transportation or not buying water in plastic bottles.

I chose these two examples, especially that of Nika, to highlight the fact that young people's relationships with consumption are not only about consumption itself, but about much more complex relationships between them and society. As Nika puts it: "I think I fit into this society. Definitely as a consumer." This quote again raises many questions, especially concerning what it is exactly that young people's relationships with consumption offer them. The suggestion here is that under the conditions of late modernity, which is characterised by plurality of choices, uncertainty and structural constraints, young people seek ways and means that will provide them with a sense that they have control over their lives. Such a feeling appears to emerge through having a choice. And yet, Nika's comment also suggests that being a consumer is not only about spending money but also about feeling less disconnected, and more being a part of this society. Nika's answer gives at least some material for us (youth researchers, especially in the Czech Republic) to rethink not only the meaning of youth consumer lifestyles in young people's lives, but also more generally to rethink what it means to be a young person in the broader context of late modernity (and especially in the contemporary Czech Republic). I propose that the answers to these types of questions lie in researching the everyday experiences of ordinary youth. But these everyday experiences and how young people interpret them should not be analysed in isolation from the broader context of the society in which they live.

The "Sheeple"

The most critical perspectives on passive conformity were articulated in terms of "herd-like" or "sheeple-like" behaviour. The expression "sheeple" is the compression of two words, sheep and people, to form one word meaning a mass of ignorant, unoriginal humans that herd together and follow one another mindlessly.[8]

> Jan: What came to my mind is foolishness and ignorance. Because a certain group of people sets some trends and indoctrinates and infects the rest of society with their ideas. And this part of society takes it. Because they fear that they won't be "in". And they wanna fit in, so they behave like sheep.

My participants brought up many examples of this, ranging from the very abstract to the very concrete. The following series of extracts comes from different phases of my research. All of them capture various representations of what my participants labelled as sheep-like behaviour, a homogeneous group or perceived as trend followers, at the same time demarcating themselves against these particular constructions, despite the fact they themselves were equally active consumers.

> Radek: What has been considered to be "cool" is changing over time. Particularly, in "mainstream consumer society" it is caused by trends. […] However, if somebody would have told us two years ago that this will be in, and we will wear it, we would scoff at him [or her]. Some people have such a compulsive and absurd need to be "cool" that they do not dress according to what they like, but to what is "in". And the most absurd fact is that they identify themselves with a particular fashion trend to such an extent, they start to like it.

This extract is taken from my series of explorative essays on the theme "What does it mean to be 'cool' in contemporary society?" collected in the first phase of the research project. The term "cool" was perceived with noticeable distrust. It encapsulates one of the common themes emerging not only from these essays but also from further discussion in focus group, a criticism of different modes of conformity. The conformists, labelled as a collective of "sheeple", were characterised as people with no personal taste or individuality. Jan's (18 years) and Radek's (22 years) descriptions

---

[8] The expression "sheeple" is borrowed from Urban Dictionary (2010). The English term "sheeple" at best captures the original meaning of Czech word *stádo* [herd] in the context in which it was used by the young people participating in this research project.

of conformity in many respects resembled the ideology and perfectionist critique discussed by academics such as Heath (2001). According to this critique, there is something wrong with what these people want. As such, these "sheeple" have manufactured desires, which means that their needs are actively cultivated primarily through the market and advertising. However, Radek, like all of my participants, was an active consumer. I started to be more sensitive to what precisely it is that this extract criticises. It appears that the subject of criticism is again not consumption itself, but whether people consume actively or passively. Radek's criticism is directed at the people who are not acting or thinking on the basis of their own desires or consideration, but rather according to ideas that have been installed in them (compare Heath 2001). This opinion was also evident in some of the focus group discussions:

> Jan: Who dictates what is and what is not "cool"? Most of people claim that those manipulators are the marketers, who set the latest trends in fashion, design or music style. But I think that the marketers are just testing us. And it is really up to us what we as the consumers accept as being cool. […] But if the majority of us succumb to advertising and media messages and we feel that we cannot live without it, then I am afraid that being cool means being a part of the herd.
>
> Interviewer: So, how do you deal with all this media and ad pressure?
>
> Jan: I guess the best I can do is that I really do not care what is now cool. You know, really, I try to be myself. To me, following what is in and dressing according to the latest trends is a kind of uniformity. I hate uniformity.

The image of a fashion conformist evoked many negative connotations, such as being manipulated, lacking personality or being a follower—an uncreative, superficial and shallow person. And yet paradoxically, despite this critique of contemporary society, the overriding message emerging during the course of these discussions was the personal desire to be a self-directed individual. In this context, the sheeple equates to a monolithic conformist mass not so much in terms of an absence of rebelliousness as an absence of individuality.

> Šárka: I think the worst brand-devotees are those who must feel they are cool all the time. This is a general expression, but I would suggest that it means that they need to fit in and so they accept and endorse only that what has been given to them on a silver platter right under their very nose. And so they go to Palace Cinemas. And basically, they just consume what they consider to be attractive and trendy.

Interviewer: Who is it that serves all these ideas on a silver platter?

Šárka: Media. MTV for example, and consequently everybody wants to be a hip hopper. I know a couple of people, who look like that, you know like the hip hoppers, but they just like this style. But you know, they are not just the followers, when they watch TV it is not like, "Oh my god I saw it on MTV so I must have this bling bling jacket." I do not know; it is really hard to explain the difference, but when, for example, my friends buy something in a hip hop style it is not only a stylisation into hip hop style. For example, Mark combines it with other styles, so in the end, it is about him. He is not shocking; he looks smart and causal at the same time. It just suits him. He is really a trendsetter. I think it is also because he just thinks about it.

There was an extensive discussion within my focus groups of the issues associated with conforming to the expectations of the wider community and the importance of wearing clothes that were deemed to be "acceptable". My participants were all too aware that clothes are used not only as material symbols of our economic, social and cultural roles in society, but also as a symbol of in-group membership. However, Šárka's (17 years old) comments are interesting with regard to how she uses different interpretations of young people's engagement with popular culture. In the broader context of living in a consumer culture, she makes a distinction between two types of conformity. The first one is defined as an unreflexive following of what is popular. In her view, in order to be popular, some young people are influenced by words and images, which are used by advertisers to jointly construct imaginary or heavily idealised worlds or "lifestyles". And yet, on the other hand, her reflection about her friend Mark provides us with a particularly useful insight into how young people can use consumer conformity in creative ways and for their own ends. She points towards her friend, who despite outwardly acting as a trend follower, does not actually succumb to the norms of a particular popular style (hip hop); but uses this source as an inspiration for mixing it with other items. His consumption simply does start and end with the act of purchasing. He buys different pieces of clothing, mixes them and creates a new look, a new image which is neither too extravagant nor too shocking, but which earns him (as Šárka mentioned) recognition and credit amongst his peers. It is through his reflexive choices that he is able to accentuate rather than lose his individuality. And this is what Šárka appears to value in him. It is not a rejection of what is popular, but further creative engagement with what consumer culture offers to him. In other words, this extract reflects the fact that young people understand and use what common culture offers them as a source of their cultural capital and they use it for their own ends.

A note with regard to my participants' reflexivity on mass media and marketing influences needs to be made. What all of the above extracts demonstrate is that my participants embody a particularly reflexive attitude of "I know what is going on" in terms of being aware of media and advertising influences. However, they do consume just as much as their friends. I concur with the commentators who suggest that young people's engagement with consumer culture does not mean that they automatically fit into the categories of the passive victims of consumer society or "consumer dupes" (Miles 2000; Nava and Nava 1992). However, as my own research did not principally focus on this issue, I do not want to underestimate the power of media and marketing industries and their strategies of influencing young people's choices. Young people are influenced by media and marketing industries, yet it appears that they do not consume these meanings uncritically and unreflexively. Arguing that young people are totally immune from the influence of the above industries would be as strong and as radical a claim as saying that "the mainstream of the young generation is to a large extent manipulated by the media and accepts the opinions and positions generated by them" (MŠMT 2007, 5). The truth lies somewhere in between. The critical perspectives on media influence and marketing strategies occurring among a majority of the young people participating in this research project and the complexity of meanings presented in their consumer choices represent at least a call for rethinking the academic orthodoxy prevailing in some Czech youth studies, especially the construction of passive, un-reflexive and manipulated "mainstream" youth (MŠMT 2007).

Neither the Sheep, Nor the Rebel

Regarding the negative conception of young consumers towards the notion of a brand-devotee, or towards sheep-like behaviour, it became obvious that its meaning was dependent upon a broader context, whether the individual used brands as a source or as a means of identity construction. The following discussion examines how much young people's mainstream lifestyles play a role in their self-construction and how young people relate to other young people through consumer lifestyles.

> Interviewer: So what about brands? Would you consider yourself as a brand-devotee type of person?

> Lenka: Definitely yes! I love brands. But I don't buy any special hip-hop brands. I prefer more commercial ones, such as Nike and Adidas, because I can mix them in a way [that] I look more like a street dancer. So I buy T-shirts and trousers in XXL size. I am definitely not into brands that are popular in hip-hop culture [...] I like a kind of extravagant look, but I hate to be a "cookie-cutter". I mean, I hate to look like every second girl.

This discussion with Lenka (21 years) raises some important issues. First of all, what appears to be at stake is an individual attitude and the need for autonomy. But here it is again looking at what an active engagement with consumer culture offers them. None of my participants could be said to be fully emancipated from consumption; their identities are rather mediated to different degrees through their consumer choices. At the same time, these young people by no means behave like unreflexive consumers; their demand for authenticity (in Lenka's case given to products through experimentation with a look) was one of the primary criteria underlying their taste preferences. Placing emphasis on one's autonomy appeared to provide my participants with self-confidence whilst also helping them to judge their friends, or in general, their contemporaries. What follows now is a discussion on how Lenka uses the cultural capital gained from her lived experience in a consumer culture and uses it further for her own ends.

> Interviewer: So can you tell me what street dance means to you?
>
> Lenka: Well, it is like I have to look cool, definitely when I teach in the class. I want to get my students inspired. You know, there are a lot of other dance schools, so I need to keep my customers interested [laugh]. So I try to invent my own street dance look. I tried to copy something from MTV clips, you know. But it does not fit here. Those clips are full of girls in bling bling jackets and tops, and also that American lifestyle in those clips is just too American. But when I buy Adidas and Nike and mix it, I can inspire my students. They can go to those stores and try to do the same thing. Makes me feel good. Makes us feel connected.

The above extract can be read as an example of how Lenka uses her cultural capital based on her experience of being an active consumer. She actively uses and combines both mainstream and spectacular/subcultural styles as a source of inspiration and as a means for inventing her own style around which she constructs her identity. As an active member of the contemporary consumer culture, she indeed appears to amass a certain kind of cultural capital. In a sense, her knowledge of what is "in", what "fits in the local context" as much as her criticism and personal taste makes Lenka an expert on the street dance style. The way in which she is expressing her identity indeed resembles what Willis calls symbolic creativity and grounded aesthetics at play (Willis 1990). Moreover, her active engagement with consumer culture appears to provide her with self-confidence. She enjoys being an inspiration for her students. What appears to be crucial for her is emphasising her own individualised consumption. As such, she does not follow the trend as a whole, but chooses, picks, processes and changes different pieces taken from different popular styles in order to create her own. However, this new style was not spectacular, nor shocking, but smart and sophisticated, focusing on small details which makes her look unique. More importantly, this style still fits into her narrative of who she is.

The above extract reflects the complexity of lifestyle choice. For her, such a lifestyle reflects not only her passion for dance and black music, her hobby and experimenting with clothes, but simultaneously a means of making a living—it became her part-time job, which she enjoys. As such, it does not appear that for my participants, consumer lifestyles presented a "freely chosen game" which "should not be confused with the way of life", as suggested by Bennett (1999, 607) or Muggleton (1997), who asserts that the contemporary identity construction of a postmodern consumer is all about a playful use of images. For Lenka, her consumer choices represent an important means of expressing her individuality as far as they appeared to her to be her own decisions. How far her choices were genuine is a matter of question. I suggest that Lenka's focus on her individuality reflects an acceptance of the norms in late modernity. And this is the paradox of conforming non-conformity. Lenka's example demonstrates that it is within her consumer lifestyles where she can feel connected to her friends, feel creative and individualistic and yet, she needs to also feel as if she is not being excluded from mainstream society. The following comment on the double meaning of the mainstream, taken from a focus group discussion, adds further weight to this argument.

> Pavlína: I think human beings are full of paradoxes. At least I am. I used to identify myself with a psychedelic trance dance culture. But my membership was actually ambivalent. I did not feel like I am a psy-trance as a whole. In many ways, I was actually conforming to mainstream society and its values. For example, I got a masters degree at the university. I had a part-time job during my studies, a very nice flat, and I paid taxes. Normal life. But I nevertheless did not feel like I fully fit into mainstream society. And I guess it is because I understand mainstream in two ways. And so it depends in which sense I am talking about mainstream. In a pejorative sense, mainstream means to me a gray monolithic crowd, average, and conformity, no provoking. Total fitting in. But I also understand mainstream in a more positive sense, like not being

so shocking and so individualistic and having values typical for our society, normal lifestyles.

Interviewer: Do you feel that you have to choose between these two lifestyles?

Pavlína: No, I actually think that it is possible to balance between these extremes. You do not have to be either a sheep or a radical. I think today it is pretty much normal to fit into society and yet be different.

The above extract tells us something about the conflicting and confusing nature of young people's everyday experience and the need to balance the tensions which appear to be a normal part of living under the conditions of late modernity. From Pavlína's (27 years) interpretation, it appears that being a part of the mainstream society does not have to always represent total conformity, but rather it reflects the construction of a "normal" and balanced life. This issue has been further explored in other group discussions in which I focused on how the young people in my research project interpreted their consumer choices in order to construct their sense of normality.

Marika: Sometimes, I have a feeling, when I watch TV or read magazines; that I have only two options of who to be. Like two extreme poles, either a herd-like obedient sheep—but this is what nobody wants to be, so the option in order to not become a sheep is acting or dressing or shocking individualistic behaviour. Everything that is between—normal behaviour, dressing or acting normally—is, according to this logic, considered not to be cool.

Marika's (21 years) critical comment demonstrates that not everything that is "in between" is automatically rejected by young people. What is at stake here is again the question of being oneself. What makes individualistic behaviour truly individualistic is not extremeness, but rather being oneself. The following discussion with Daniel (21 years) and David (22 years) elaborates the issue of what my participants considered being "normal" and how they themselves maintained their sense of normality.

Daniel: Well, I guess that I am quite normal [laugh all]. I mean brands do not bother me as much, but I have some favourites; of course, I do. I am not an anti-consumer. Like the punks. Sometimes I wish I could say I fight against consumer lifestyles and consumer society, it would be cool, or maybe not, but it is simply not the truth. I think you need to find a balance. This is what I think is normal.

David: I think that being normal does not mean being average. I think there are so many fashion styles today, that you do not have to be extreme and to shock and still you can be really outside of that hard-core mainstream. You know, like you do not rebel, but not totally conform.

The above extracts demonstrate that young people in general tend to establish both—their feeling of belonging to the mainstream, and at the same time a sense of their authenticity and individuality (Miles 2000). Of a particular interest is David's notion that "being normal does not mean being average". This notion is developed in the following extract taken from a group discussion. As I will show, young people tend to challenge the conventional dress code (typical for the norms of a particular setting), but never to such an extent that would be beyond acceptable and normal in the given context. However, this does not mean that young people do not find space for creative expression and for an exploration of these boundaries. The following discussion on the dress appropriate code for a typically formal event, such as going to the theatre, is a good example.

Interviewer: Have you ever bought some clothes in order to fit in?

Katka (17 years): Yes, for an occasion such as the theatre or a dance class. But everybody does it. I personally do not know whether it is better to keep this dress code, or to be more relaxed and casual.

Milan (18 years): I like when you keep a dress code. It is like another world. I personally feel like a celebrity while wearing a suit. And it is a part of that atmosphere.

Katka (17 years): Yeah, slightly-prim atmosphere [laugh]. But kind of ceremonial, people feel extraordinary…

Dáša (16 years): Yeah I know what you mean. You wear jeans normally, and sometimes you get tired of all those different styles you see at school. But when you go to a theatre, everybody gets dressed up. It is kind of being uniform, I know, but still, it happens so rarely that it is somehow amazing. I think it is cool, seeing my classmates in suits and dresses and high heels. Everybody is in a trance. We all feel somehow extraordinary.

Milan: I really like being dressed in a suit. It does not happen every day. But at the same time, I like to add something to it. Something slightly provocative, but not too much. But more in a sense of being hip. Last time I had this combination, a black classy suit, white shirt and Converse shoes. Black Converse shoes. No let me put it this way, footwear in slightly punk-style [laugh]. And I felt great!

It appears that despite their tendency to consume individualistically, the young people in my focus group enjoy an occasional conformity to the norms. This extract also demonstrates how young people use their cultural capital creatively. For example, Milan's (18 years) notion of wearing Converse shoes in a punk-style does not appear to violate the norms of a formal dress code. On the contrary, it appears that this is an example of what Willis (1990) calls symbolic creativity. Milan changes the meaning of the dress code for this occasion and simultaneously, he gives a new meaning to punk shoes. However, this is a long away from rebellion. And even Milan does not seem to intend to be provocative, but prefers rather to stimulate others and himself as well. It also appears that his ability to sustain a balance between formal norms and the expression of his individuality gives him a feeling of pleasure and satisfaction.

The Pros and Cons of Social Change

Although the above extract suggests that consumption provides young people with the means of maintaining their sense of balance between what they perceived as normal and unacceptable, my data also demonstrate that life in contemporary consumer society can sometimes represent a disorientating experience for many of the young people I interviewed. To understand this contradiction we need to again interpret the above data in a broader context of living under conditions of late modernity. This is partially because my participants' experiences are different from those of their parents when they were young. My participants had no, or very limited, personal experience of life under socialism, but they are told about what it was like. They know that living twenty years ago would have meant having little choice or control over their lives. Today, they live under circumstances offering them comparatively unlimited choice. Yet it does not mean that they have genuine control over their lives. Macháček (2004), Roberts (2009) and other commentators argue that young people in post-communist countries live under conditions which offer them significant options in domains of life where there used to be no options: what kind of education to get, what kind of job to have, whether to marry or have children, all become a matter of a personal choice (Pyšňáková and Miles 2010). Indeed, not only can people now choose, but they are encouraged to do so. Throughout the course of this article, I have focused on the paradoxical nature of conformity in late modernity, on its pros and its cons and how this paradox is reflected in "mainstream" youth's day-to-day lived experiences. And the same paradox can be applied to the notion of choice. My participants were aware of their contradictory experiences with reality, as despite being encouraged to be, or at least to believe they can be, who they want to be, they had to often face many constraints. However, despite its paradoxical nature, it is nonetheless certain that having choice in itself represents a remarkable shift in the experience of contemporary young people in the Czech Republic.

> Jan: I think that what has changed is that people are more used to diversity. Like when I put my weird hat on and go to the city, many people in the street just don't care. I mean they look at me, but they are not shocked. So I wear a weird hat, but I don't feel like I am a weirdo [laugh]. I think people started to perceive that change and diversity is something more natural.
>
> Interviewer: And what do you really love about living in today's society?
>
> Lenka: Extravagance. Finally, people have started to experiment a bit more. I mean like with fashion. It feels good; I cannot imagine living in a grey, dull world. I mean, lots of buildings are still grey, and people have frowning faces. And you still have to deal with lots of problems in your life, school, work, relationships. Lots of responsibility. Nobody tells you what to do. But my theory is that if everybody would wear a red jumper and yellow pants, or something like that, the world around us wouldn't seem so serious [laugh].
>
> Interviewer: And what you don't like?
>
> Lenka: Hmmm, poseurs. And overcrowded malls. [laugh]. And stress. But in many respects, I think I fit into the group of consumers. Well, I spend an awful lot of money on clothes, brands and cosmetics. But you know, it is a matter of the heart. Actually, I haven't realised how much I am dependent on shopping until this year. Shopping comforts me. It's my relaxation, my addiction, and I like it. And Nika [Lenka's friend] likes it as well.

The above extracts reflect that in contemporary Czech society, consumption is increasingly an arena within which emotions and rationality are combined. As Lenka (21 years) pointed out, however short-lived the experience of pleasure in a consumer society might be, for young people in that moment such pleasure is not illusory; it feels real and, as such, it is real. What appears to be important is that indeed the ubiquity of choice and the need to take full responsibility for such can be for many Czech young people today potentially as stressful an experience as having limited choice. Lenka's comments on how she copes with the problems in various areas of her life and how she perceives all that responsibility on her shoulders to be normal, tells us a lot about the everyday experiences of contemporary young people in the Czech Republic. The above quote suggests that young people appear to accept the condition of late modernity in which living with uncertainty on a daily basis has become a norm. However, despite that fact, Lenka appears to be an exemplary case of a person who seems to conform to this cultural norm; she does not seem to take a passive stance. It is within the context of her consumer practices that she is able to actively negotiate and deal with the circumstances of the conditions she is exposed to. In this sense, it might be suggested that many young people are attracted to consumption for its apparently positive and soothing effect.

Common Biographies

The above extracts might imply that consumer lifestyles represent for young people nothing more than a form of escape from the cruel reality of the social world. However, this final section attempts to demonstrate that consumer lifestyles mean something more to young people than just running away from reality.

Interviewer: Can you tell me what you really like about contemporary society?

Marek (20 years): I don't know. Really I don't know… Maybe that today's people have more opportunities and freedom. You know you can choose. Like 20 years ago, people would say: Jeeeeesus, I cannot afford it. I mean not only because they didn't have money, but because it was not available. Because many things just did not exist here. And I like that people started to take care of themselves, especially in regard to fashion. You know, they are not wearing the same pair of jeans and old T-shirt all the time. But I don't know, even older people look younger and youthful. And maybe it is not just because of their clothing; maybe it is also an attitude.

Filip: Yeah, It might sound weird, but my parents don't know how to dress. So my sister and I showed them how to look better. It was actually by chance. Nothing planned. Once, sis and I went to a skate shop to buy some jumpers and T-shirts, and our parents went with us. And I said: Mum, dad! Try this! And they put on T-shirts with crazy pictures on them but my parents looked just great [laugh].

Interviewer: So you shared your knowhow with your parents?

Filip: [laugh] It was actually fun, but also a great feeling. You know usually it is like your parents tell you what you should do. But this was the reverse. Teaching my parents felt good [laugh]. But I mean mum and dad look really great.

This extract shows again that despite young people often lacking economic capital, such a disadvantage can be compensated to an extent through their cultural capital. In relation to their parents, being in the know as to what is in, what looks good, what is the difference between brands, and why a particular brand might be socially significant, is all knowledge that makes young people in many regards *cultural experts* in the area of consumer culture. And it also seems that this is expert knowledge that matters to contemporary youth, because, as Filip (16 years) mentions, it provides an occasion and an arena within which they can be taken seriously. From this perspective, consumption gives young people the opportunity to actively experience their autonomy and equality. Consumer lifestyle as an arena of shared experiences was one of the frequent themes among my participants. The general feeling among the young people I interviewed was that, although they want to be independent individuals, by no means did they prefer living in isolation; on the contrary, friendships played a key role in their lives, and in this context, consumption served as an arena of shared experiences and feelings.

Eva (17 years): I think friends are really important. They influence us in everything, not only in brand choice. But on the other hand, it is still possible to have one's own individual style. I have a very good friend and we really understand each other, despite having totally different tastes and styles. When we go out, I take my jumper, jeans and trainers and she goes in her high-heeled shoes and mini-skirt, but we get along with each other perfectly. Sometimes we argue about our styles, but it's a part of our friendship. We actually respect each other's style. Yeah, we truly get along with each other perfectly, even through brands and clothes.

The suggestion here is that however much young people feel the need to differentiate themselves, they are united through the common biographies made available to them through consumption, and in this sense, they are emotionally connected to others through consumption. As one of my participants put it:

Patrik (18 years): Yeah. Sometimes I walk down the street and I see a person with the Koss headphones, and I see how he gives himself airs and graces. So I must laugh at him. Because Koss is cheap rubbish. But if I see a person with unknown, Japanese Stax, I know that he invested into something that is not trendy. Which is unknown yet of a high quality. So I would stop him and start chatting about music. And even for 12 hours, cos we will have something in common. This is my experience.

This connection provides an invaluable means by which young people can negotiate a period of rapid social change. It is in this regard that the focus on the more ordinary, or as I prefer "mainstream", youth and their relationship with consumer lifestyles might provide us with a useful lens for understanding what it means to be a young person today. The ordinary provides a means by which young people cope with the extraordinary rapidity of social change.

Discussion

This article put forward the proposition that an empirical understanding of the "mainstream" youth, particularly as it is manifested through consumer lifestyles, may provide an effective means by which youth researchers, and sociologists of youth in the Czech Republic in particular, can more effectively understand Czech young people's relationship with the key elements of social change. The suggestion underlying this proposition is that consumer lifestyles help young people amass resources (Giddens 1984) for successful integration into what has been described as an increasingly risky society (Beck 1992; Beck and Beck-Gernsheim 2002). Furthermore, such lifestyles may well play a particularly prescient role in what continues to be such a transient and relatively uncertain period in Czech history. My intention, however, is not to put researching young consumer on a pedestal within the youth research agenda in the Czech Republic. Neither am I suggesting that consumption is the most important element in young people's lives. However, as my data suggest, researching young people's relationship to consumption is sociologically relevant, because consumption constitutes a ubiquitous and natural part of their day-to-day experience. And this has been underestimated in contemporary youth research in the Czech Republic. Thus, the notion of "mainstream" youth provides a particularly useful lens for understanding the conflicting nature of young people's experiences in a risk society on a day-to-day basis. Researching the meaning of consumer lifestyles might be significant for understanding how young people actively deal with the conditions of late modernity. From this perspective, a vital part of the re-conceptualisation of "mainstream" youth involves going beyond equating them with a homogeneous group or using this expression as a label, but rather to understand it as a lived experience. My research offers an insight thanks to the young people who were willing to share with me their interpretations of what it means to be a young person in contemporary society. Their openness allowed me a partial understanding and knowledge of their day-to-day experience of living under the conditions of late modernity, with all of its pros and cons. The concept of "mainstream" youth which I propose in this article challenges the taken-for-granted representation of mainstream youth in terms of being a passive and conforming majority.

One of the aims of this article was to discuss the paradox of conforming non-conformity and its relevance for the concept of "mainstream" youth. Drawing on theories of late modernity (Giddens 1991; Beck 1992; Beck and Beck-Gernsheim 2002), the paradox of conforming non-conformity captures the tensions between the normative demands of what appears to be an increasingly individualised society and the ways in which "mainstream" young people endeavour to sustain a sense of their own autonomy, individuality and normality. In late modernity, it is suggested by commentators such as Giddens (1991), Beck (1992) and Beck and Beck-Gernsheim (2002) that individuality, self-responsibility and the active management of one's biography is not a choice, but rather an obligation. According to Giddens, one risk in late modernity is for people to lose their self-identity and self-confidence, as these present the most important competencies of social integration in late modernity. This article examined how young people participating in my research project used their consumer lifestyles as a means of social inclusion under the conditions of late modernity.

My participants were undoubtedly active consumers. This should not, however, imply that they simply accepted the nature of the consumer society. Their emphasis on individual consumption and the choices they made as consumers made them feel as if they were not participating in what they call "sheep-like behaviour". Heath and Potter (2005) argue that this is exactly what contemporary late modern conformism is, as capitalist society enforces conformity through emphasising one's individuality, especially through the consumer market. Mainstream culture becomes about maintaining a distinct cultural identity (ibid.). However, many of the young people I interviewed were critical about consumption and they were well aware of the influences of media, advertising and marketing industries on their own consumption patterns.

This situation appears paradoxical. Rather than conformity, I suggest framing young people's relationships with consumption as a "paradox of conforming non-conformity". The young people in my study criticised certain aspects of consumer society, such as blindly following trends, passive consumption of media or obsession with brands. However, at the same time, they themselves are active consumers. My data suggest that young people use consumption as a means of dealing with everyday aspects of social change. As such, it seems that a rebellious approach to consumption would jeopardise their own sense of belonging to a society (Pyšňáková and Miles 2010). As one of my participants put it, "I think I fit into this society. Definitely as a consumer." They used their own conformity reflexively and for their own ends. It was their active engagement with consumer culture which provided them with a sense of being relatively free agents. They used this conformity creatively. Combining different items implied further symbolic work with the meanings of the items which they purchased, and sometimes it involved inventing their own styles. However, their active involvement with consumer culture provided my participants with something more than just a new look. It was through their consumer lifestyles that they related to each other, shared something in common, getting self-confidence and also recognition from their peers. The suggestion is that consumer lifestyles help young people amass resources (Giddens 1984) for successful integration to what has been described as an increasingly risky society (Beck 1992; Beck and Beck-Gernsheim 2002). Furthermore, such lifestyles may well play a particularly prescient role in what continues to be such a transient and relatively uncertain period in the Czech Republic's history.

From this perspective, it can be argued that although young people appear to conform to the conditions of late modernity, such conformism does not necessarily represent passivity, but a form of active agency and a calculative attitude to one's life (Giddens 1991). It is in this sense that an examination of the consumer lifestyles of ordinary youth might challenge the taken-for-granted assumption, generally evident in the Czech sociology of youth, that young people have an unreflexive and passive engagement with consumption. In the context of youth research in the Czech Republic, it is suggested that a focus on the "mainstream" youth might offer a perspective, or a useful lens, on young people, as it allows us to focus upon the ways in which they are blending old and new patterns of identity construction and are actively shaping new approaches to life. From this perspective, it is also suggested that an empirically informed understanding of young people's relationships to consumption might provide a means of understanding the social and cultural implications of the post-socialist transition on young people in the Czech Republic and a useful lens for understanding how they interpret, construct and maintain their sense of belonging to contemporary society. My data suggest that in the Czech Republic, young people's use of consumption serves not only as an arena of self-expression that was previously unavailable, but also as a means by which they actively navigate their way through a life experience that appears to offer choice and yet simultaneously constrains such choice. It is within the context of consumer practices that young people are able to actively negotiate and deal with the circumstances of the conditions they are exposed to.

References

Bauman, Zygmunt. 2001. *The Individualized Society.* Cambridge: Polity.

—. 2007. *Consuming Life.* Cambridge: Polity.

Beck, Ulrich. 1992. *Risk Society: Towards a New Modernity.* New Delhi: Sage.

Beck, Ulrich, and Elisabeth Beck-Gernsheim. 2002. *Individualization: Institutionalized Individualism and Its Social and Political Consequences.* London: Sage.

—. 2009. "Global Generations and the Trap of Methodological Nationalism For a Cosmopolitan Turn in the Sociology of Youth and Generation." *European Sociological Review* 25 (1): 25–36.

Bennett, Andy. 1999. "Subcultures or Neo-Tribes? Rethinking the Relationship Between Youth, Style and Musical Taste." *Sociology*, 33 (3): 599–617.

Brown, Phillip. 1987. *Schooling Ordinary Kids: Inequality, Unemployment and the New Vocationalism.* London: Tavistock.

Brubaker, Rogers. 2002. "Ethnicity Without Groups." *Archives Européennes de Sociologie* 43 (2): 163–189. http://works.bepress.com/wrb/7.

Charmaz, Kathy. 2005. "Grounded Theory in the 21st Century: Applications for Advancing Social Justice Studies." In *The Sage Handbook of Qualitative Research*, edited by Norman K. Denzin, and Yvonna S. Lincoln, 507–535. Thousand Oaks: Sage.

—. 2006. *Constructing Grounded Theory: A Practical Guide Through Qualitative Analysis.* London: Sage.

Denzin, Norman, K., and Yvonna S. Lincoln, eds. 1998. *Strategies of Qualitative Inquiry.* London: Sage.

France, Alan. 2007. *Understanding Youth in Late Modernity.* Buckingham: Open University Press.

Giddens, Anthony. 1984. *The Constitution of Society: Outline of the Theory of Structuration.* Cambridge: Polity.

—. 1991. *Modernity and Self-identity: Self and Society in the Late Modern Age.* Cambridge: Polity.

Griffin, Christine. 1993. *Representations of Youth: The Study of Youth and Adolescence in Britain and America.* Cambridge: Polity.

Heath, Joseph. 2001. "The Structure of Hip Consumerism." *Philosophy & Social Criticism* 27 (6): 1–17.

Heath, Joseph, and Andrew Potter. 2005. *The Rebel Sell. How the Counterculture Became Consumer Culture.* Chichester: Capstone.
Hollands, Robert. 2002. "Divisions in the Dark: Youth Cultures, Transitions and Segmented Consumption Spaces in the Night-time Economy." *Journal of Youth Studies* 5 (2): 153–171.
Huberman, A. Michael, and Matthew B. Miles, eds. 2002. *The Qualitative Researcher's Companion.* London: Sage.
Jenkins, Richard. 1983. *Lads, Citizens, and Ordinary Kids: Working-class Youth Life-styles in Belfast.* London: Routledge & Kegan Paul.
MacDonald, Robert, and Frank Coffield. 1991. *Risky Business? Youth and the Enterprise Culture.* Basingstoke: Falmer Press.
Macháček, Ladislav. 2004. *Youth in Slovakia and European Identity.* Bratislava: Institute for Sociology of Slovak Academy of Sciences. http://www.vyskummladeze.sk/images/stories/iuventa/DAVM_003/pdf/YOUTH_and_Identitty.pdf.
Miles, Steven. 2000. *Youth Lifestyles in a Changing World.* Buckingham: Open University Press.
Mills, Jane, Ann Bonner, and Karen Francis. 2006. "Adopting a Constructivist Approach to Grounded Theory: Implications for Research Design." *International Journal of Nursing Practice* 12 (1): 8–13.
MŠMT. 2007. *State Youth Policy Conception for the Years 2007–2013.* Praha: MŠMT. http://www.msmt.cz/mladez/state-youth-policy-conception-for-the-years-2007-2013.
Muggleton, David. 1997. "The Post-subculturalist." In *The Clubcultures Reader: Readings in Popular Cultural Studies*, edited by Steve Redhead, Derek Wynne, and Justin O'Connor, 167–185. Oxford: Blackwell.
Nava, Mica, and Orson Nava. 1992. "Discriminating or Duped? Young People as Consumers of Advertising/Art." In *Changing Cultures: Feminism, Youth and Consumerism*, edited by Mica Nava, 171–183. London: Sage.
NIDM MŠMT. 2000. *Mládež na prahu 3. tisíciletí.* Praha: NIDM MŠMT. http://www.vyzkum-mladez.cz/zpravy/1135332867.pdf.
Pilkington, Hilary. 2004. "Youth Strategies for Glocal Living: Space, Power and Communication in Everyday Cultural Practice." In *After Subculture: Critical Studies in Contemporary Youth Culture*, edited by Andy Bennett, and Keith Kahn-Harris, 119–134. Basingstoke, New York: Palgrave Macmillan.
Potůček, Martin et al. 2002. *Průvodce krajinou priorit pro Českou republiku.* Praha: Guttenberg.

Pyšňáková, Michaela, and Barbora Hohnová. 2010. "Od monolitické masy k neomezenému individualismu? Význam spotřeby v každodenním životě 'mainstreamové' mládeže." *Sociologický časopis* 46 (2): 257–280.
Pyšňáková, Michaela, and Steven Miles. 2010. "The Post-revolutionary Consumer Generation: 'Mainstream' Youth and the Paradox of Choice in the Czech Republic." *Journal of Youth Studies* 13 (5): 533–547.
Roberts, Ken. 2009. *Youth in Transition: Eastern Europe and the West.* Basingstoke: Palgrave Macmillan.
Roberts, Steven. 2011. "Beyond 'NEET' and 'Tidy' Pathways: Considering the 'Missing Middle' of Youth Transition Studies." *Journal of Youth Studies* 14 (1): 21–39.
Šafr, Jiří. 2006. "Sociální třídy a (ne)okázalá spotřeba v ČR 2004." Paper presented at the conference *Sociální reprodukce a integrace: ideály a meze*, Institut pro výzkum reprodukce a integrace společnosti, Fakulta sociálních studií Masarykovy univerzity, Brno, November 9–10.
—. 2008. *Životní styl a sociální třídy: vytváření symbolické a kulturní hranice diferenciací vkusu a spotřeby.* Praha: Sociologický ústav AV ČR.
Sak, Petr. 2000. *Proměny české mládeže.* Praha: Petrklíč.
Sak, Petr, and Karolína Saková. 2004. *Mládež na křižovatce.* Praha: Svoboda Servis.
Sassatelli, Roberta. 2007. *Consumer Culture: History, Theory and Politics.* London: Sage.
Shildrick, Tracy. 2006. "Youth Culture, Subculture and the Importance of Neighbourhood." *Young* 14 (1): 61–74.
Silverman, David. 1993. *Interpreting Qualitative Data. Methods for Analysing Talk, Text and Interaction*. London: Sage.
Slater, Don. 1997. *Consumer Culture and Modernity.* Cambridge: Polity.
Smolík, Josef. 2010. *Subkultury mládeže. Uvedení do problematiky.* Praha: Grada Publishing.
Šťastná, Lenka, and Matúš Šucha. 2010. *Drogy a ohrožené skupiny mladých lidí.* Praha: Centrum adiktologie, Psychiatrická klinika, 1. lékařská fakulta, Univerzita Karlova v Praze.
Threadgold, Steven, and Pam Nilan. 2009. "Reflexivity of Contemporary Youth, Risk and Cultural Capital." *Current Sociology* 57 (1): 47–68.
Truhlářová, Zuzana, and Martin Smutek, eds. 2006. *Riziková mládež v současné společnosti.* Hradec Králové: Katedra sociální práce a sociální politiky Pedagogické fakulty Univerzity Hradec Králové.
Urban Dictionary. 2010. "Sheeple." Accessed October 3. http://www.urbandictionary.com/define.php?term=sheeple.

Vanžurová, Lenka. 2006. "Příčiny krizového chování mladé generace." In *Riziková mládež v současné společnosti*, edited by Zuzana Truhlářová, and Martin Smutek, 82–86. Hradec Králové: Katedra sociální práce a sociální politiky Pedagogické fakulty Univerzity Hradec Králové.
Willis, Paul. E. 1990. *Common Culture: Symbolic Work at Play in the Everyday Cultures of the Young*. Buckingham: Open University Press.
Wyn, Johanna, and Rob White. 1997. *Rethinking Youth*. London: Sage.

SUSTAINABILITY AND THE "URBAN PEASANT": RETHINKING THE CULTURAL POLITICS OF FOOD SELF-PROVISIONING IN THE CZECH REPUBLIC

PETR JEHLIČKA AND JOE SMITH

Introduction

The system changes in 1989–1990 that saw the end of state socialism in Central and Eastern Europe (CEE) and the initiation of what has widely been figured as a "transition" coincided with a high-tide mark for discourses of sustainable development within international political discourses. The UN Earth Summit of 1992 proclaimed sustainable production and consumption as key areas for attention.

Food systems are a prominent feature of these discourses about progress towards sustainability. The impacts associated with production, distribution and consumption and waste were all identified as requiring urgent attention in Western societies. While agro-industrial efficiency has long been seen as one component of sustainable food systems, more recently there have been efforts—such as those within the UK Transition Town movement—aimed at the promotion of food self-provisioning as a form of sustainable production and consumption.

Given the concurrence of the "transformations" in CEE with the dramatic explosion of mainstream political enthusiasm for "sustainable development" it might have been expected that, as part of CEE countries' accession to the European Union (EU) the policy community in CEE and EU institutions might have paused to reflect on those aspects of CEE societies that sustained or nurtured sustainable societies, in particular those aspects of transport and food provision that Western societies were seeking to advance. These included extensive collective transport systems and relatively high rates of walking and cycling in the transport sector and dramatically higher rates of food self-provisioning in the food sector.

Alber and Kohler's (2008) Europe-wide research shows that, with a few exceptions, the proportion of the population in west European countries growing their own food does not exceed 10%. By contrast between 35 and 60% of the population in CEE countries grow some of their own food. But rather than being studied and protected by an EU whose constitution was the first in the world to integrate sustainable development as a goal, or by CEE polities that were designed at precisely the time that international political community was casting around for "paths to sustainability" these practices were ignored or met with disdain. "Plan SAPARD—The Plan for the Development of Agriculture and the Countryside for the Period 2000–2006" prepared in 2000 by Western consultants under the auspices of the EU-sponsored Programme SAPARD[1] for the Czech Ministry of Agriculture and Ministry of Regional Development is a case point. On three occasions the document mentions food self-provisioning, always in a negative light:

> Ineffective self-provisioning habits (eggs, poultry, potatoes, vegetables, fruit) hang over from the past, which contributes to the relatively low purchasing power of the countryside (Ministerstvo pro místní rozvoj a Ministerstvo zemědělství 2000, 18).

> Food self-provisioning, which provides households involved in this activity with a basic livelihood, can sometimes contribute to decline and exclusion (ibid., 43).

> Statistics do not include occasional self-provisioning carried out by rural populations, the unemployed, women and the retired (ibid., 53).

Research in this field has more often than not followed these readings, framing these practices as backward, and contrasting them with Western modernity. Food self-provisioning is read as an index of path dependency, an economic coping strategy or as a faintly embarrassing cultural remnant. The chapter will track back to see how CEE food self-provisioning has come to be understood as a survival strategy of the poor. We identify entrenched Western readings of Eastern Europe and specific developments in post-socialist Russia as being significant. Over a century of "othering" of Eastern Europe has combined with a more recent Western myth of the Russian "urban peasant". Despite the lack of evidence or justification we argue that these framings have proven influential in shaping interpretations of CEE food self-provisioning in policy and academic discourses.

---

[1] SAPARD stands for Special Accession Programme for Agriculture and Rural Development.

Far from being a necessity, our case shows how self-provisioning is rather a complex bundle of practices that hold cultural and social significance that far outweighs economic explanations. These practices support and are supported by extensive networks based in sharing. Food hence reinforces community and family bonds and cooperation. We find it interesting, and of significance to sustainability debates in Western Europe and North America, that sustainability is clearly not a motive for these growers and sharers, despite the fact that there are clearly substantial environmental benefits that can result. We conclude the chapter by proposing that the new framing of food self-provisioning in CEE we present is of significance to sustainability debates far more widely. By contrast with technocratic or constraining accounts of sustainability the food culture we explore points to an attractive, exuberant and socially inclusive version of sustainability.

Urban Peasants? Othering the East

The notion of food self-provisioning as survival strategy had its origins in survey data that showed that two-thirds of Russian households, 48% of Polish households, and 62% of Bulgarian households grew some of their food in the years immediately after the end of state socialism (Clarke et al. 2000; Rose and Tikhomirov 1993). It is worth noting that we do recognise that there are circumstances where food self-provisioning is one element of a coping strategy for the lowest income groups in CEE countries, and that this involves a blurring of boundaries between capitalism "and its outsides" (Smith and Stenning 2006). Smith and Rochovská:

> emphasise the continuing importance of the economic practices of food production in both providing resources for domestic consumption and, in doing so, enabling other engagements in the formal economy—such as higher expenditure—than might otherwise be possible (Smith and Rochovská 2007, 1174).

Nevertheless, the media have tended to tell the story of this "economy of jars" (Cellarius 2004) purely in terms of the "rise of the urban peasant". This representation has fed directly into public policy, such as the structuring of social assistance provision funded by the World Bank's loan in Russia (Clarke et al. 2000). The highly influential Western consultants who did so much to shape the post-socialist "transition" tended to view post-socialist societies as an undifferentiated mass (a "bloc"). Their prescriptions for treating the patient assumed not just Eastern otherness, but also backwardness, and food self-provisioning was considered a marker of this.

Influential research in public policy, development and economics (e.g. Rose and Tikhomirov 1993; Seeth et al. 1998; Alber and Kohler 2008) followed the same lines. Alber and Kohler (2008) drawing on Rose and Tikhomirov's (1993) used a Europe-wide survey of 27 countries to conclude that CEE food self-provisioning was a coping strategy with direct descent from the socialist past. We want to suggest however that to portray CEE food self-provisioning as anti-modern and as a survival strategy is both inaccurate, and potentially very harmful to attempts to promote more sustainable food systems. We want to draw attention to the fact that self-provisioning by CEE household food systems can and should be respected both as a valid form of modernity, and one with substantial claim to being much more sustainable than its Western variants.

A starting point for understanding the limited vision that we are critiquing is to recognise the maintenance of a mental separation of Europe and Eastern Europe. Kuus (2004) identifies an orientalist discourse founded in an assumption of an essential difference between Europe and Eastern Europe. Such othering of Eastern Europe has long influenced the construction of European identity, with the region being figured as "not yet European". Wolff (1994) points to more than two hundred years of "advice" flowing from West to East. Kuus finds that these portrayals do not dismiss Eastern Europe out of hand "as irredeemably alien but as halfway house between Europe and Asia" and that "Eastern Europe was not simply backward, but a learner, an experiment and testing ground" (2004, 474). These accounts are not held only outside the region, but also widely shared in CEE societies. The collapse of state socialism in Eastern Europe in 1989 served to dramatically reinforce the region's latent status, and its role as needy recipient of Western advice:

> In the early 1990s, East-Central Europe was indeed not upgraded but "downgraded" in the scale of development. It was no longer treated as a second world—antagonistic but capable of industrial innovations—but as a variant of third world and hence a space under Western tutelage (Kuus 2004, 475).

Hence where we have approached CEE's cultural politics of food as being a resource of ideas and practices of value to any pursuit of social and ecological sustainability the dominant regional and Western accounts of the same have been at best dismissive.

The trope of the urban peasant supports the representation of food self-provisioning as backward and anti-modern. The figure of the peasant has long troubled attempts to give account of social progress and the development of capitalism. Leonard and Kaneff (2002, 6) suggest that peasants "embody a mode of production and a way of thinking that was felt to be antithetical to capitalist and socialist development alike". Food self-provisioning in CEE countries does not equate to professional farming. Nevertheless, the association with cultivation, growing and sharing and barter is strongly redolent of peasant practices and offers the "modernisers" a short step to the generation of negative representations of food self-provisioning.

Despite the dominance of economistic and Western framed and focused accounts of appropriate development path alternative approaches to research have worked to explore food self-provisioning via more cultural informed approaches to understanding habits, practices and identities. These have tended to be based upon qualitative research at the "micro" level, most notably social anthropology. These less deterministic approaches are showing results that contradict the previously accepted explanations.

Anthropologies of Food Self-provisioning

The high levels of food self-provisioning and sharing of fruit and vegetables in CEE have consistently puzzled researchers both during (Gábor 1979; Hann 1980) and after the state socialist period (Sik 1992; Skalník 1993; Czegledy 2002; Torsello 2005; Acheson 2007). Acheson's (2007) work on household food production and exchange networks in Slovakia between 1993 and 2006, noted that the phenomenon could be considered to be anomalous, given that exchange networks are a feature of tribal and peasant societies, and are not anticipated in a modern industrial society such as Slovakia. She concluded that these exchanges are motivated by a mixture of altruism and self-interest. They embody egalitarianism and some deeply rooted moral norms, including the stigmatisation of self-centredness and the promotion of mutual help and sharing. Similarly Torsello's (2005) research conducted in a rural Slovak village showed how food self-provisioning plays a role in creating and maintaining strong ties between kin members and friends by establishing mutuality, reciprocity, task sharing and trust.

In similar vein anthropologist Snajdr's (2008) research into the relationship between Slovak urban dwellers and their access to gardens on the fringes of cities shows how, on these:

> tiny garden plots, which were often within sight of a factory or along railroad tracks, they grew a variety of vegetables, fruits, and herbs [...]

> Most gardens included small *domčeky* or *chaty* [cabins] that were built by the owners. Gardens [...] were often quite elaborate, with trestles supporting grape vines, or rows of slender fruit trees so skilfully pruned that their curling branches formed a virtual wall along the footpath. If a family did not own a garden plot themselves, they had access to one through relatives. Whether elaborate or bare bones, these private spaces were visited frequently, to tend to vegetables, have a family cook-out, or throw a small evening party. The garden was a sanctuary, if only for a few days, that provided relief from the city and from the system (Snajdr 2008, 34–35).

Snajdr quotes Paulina Bren's conclusion that cottage culture "thrived on the fantasy of the weekend getaway as a private retreat where one was left to one's own devices" (Bren 2002, 127; quoted in Snajdr 2008, 35).

This point allows us to dwell on what we think is one of the most important "exportable" findings about food and sustainability in CEE. Where Acheson and Torsello focus on how familial obligation plays a role in supporting self-provisioning, Czegledy's interpretation of Hungarian food self-provisioning and sharing allows pleasure to play a more central role. Home grown food and drinks (including wine and fruit brandy) are shared with guests and friends. This sharing celebrates the relationship of hospitality, but it also serves as an opportunity to appreciate the time, effort and skills invested in growing and preparation. Sharing these goods is to share "a distinct colour, a specific texture, and certain taste" that shop-bought produce cannot offer (Czegledy 2002, 213). Enthusiasm for these appears to relate to how they can support a reaffirmation of cultural identity and help people to cope with the unrootedness of international capitalist production (ibid., 214).

We want to go further than these anthropological studies and propose that these practices have far wider significance in pointing to some of the ways that sustainable practices might be valued and nurtured elsewhere.

Food Self-provisioning as a Sustainable Practice: The Czech Evidence

We cannot argue for food self-provisioning as a leading sustainability practice without demonstrating that it is not a coping or even survival strategy, as Rose and Tikhomirov 1993, Seeth et al. 1998 and Alber and Kohler 2008 have posited. Our counter-argument is drawn from the findings of long-term qualitative and quantitative research (2004–2010) into household food production conducted in Czechia. Our conclusions fall more closely into line with Czegledy's (2002) than Acheson's or

Torsello's. Where their work was based in anthropological qualitative research in a single or a small number of locations we have combined quantitative surveys of a representative sample of the Czech population with a limited number of in-depth interviews. These interviews have been conducted in a range of places from the national capital to a small village. Our goal with this mixed methodology approach has been to derive from the qualitative data underlying motivations and to probe causalities and explanations behind some of the data gathered in quantitative surveys.

The research characterises Czech household food production as primarily a voluntary activity imbued with deep social and cultural meanings and associated with feelings of exuberance, joy and a sense of achievement rather than with constraints, necessity and a sense of obligation. On the basis of three surveys of representative samples of the Czech population (2005, 2009 and 2010) we are convinced that 15–20 years after the fall of the Czechoslovak communist regime food self-provisioning should not be understood as a "coping strategy of the poor". Our evidence comes most directly from the reasons identified for self-provisioning by the respondents to the 2005 and 2010 national surveys. On both occasions, the main reason was not financial saving (which in 2005 came only as the third and in 2010 the fourth most important reason), but fresh food (the first reason in both 2005 and 2010) and secondly food self-provisioning was valued as a hobby (the second reason in both surveys). The third reason given in 2010 was "healthy food".

We were able to investigate these findings further via in depth interviews. The respondents consistently placed emphasis on "healthy food" which to them primarily meant food grown with no or limited use of pesticides and other industrially produced chemicals and which contain, as a result, the least possible residua of industrially produced chemicals:

> It's more like organic farming. We use almost no chemicals. We fertilise the garden with rabbit manure. And we hoe up weeds, for that we don't use any chemicals (Interview, Polička, 4/4/2005).

> The reason why we grow our own food is that we do not use any sprays. Yes, the fruit is spotty, it certainly does not look like the fruit in shops. We are now running out of our own apples, so I wanted to buy some in the shop but my husband said: "Don't buy those chemical balls" (Interview, Stěžery, 29/3/2005b).

> We can buy food with chemicals in shops. The point of growing food at home is to do it without chemicals (Interview, Stěžery, 29/3/2005a).

The notion of healthiness is related to food's provenance and freshness:

> When I grow that tomato in my own garden, I consider it to be healthy (Interview, Stěžery, 29/3/2005b).

> My family grows food because it's fun and because it gives us fresh food (Interview, Polička, 5/4/2005).

Self-provisioning of a range of commodities is very high compared, for example, to West European rates. The February 2005 survey showed that among productive gardeners about two thirds of the consumption of currants, strawberries and apples is accounted for by people's own production (see Table 3-1). These productive gardeners also emphasise the natural state of their produce, and the absence of additives, for example:

> The non-alcoholic cider we make from our apples is without added sugar. It is something different to the cider bought in shops. Ours is naturally sweet (Interview, Pardubice 30/3/2005).

Table 3-1: Proportion of self-grown produce in the total gardeners' household consumption of the fruit or vegetable (%) as reported by respondents to the February 2005 national survey

Fruit or vegetable	Percentage	Fruit or vegetable	Percentage
Currants	73	Carrot	52
Strawberries	68	Plums	49
Apples	62	Onion	44
Cherries	55	Potatoes	44
Tomatoes	53	Pears	41

These results are confirmed in more extensive official data (see Table 3-2 & 3-3). The Czech Statistical Office carries out an annual survey of household budgets using a quota sample of 3,000 households that is representative of the Czech population. One category of data gathered within the framework of household budgets is "consumption in kind". This denotes consumption of food that is not purchased but is either provisioned within the household (self-provisioning, foraging berries and mushrooms) or obtained as a gift. Hence consumption in kind does not equate with volumes of food produced by households, but the majority of the food in this category is the result of self-provisioning.

Although in the last decade the trend in the overall volume of consumption in kind has been mildly declining, this non-market source of food is still highly significant. In 2007, consumption in kind accounted for

34% of the overall consumption of fresh fruits in Czech households (restaurants and canteens are excluded from this statistics), 32% of eggs, 27% of potatoes, 24% of lard and 22% of vegetables (Štiková, Sekavová and Mrhálková 2009). In terms of absolute indicators of consumption in kind, the data for Czech households in 2010 were as follows (in kg per person per year): potatoes 12.5 (15.4 in 2000), fresh vegetables 8.2 (12.9 in 2000), fresh fruit 11.1 (22.0 in 2000); and 67 eggs per person per year (71 in 2000). The figures for fruit and vegetables are affected by weather conditions—consumption in kind of fresh fruit in 2010 was markedly lower (11.1 kg per person per year) than the previous year (16.7 kg) (Štiková, pers. comm., October 3, 2011).

With the exception of apple trees and sour cherries, the proportion of the number trees in households is higher than in the commercial sector (between 50% [currants] and 96% [gooseberry and walnut trees]). In terms of the volume (tonnes) of produced fruits, with the exception of apples and sour cherries, Czech households produce over 80% of the domestic production of all fruit commodities.

Czech households account for 30% of the total area used for growing vegetables in the country, commercial farmers account for 70%. In terms of the volume of produced vegetables, Czech households produce more than 50% of the following commodities grown in the country: strawberries, kohlrabi, pickled cucumbers, cucumbers, tomatoes and garlic, ranging from 50% (tomatoes) to 95% (garlic).

The data on living standards and income levels helps us understand who is growing this food and why. It is striking to us, given the dominant framing of these practices, that it is economically secure rather than insecure households who are predominantly growing their own food. For instance, 48% of respondents who indicated in 2010 that the living standard of their households was "good" (44% in 2005), are self-provisioning, whereas the percentage of respondents from households whose living standard was "neither good, nor bad" and from households with a "bad" living standard, were 43 and 33% (42 and 35 in 2005). Similarly, the most affluent quartile (according to household income declared by respondents) in the 2010 data contained 41% self-provisioners and in the second highest quartile the figure was 46%. In the lowest quartile, the rate of self-provisioning was 34% and in the second lowest it was 43%. Table 3-4 shows that in the second half of the 2000s more than 40% of Czech households were growing food to eat and share.

Table 3-2: Czech households producing fruit

Fruit	Proportion of households with fruit trees		No trees in Czech house-holds	Harvest of fruits in Czech house-holds (in tonnes)
	Percentage of all households which grow their food	Percentage of the total number of households		
Apple trees	81.3	32.5	7,157,000	127,871
Pear trees	42.7	17.1	1,061,000	10,675
Peach trees	30.5	12.2	125,000	16,209
Apricot trees	28.4	11.4	998,000	17,056
Plum trees	43.5	17.4	713,000	30,289
Other types of plum trees	32.2	12.8	983,000	10,652
Cherry trees	46.7	18.7	1,031,000	13,213
Sour cherry trees	22.9	9.1	469,000	3,564
Currant trees	71.8	28.7	4,631,000	8,884
Gooseberry trees	41.1	16.4	1,421,000	2,057
Walnut trees	30.2	12.1	755,000	9,211

Source: Czech Statistical Office, 2006

Despite the fact that the poorest in Czech society appear to be growing less, the fact that around a third of the lowest quartile are self-provisioning demonstrates that this remains a socially inclusive activity. This also applies to educational levels: respondents with the lowest (9 years of school attendance up until the age of 15) and with the highest (university degree) educational level were equally likely to grow their food; 35% of these respondents declared in 2005 that they did so. The percentages of respondents with secondary education, without and with the school leaving exam (usually taken at the age of 18), growing their food were also similar: 45 and 44% respectively. There is also fairly even distribution of the practice across urban and rural areas: of the respondents, self-provisioning takes place in villages (65% of our 2005 respondents living in settlements with less than 2,000 inhabitants grew their food), in mid-size towns (41%) yet also in the capital Prague, albeit at reduced rates (21%). We know from the qualitative research that some households do not grow food in their primary dwelling, but rather in gardens at their recreational cabins and cottages. The social inclusiveness of self-provisioning is an essential component of our argument that these practices promote both social and ecological principles of sustainability, including the strengthening of local bonds of trust (Smith and Jehlička 2007) beyond family relations.

In terms of environmental sustainability, barter or gifting of self-provisioned food serves as a way of distributing surplus production which might otherwise go to waste. The Czech household interviews from 2005 established that there was a lot of barter going on:

> I have plenty of eggs and rabbits and it is quite unhealthy to eat too much of these. As I have a lot of friends, I give a couple of eggs or a rabbit and exchange them for, say, lettuce and other vegetables or for leftovers which I then feed to the rabbits (Interview, Stěžery, 29/3/2005).

This is going on through family and friendship networks in large cities as much as rural areas. Furthermore both urban and rural dwellers forage for wild berries (for example bilberries and alpine strawberries) and mushrooms. When explaining the role of foraging, self-provisioning, allotments or smallholdings, people emphasised that these practices "help to sustain dense webs of connection between the rural and urban in ways that are now comparatively rare in Western Europe" (Jehlička and Smith 2011, 367) (confirming Stenning 2005, 122–123):

> We grow leek, lettuce, radish, peas and spinach... Some fruits do not grow well here, so we get it from relatives, from my mother-in-law, or we bring it from Moravia. Apricots and plums. We have relatives there, so we go there quite regularly. I make compotes. This year [I made] about 15 kg [of compotes], I freeze some of it and I also made marmalade this year. We also grow tomatoes-we have plenty-and also cucumbers... My mother-in-law lives 5 km away from us and there are slightly different climate conditions, so they have cherries, pears that we do not have because the conditions here are not favourable to them (Interview, Polička, 4/5/2005).

Table 3-3: Czech households producing vegetables

Vegetable	Proportion of households with land for growing vegetables		Total area for growing vegetables in Czech households (in hectares)	Harvest of vegetables in Czech households (in tonnes)
	Percentage of house-holds which grow their food	Percentage of the total number of households		
Potatoes	46.3	18.5	8,523	144,440
Strawberries	72.0	28.2	1,972	15,429
Root celery	35.1	14.0	207	3,238
Carrots	59.2	23.7	556	8,789
Root parsley	42.4	17.0	282	2,977
Kohlrabi	41.0	16.4	349	5,847
Sprout	12.4	5.0	71	1,185
Cauliflower	9.0	3.6	81	1,262
Cabbage	14.2	5.7	200	5,113
Pickled cucumbers	45.4	18.1	1,151	19,529
Cucumbers	39.6	15.8	383	10,295
Tomatoes	68.5	27.4	1,042	23,120
Onion	53.2	21.3	735	9,489
Garlic	22.4	9.0	301	1,982
Garden pea	34.3	13.7	327	1,497
Lettuce	13.2	5.3	93	1,553
Radish	8.6	3.4	34	410
Peppers	19.5	7.8	246	3,501
Courgette	16.3	6.5	308	7,453
Green bean	8.6	3.4	83	605
Other	5.7	2.3	53	118
Herbs	6.2	2.5	28	119

Source: Czech Statistical Office, 2006

Table 3-4: Percentages of respondents growing some of their food in the Czech Republic

Country	1991	2003	2005	2009	2010
Czechia (Czechoslovakia)[a]	70[a]	30	42	43	43

Sources:
1991: Rose and Tikhomirov (1993)
2003: Alber and Kohler (2008) (our reading of the chart in the article)
2005 and 2010: National surveys commissioned by us
2009: National survey conducted by Median Agency

Only one respondent out of 15 household interviews was not involved in such networks of food exchange. The exchanges are not restricted to extended families: neighbours, friends and co-workers frequently participate. The 2010 interviews gave us a chance to probe the extent and meaning of sharing and barter further. They provided rich evidence:

> We consume the produce from our garden when it's fresh, and all surplus is preserved as marmalades, jams and syrups. And we have so much that we don't manage to preserve everything: we give it to friends and other people including work colleagues (Interview, Dolánky, 12/11/2010).

> When you have, you give (ibid.).

> We don't have cherries, but we don't buy them. We usually get them from friends… We don't have plums either, but I almost never buy them. I get them from friends (Interview, Boskovice, 20/11/2010).

> When I have a surplus of, say lettuce, I give it to the (extended) family, to my female colleagues at work (altogether fifteen per cent) and a small part (five per cent) for sale in the shop of the Gardeners' Union (ibid.).

> It is not a (formalised) exchange. It depends on what people have, and they simply suggest in a conversation—"would you be interested?" (ibid.).

> Why don't I sell all the surplus? I have friends who I know will be pleased to get apples for free. I do not need to profit from this… (ibid.).

> We don't buy pears—the family helps each other. We get pears. And sour cherries we get from our neighbour's garden, so although we don't have our own, we do not buy them (Interview, Boskovice, 21/11/2010).

> [Exchanges are not organised], it's quite random, when something ripens and becomes available, when people have enough of it, so they give each other a ring… (ibid.).

> For example, we send something to my brother-in-law in Litomyšl, or sometimes we exchange things, he sends us cucumbers and we send something else in return (Interview, Telecí, 21/11/2010).

> For example, there was a lot of plums this year. So I gave some to my (female) colleagues at work. They were pleased and cooked plum dumplings… (Interview, Prague, 8/11/2010).

> There was a huge boom of cucumbers in the summer, so I picked them and took them to work… I did not want them to go to waste… (Interview, Prague, 6/12/2010).

The amounts that self-provisioners give away varies: 26% of growers give away less than 10% of their produce; 30% of growers give away 11–50% of their produce and 4% give away more than 50% of their produce. Forty per cent of growers do not give away anything. But it should be noted that some respondents do not consider sharing their produce with the family (daughters etc.) to be sharing. These findings confirm Acheson's (2007) research in eastern Slovakia (undertaken in 1993 and 2006). Although these networks around growing and sharing were well-established during the state socialist period (Torsello 2005), they pre-existed state socialism (Acheson 2007). The fact that they have been very resistant to change in the years of the post-1989 social and economic transformation in some senses provided the starting point for our research. We want to suggest that, by reinforcing family and community networks in ways that are not reliant on the formal economy or on the consumption of material goods, these practices serve a body of social as well as environmental dimensions of sustainability.

The perishability of much produce offers at least part of the reason for the high levels of sharing, but not all. Acheson's Slovakian research (ibid.) showed that exchanges were not confined to self-provisioned food, but that they also involved goods purchased in shops or commodities to which they have special access. People also exchanged labour, for example when building a house. The same practices were revealed in our 2005 interviews. The sharing and exchanging of food, and other commodities and services may be rooted in shared but implicit norms around egalitarianism and the negative perception of selfishness and self-centredness. We sense that further focused research into the positive associations people hold regarding mutual help and the sharing of resources will be productive and important.

Another area that we feel would benefit from further research is the analysis of the environmental benefits of household food production. This is not easy, nevertheless even on the basis of our work to date we feel there are reasons to be confident that in comparison with conventional food marketing home-growing results in significantly reduced environmental impacts (Jehlička and Smith 2011). We knew from both the 2005 and 2010 surveys and the in-depth interviews of 2005 that most growers valued chemical-free cultivation (hence the emphasis on healthy food). Our 2010 survey addressed these environmental dimensions directly. The results confirmed that in terms of pesticide and fertiliser inputs and in terms of transport energy intensity in production and sharing, food self-provisioning greatly reduces the environmental impact of the food system (Jehlička and Smith 2012).

We want to suggest that one of the reasons this may be interesting and important is precisely the fact that these environmental virtues go unmentioned by the self-provisioners. This hints at one of the reasons why it may be that the promotion of environmentally beneficial behaviours has often proven difficult when they are presented in these terms, rather than being justified by reference to other or wider social norms or benefits.

Elsewhere we have explored in some depth the puzzle as to why the sustainability policy communities at local, national and international levels have failed to protect, promote or even acknowledge these sustainability-compliant practices in the development of policy initiatives (ibid.). Our purpose in this chapter has been to further explore the data on self-provisioning to demonstrate its extent and socially inclusive and diverse nature. All of this data points to the potential for self-provisioning to continue to play an important role in environmental protection and social solidarity. However we want to go further and suggest that it serves as an exemplar that other developed world societies can study and seek to follow.

Conclusion

When international (i.e. Western) academia has approached the evidence of widespread household food production in post-socialist societies their accounts have tended to be subject to several myths about Eastern Europe. Development, social policy and economics disciplines (with their close links to policy worlds) have represented self-provisioning practices not as leading exemplars of localised food production and social capital, but rather as backward anomalies that need to be "brought in line" with Western trajectories of development. They have occurred in the "wrong" place, and have to some degree originated in the "wrong" time.

We have drawn on work conducted by social anthropologists and on our own quantitative and qualitative research in Czechia to challenge this account. Our findings demonstrate that people's self-provisioning is a component of their own construction of modernity, and one that valorises historical and cultural references that have been otherwise erased in the aggressive pursuit of "transition". Western official environmental policies, as well as environmentalist movements such as Transition Towns all promote self-provisioning as one strand in the development of a more sustainable society. Yet in Czechia the proportion of self-provisioners exceeds that in Western Europe by several factors. Rather than seeking to depict these sustainable practices as backward to make them fit with the stereotypical image of Eastern Europe, we argue that this model should be nurtured, promoted and transferred to new social contexts.

Bockman and Eyal argue for a more open sense of the flow of ideas and policies in terms of understanding neoliberalism and post-socialism. They propose that:

> it is impossible to divide this transnational dialogue into an active, Western "author" of neoliberal ideas and policies and a passive, East European "recipient". Neoliberalism was not simply disseminated from West to East, but was made possible and constructed through the dialogue and exchanges that took place within this transnational network (Bockmann and Eyal 2002, 311).

In similar, but far more positive, vein we propose that the "actually existing sustainability" demonstrated in the resilient high levels of self-provisioning and gifting/barter in CEE countries can and should form part of a flow of ideas and experiences from East to West.

Most obviously these practices help to reduce the environmental impact of food systems. The percentages of production in some categories (e.g. soft and orchard fruits) demonstrate how self-provisioning can make a substantial contribution to the reduction in food miles, packaging and industrial agricultural inputs, even in a country that is capitalist, "modern" and, in the consultants and economists' terms "post-transition". The socially diverse make-up of these self-provisioners shows that these are practices that are not driven by economic need.

On the contrary: our evidence points to these practices fulfilling a broader body of social benefits, including the expression of moral norms (Acheson), and enjoyment at cooperation and interaction with other people through food (Czegledy). To understand, protect and extend these practices requires some practical policy measures, including planning protection for allotments and productive gardens, but it is also necessary to engage with the underlying norms that seem to be supporting them. These include the stigmatisation of selfishness and the extolling of mutual help and sharing. In other words food self-provisioning, despite its outward appearance as a "trivial" individualised and inner-directed hobby, seems to directly relate to the tending and nurturing of values that are of great significance to any discussion of how developed world societies might become more sustainable.[2]

References

Acheson, Julianna. 2007. "Household Exchange Networks in Post-Socialist Slovakia." *Human Organization* 66 (4): 405–413.

Alber, Jens, and Ulrich Kohler. 2008. "Informal Food Production in the Enlarged European Union." *Social Indicators Research* 89 (1): 113–127.

Bockman, Johanna, and Gil Eyal. 2002. "Eastern Europe as a Laboratory for Economic Knowledge: The Transnational Roots of Neoliberalism." *American Journal of Sociology* 108 (2): 310–352.

Bren, Paulina. 2002. "Weekend Getaways: The Chata, The Tramp, and the Politics of Private Life in Post-1968 Czechoslovakia." In *Socialist Spaces: Sites of Everyday Life in the Eastern Bloc*, edited by David Crowley, and Susan E. Reid, 123–140. London: Berg Publishers.

Cellarius, Barbara A. 2004. *In the Land of Orpheus: Rural Livelihoods and Nature Conservation in Postsocialist Bulgaria.* Madison, WI: The University of Wisconsin Press.

Clarke, Simon, Lena Varshavskaya, Sergei Alasheev, and Marina Karelina. 2000. "The Myth of the Urban Peasant." *Work, Employment and Society* 14 (3): 481–499.

[2] Acknowledgments: We wish to thank Jiří Vinopal for advice concerning the construction of the Czech national survey questionnaires, the Public Opinion Research Centre (CVVM) in Prague for conducting the 2005 and 2010 surveys and Tomáš Kostelecký for assistance with the analysis of the survey results and for conducting some of the interviews. We gratefully acknowledge research funding support from the Open University's Department of Geography and OpenSpace Research Centre as well as from the Czech Science Foundation via grant No. 404/10/0521, entitled *Environmental Values, Beliefs and Behavior in the Czech Republic in Historical and International Perspective.*

Czech Statistical Office. 2007. "Zemědělská produkce domácností v roce 2006." http://www.czso.cz/csu/2007edicniplan.nsf/t/7C002F5667/$File/213207a02.pdf.

Czegledy, Andre. 2002. "Urban Peasants in a Post-Socialist World: Small-Scale Agriculturalists in Hungary." In *Post-Socialist Peasant? Rural and Urban Constructions of Identity in Eastern Europe, East Asia and the Former Soviet Union*, edited by Pamela Leonard and Deema Kaneff, 200–220. Basingstoke and New York: Palgrave Macmillan.

Gábor, István R. 1979. "The Second (Secondary) Economy." *Acta Oeconomica* 22 (3–4): 291–311.

Hann, Chris M. 1980. *Tázlár: A Village in Hungary.* Cambridge: Cambridge University Press.

Jehlička, Petr, and Joe Smith. 2011. "An Unsustainable State: Contrasting Food Practices and State Policies in the Czech Republic." *Geoforum* 42 (3): 362–372.

—. 2012. "Shelf Life: Food and the Politics of Sustainable Consumption." In *Atlas: Geography, Architecture and Change in an Interdependent World*, edited by Renata Tyszczuk, Joe Smith, Nigel Clark, and Melissa Butcher, 56–63. London: Black Dog Publishing.

Kuus, Merje. 2004. "Europe's Eastern Expansion and the Reinscription of Otherness in East-Central Europe." *Progress in Human Geography* 28 (4): 472–489.

Leonard, Pamela, and Deema Kaneff. 2002. "Introduction: Post-Socialist Peasant?" In *Post-Socialist Peasant? Rural and Urban Constructions of Identity in Eastern Europe, East Asia and the Former Soviet Union*, edited by Pamela Leonard and Deema Kaneff, 1–43. Basingstoke and New York: Palgrave Macmillan.

Ministerstvo pro místní rozvoj a Ministerstvo zemědělství. 2000. "Plán SAPARD: Plán rozvoje zemědělství a venkova České republiky na období 2000–2006." http://eagri.cz/public/web/mze/dotace/dobihajici-a-ukoncene-dotace/sapard/programove-a-jine-dokumenty/plan-sapard.html.

Rose, Richard, and Yevgeniy Tikhomirov. 1993. "Who Grows Food in Russia and Eastern Europe?" *Post-Soviet Geography* 34 (2): 111–126.

Seeth, Harm T., Sergei Chachnov, Alexander Surinov, and Joachim von Braun. 1998. "Russian Poverty: Muddling Through Economic Transition with Garden Plots." *World Development* 26 (9): 1611–1624.

Sik, Endre. 1992. "From the Second Economy to the Informal Economy." *Studies in Public Policy*, no. 207. Glasgow: Centre for the Study of Public Policy, University of Strathclyde.

Skalník, Peter. 1993. "'Socialism Is Dead' and Very Much Alive in Slovakia: Political Inertia in a Tatra Village." In *Socialism: Ideals, Ideology and Social Practice*, edited by Chris M. Hann, 218–226. London: Routledge.

Smith, Adrian, and Alena Rochovská. 2007. "Domesticating Neo-liberalism: Everyday Lives and the Geographies of Post-socialist Transformations." *Geoforum* 38 (6): 1163–1178.

Smith, Adrian, and Alison Stenning. 2006. "Beyond Household Economies: Articulations and Spaces of Economic Practice in Postsocialism." *Progress in Human Geography* 30 (2): 190–213.

Smith, Joe, and Petr Jehlička. 2007. "Stories around Food, Politics and Change in Poland and the Czech Republic." *Transactions of the Institute of British Geographers* 32 (3): 395–410.

Snajdr, Edward. 2008. *Nature Protests: The End of Ecology in Slovakia.* Seattle, WA: University of Washington Press.

Stenning, Alison. 2005. "Postsocialism and the Changing Geographies of the Everyday in Poland." *Transactions of the Institute of British Geographers* 30 (1): 113–127.

Štiková, Olga, Helena Sekavová, and Ilona Mrhálková. 2009. *Vliv socio-ekonomických faktorů na spotřebu potravin.* Praha: Ústav zemědělské ekonomiky a informací.

Torsello, Davide. 2005. "Neviditeľné základy dôvery. Domáca produkcia, práca a výmena na slovenskej dedine." *Slovenský národopis* 53 (1): 5–18.

Wolff, Larry. 1994. *Inventing Eastern Europe: The Map of Civilization in the Mind of the Enlightenment.* Stanford, CA: Stanford University Press.

MULTIPLEXES AS THE LIMES OF "GLOBAL HOLLYWOOD"

MARCIN ADAMCZAK

Welcome to "Global Hollywood" or After "the Last Picture Show"

The film studies of the 1990s brought many voices about "the death of cinema" threatened by the new media that drove away filmgoers and undermined the economic stance of the film industry. The metaphor of "the last picture show" from Bogdanovich's movie was frequently referred to in such opinions. It seems from the perspective of the end of the first decade of the 21st century that the rumours about "the death of cinema" can still be treated as exaggerated. The title of an edited collection published a few years ago and devoted to the American cinema of the 1990s is quite characteristic for the current situation of the Tenth Muse. The editor of the volume chose the title *The End of Cinema*, but he supplemented it with the following subtitle written in smaller letters *As We Know It* (Lewis 2001). Indeed, it may be the end of cinema as we know it, but not the end of cinema in general.

As compared to other visual arts, cinema seems to have always undergone faster changes and transformations. Stylistic conventions and the language of artistic expression have evolved faster in accordance with the dromologic nature of this medium. However, it was the institutional and market circumstances of the Tenth Muse that transformed particularly rapidly in the last two decades of the 20th century. The changes were significant enough to justify a thesis that the cinema after 1980 has been "something else", something significantly different from the cinema of the 1960s, for example. The transformations pertained to its language, reception practices, consumption models, and especially the film market, the character and the scale of world production. These transformations stem from broader economic, political and cultural processes related to globalization[1] and comprise a few processes, such as: the appearance of powerful media and entertainment concerns and the inclusion of Hollywood studios in their corporate structure, the dramatic increase of film budgets, including in particular advertising and marketing budgets, the robust development of the new media, the global domination of Hollywood cinema and, last but not least, the development of multiplexes. All these factors led to the treatment of films increasingly as commodities and determined the dominance of economic logic in cinema at an unprecedented scale.

The 1980s in the United States were the period of Ronald Reagan's administration. It brought a definite neoliberal turn in internal and economic policies (sometimes referred to as Reaganomics). After 1980, the market deregulation policy removed or reduced many previous limitations regarding mergers and the creation of conglomerates that raises the threat of market monopolization. The economic liberalization brought benefits also to the Hollywood studios and large mass media and entertainment concerns. In the 1980s, many studios were taken over or merged with powerful media concerns or even corporations with core business beyond the area of media and entertainment, so close to the film industry. The "Big Six" studios thus became part of larger corporations and started operating under slightly different names. However, what is most important is the significant expansion of their business operations to include other areas of popular culture and entertainment. As a result, they could diversify their business to an even greater extent, reaping profits from various film-related sectors and gaining easier access to various distribution channels for the same film. This "horizontal integration" reduced the risk of operations performed by the studios and strengthened their global domination. As a result, Warner Brothers became part of Time Warner-Turner (controlled by Ted Turner), Disney became part of Disney-ABC, 20th Century Fox became part of News Corporation (owned by

---

[1] Mark Shiel claims that the transformations in contemporary cinema are not so much the results of globalization processes, but rather their central and co-creating elements. The British cinematologist states that "cinema, of course, is an excellent means to an understanding of globalization for a number of reasons. […] not only may cinema—particularly Hollywood cinema—be described as having always been postmodern, even before postmodernity, because of its peculiar combination of both sign and image (culture) and manufactured goods (industry, technology, capital), it may also be recognized as central to, rather than merely reflecting, the process known as globalization. In today's context, it isn't that films or the Hollywood film industry reflect globalization but that films and the Hollywood film industry effect globalization. Films are globalization, not its after-effects" (Shiel 2001, 10–11).

Robert Murdoch), Columbia is controlled by Sony, Paramount by Viacom, while Universal belonged to Matsushita/MCA in the 1990s as is now part of the corporate structure of General Electric.

The incorporation of the Hollywood studios into large businesses in the late 1970s and the early 1980s was also related to many changes in management. A completely new type of executives took the control over the largest studios. These were usually people previously unrelated to the film industry. As Hozic wrote:

> Thus, when declining corporate profits forced Hollywood moguls to leave the studios, they were replaced by the quintessential "office boys"—the men who understood well the intricacies of financing and sales but knew little and cared little about film production or about the films themselves (Hozic 2001, 103).

Even if those people advanced to the managerial level through the corporate structure of the film studios from the lowest level in the hierarchy, they usually came from the distribution departments. They drew upon their experience and realized better than anyone else that the success of a film is little determined by its artistic value and largely depends on artistic qualities in distribution and marketing. It was natural for the new generation of studio managers to perceive the film through economic logic. Simultaneously, the discourse of marketing and management was based on the assumption that the rules and mechanisms were universal regardless of the industry. A good manager will be successful in managing a company from the automotive, footwear or cosmetic industry. Thus, the film studios were more and more like corporations managed similarly to concerns in other industries: automotive, footwear, cosmetic or any other.

> [Hollywood became] an industry town dominated by media conglomerates more comfortable with MBAs than with movie moguls. The new breed of studio executive already spoke the language of market research. Several marketing firms moved to Hollywood to take advantage of what promised to be a booming business opportunity (Lerner 1999, 18; quoted in Miller et al. 2005, 260).

Marketing and distribution departments had a very strong position in Hollywood's corporate structure. It was an open secret that it was them, not the production departments that took decisions about implementing certain projects. Such decisions were based mainly on the assessment of the marketing potential related to the sales of merchandise and opportunities for multiple profits brought by the film through various distribution channels.

The transformation of Hollywood into corporate structures or their parts, and changes in the management of studios created a huge market of marketing and advertising services related to the promotion of specific films. The above mentioned increase in budgets was greatly reflected mainly in the area of film marketing and the figures show that the current promotion costs of a Hollywood film equal the production costs of, for instance, six French films or seven Italian films. In 1999 alone, Hollywood spend USD 2.55 billion on advertising its products, which made it the third largest industry in the US as regards expenses on advertising, following the automotive industry and retail sales of food products (Miller et al. 2005, 261).

The robust growth of film budgets, which influenced the film itself and the global market, began in the late 1970s and the early 1980s. This growth was one of the major factors leading to the isolation of smaller (mainly European and independent) producers, pushing them to an ever narrowing and less profitable niche of *auteur* or "artistic" cinema. In 1980–1994, the production costs of an average Hollywood film increased from USD 9.4 million to USD 34.3 million, while distribution and marketing costs for one title grew from USD 4.3 million to USD 16.1 million (Hozic 2001, 114). The average marketing costs for a Hollywood production reached as much as USD 21 million in 1999 (ibid., 95). In 2006, the average production budget for a Hollywood film stood at USD 65.8 million, whereas the average budget of a British film (frequently co-produced with Hollywood, which increased the costs) was USD 13.6 million, and the average budgets of French productions did not exceed USD 6.6 million and those of Italian films—USD 4.9 million (Newman-Baudais 2007, 7). In the same year, Hollywood studios spent the average of USD 34.5 million on advertising and marketing of a single title (the amount was USD 36.1 million a year before) (ibid., 37). A few factors led to such a robust growth in costs. First, the remuneration for the so-called "above-the-line talents", which is a Hollywood term for star actors and, to a certain extent, directors. Second, the necessary lavishness in the production and setting of blockbusters. However, the highest growth pertained to the costs of marketing and advertising campaigns, which have been of key significance for the Hollywood model in recent decades. The majority of costs were incurred mainly because of intensive TV advertising campaigns, including commercial spots and trailers, the costs of the *blanket strategy*, i.e. simultaneous premieres of a film on hundreds of screens during the opening weekend, which required huge numbers of celluloid copies.

From a purely economic point of view, such a huge increase in production costs in the 1980s should be a source of the producer's concern, rather than satisfaction. However, the costs increase in the "dream factory" entailed increased profits and the 1980s turned out to be a very prosperous period. It was not overshadowed by another potential source of the producers' concern, i.e. the appearance of competition for the "older" medium of cinema in the form of robustly developing new media. After 1980, Hollywood studios faced opportunities, later fully exploited, for increasing revenues and expanding their domination on the international film market, i.e. the appearance of "global Hollywood", to use Toby Miller's term, or "Hollyworld" (a term coined by Aida Hozic).

After the Second World War, the US and Europe experienced a continuous decrease in the number of filmgoers. In 1960–1990, the number of cinema tickets sold in Europe fell from 2.9 billion to 564 million per annum. The number of cinemas decreased by 60% in the same period (Miller et al. 2005, 306–307). However, the statistics show that for the period beginning in the 1980s this decrease pertained to viewers of European films, while the number of tickets sold for American films remained relatively stable. Between 1980 and the mid 1990s, the number of tickets sold in European cinemas for American films dropped from 425 million to 420 million per annum, while the number of tickets for European films sold in Europe fell from 475 million to 120 million (Vasconcelos 1994, 17). Thus, the decreased number of viewers of European productions led to the constant growth in the dominance of Hollywood studios on European markets. In 1968, 60% of filmgoers on the Old Continent were attracted by European productions and only 35% chose American films. In the late 1970s, the share of the Old Continent films in the European market amounted to 55%, while the share of overseas pictures was 44%. Meanwhile, in 1994, European producers had only a 20–30% share in their own internal market and all the rest (i.e. 70–80%, or even 90% in some countries) was controlled by American films (ibid., 17). This continuous weakening of the European industry and the growing domination of Hollywood intensified in the 1980s. Additionally, Europe's deficit in trade with the United States grew from USD 2 billion to USD 5.6 billion per annum in the whole audiovisual sector (film, television, VHS/DVD market) in 1989–1997. The period 1989–1997 brought the EU Television Without Frontiers Directive that was to strengthen the European audiovisual industry. Paradoxically, it turned out that the European audiovisual market had no frontiers only for American expansion. When the long-term downward trend in the number of filmgoers was blocked in the 1990s (the number of filmgoers in the

European Union Member States reached 756.5 million per annum in 1997), Hollywood studios were once again the biggest beneficiaries, which resulted from the influence of the overall and significantly transformed "film culture".

The last process discussed here, and the one responsible for transforming the cinema after 1980 into "something else" and for "the end of cinema as we know it", is thus the significant strengthening of Hollywood's domination on foreign markets, and the European one in particular. This was happening when the value of the total audiovisual market (including traditional distribution channels, such as cinema, with new ones, such as cable television, pay-per-view television, VHS/DVD) was growing robustly[2] and the decrease in the number of cinemagoers, continued since the end of World War II, was stopped. But the benefits of this increase were mainly reaped by Hollywood and filmgoers returning to cinemas came back to see Hollywood films. The exorbitant increase in the Hollywood film budgets (both in production and marketing) and the transformations of the overall film culture favourable to the Hollywood model belittled European producers, created difficulties they had to face or even made it impossible for them to compete with Hollywood. They were largely pushed to the narrow market niche of "artistic cinema" and art houses. This meant small audiences and low profitability. On the other hand, the contemporary film culture is based on the Hollywood model and the *look, hook and book* rule used frequently by Hollywood marketing experts. The reality is thus that blockbusters reap the lion's share of all the profits. These blockbusters have the *look* i.e. the Hollywood glamour, lavish production, large scale and high expenses, the *hook* i.e. the attention grabbers, such as star actors, and, last but not least, the *book* i.e. the above described opportunity to sell through various distribution channels and, first of all, to gain significant profits from selling related merchandise, various licenses and tie-ins.[3] Low-budget and fragmented European

---

[2] The value of the so-called "copyright industry", which is a term suggested by researchers related to Toby Miller to be used to denote "the culture industry", is estimated at USD 387.9 billion per annum, and its most crucial sector is traditionally the audiovisual industry.

[3] Tie-ins are large advertising campaigns in which a given film is most frequently advertised together with a large chain of restaurants (Burger King, McDonald's, Pizza Hut) or a beverage producer (Coca-Cola, Pepsi and their proprietary brands). TV commercials, press ads and billboards advertise a given film and a given food product simultaneously. However, tie-ins are not just limited to cooperation with restaurant chains and beverage producers. *Four Weddings and a Funeral* had a campaign with a French airline and travel agency to promote a honeymoon on Tahiti. In Italy, *Shrek* was advertised together with Barilla pasta, and *Terminator 3*

productions with low advertising budgets cannot compete with Hollywood super productions, skilful and complex profit-generating machines.

The above described combination of factors that has shaped the reality of world cinema after 1980 has led to the treatment of film as a commodity and the greater than ever domination of the economic approach to cinema, which means that a film has simply become a corporate product. It is not only a commodity to be traded numerous times, created for a predefined and existing market, but also a commodity used to sell other goods. Thomas Elsaesser writes that contemporary films are like advertising billboards extended in time (Elsaesser 2001, 11). This simile is close to another metaphor applied to a contemporary film, that of a "locomotive" or an "engine" that drives the machinery of audiovisual industry, even if the engine itself is not the largest part of it. A cinema show is a "billboard" that presents "the classics of tomorrow", available in DVD shops and rentals and on scrambled television channels, and then on cable TV.[4] Elsaesser puts forward another metaphor in the same text. He compares the workings of a film in the circumstances of "global Hollywood" to pinball. A film would be a metal ball earning extra balls and replays thanks to keeping it in play on a playfield of the pinball machine. This metaphorical playfield would include cinema screens, shops, VHS/DVD rentals, theme parks, TV stations, advertisements, toy shops, restaurant

---

was promoted in the US alongside Toyota T-3. Volvo advertised its new C70 model by joining efforts with producers of *The Saint* (1997). In Great Britain, British Telecom and the distributor of *102 Dalmatians* (2002) organized a tie-in that included such products as, for instance, a special issue of phone cards related to the film.

[4] It seems that the treatment of a film as a commodity is so developed that Elsaesser's metaphor may be expanded to show a broader range of products promoted in "a cinema film as a billboard". Since the 1920s Hollywood lobbyists working in Washington have, in harmony with officials from the Department of Trade and the Department of State, paraphrased the famous British colonial maxim "trade follows the flag", claiming that currently "trade follows the film". The phrase was used for the first time in 1927 by William Hays during his guest lecture in Harvard Business School. A few years later, Hays calculated that each 30 cm of celluloid tape of a film exported from the US translated into one dollar from sales of goods other than the film itself. Similar views were presented by Senator Joseph P. Kennedy, father to the later US President. He claimed that a film serves as "a silent merchant" of other American industry products. Toby Miller emphasizes the intensification of such a type of film productions in the late 20th century: "Films, especially blockbusters, have come to be judged in terms of their capacity to act as logos or have a distinct product image. In these cases, the film sells records, clothes, toys, video games, books, magazines, drinks and food" (Miller et al. 2005, 244).

chains, bookstores or music stores (ibid., 18). Representatives of the "dream factory" are pinball champions, while Europeans manage to keep the celluloid "metal ball" in play for a very short time and score few points in one or two locations of the playfield or, like independent producers, they do not own the distribution rights and can only watch as someone else is playing the "ball" they produced, winning extra balls and replays.

Thus, time has come to focus on one of many locations, but still of key importance, on the playfield of the pinball machine. This place offers the player many extra balls and determines whether the "metal ball" will be kept in play or will be lost.

Reprise of Vaudeville Bill

Multiplexes[5] widely appeared in the US in the 1980s, in Western Europe—in the early 1990s and in Central Eastern Europe—in the late 1990s. They are related to huge investments in film infrastructure and the prevention of gradual dereliction of cinema theatres, which meant that, according to Martin Dale, in 1980s watching films in Europe was becoming a slums-like activity performed in slums-like surroundings (Dale 1997, 173). The impact of multiplexes on reception practices, filmgoers' experience and social perception of the medium seems so significant that, in my opinion, we can talk about the Tenth Muse's moving from a film club to a multiplex. Unseen by many cinematologists, the Tenth Muse moved from small theatres in side streets of city centres to the reality of suburban multiplexes, large theatres with fantastic picture and sound quality, surrounded by restaurants, bards, billiard clubs, or even hairdressing studios—all in an economic symbiosis. It is multi-screen cinemas that now dominate the cinema landscape.

Looking at the simplest and basic level, the appearance of multiplexes stopped the decrease of filmgoers, gradually happening since the post-war years. Then, for the first time in fifty years, the number of filmgoers actually increased, the number of cinema screens grew[6] and the quality of

[5] A differentiation is sometimes made between multiplexes and megaplexes. The former are multi-screen cinemas located in large shopping malls, usually in city centers. The latter are separate complexes, much larger than multiplexes, located outside city centers. A large cinema complex is constructed alongside other facilities, such as restaurants, bars, arcade game centers, billiard clubs and a wide range of other entertainment options.

[6] According to the data of the European Audiovisual Observatory, the number of cinema tickets sold in Europe increased from 765 million to 926 million per annum

cinema screens improved immensely. Looking at the deeper and what seems like a frequently unnoticed level, this brought a redefinition, cultural reformulation and transformation of the social practice of "cinema-going" and the experiences of a viewer participating in a film show.

The data referring to the growth of multiplexes lead, in my opinion, to the reassessment of views about the "death" (anachronism and decline) of cinema. It seems however that the image of the "global Hollywood" varies from the "cannibalistic" model of relations between mass media, according to which the new media "devour" (belittle and isolate) the older medium, i.e. the cinema. This image is also at a variance with the "paragons" (similarly to the "paragons" of Leonardo da Vinci who proved the absolute superiority of painting over sculpture, poetry and music) which attempt to show the superiority, greater significance or the range of new media forms in competition and opposition to the medium of cinema. Meanwhile, the cinema appears to be a certain culture-conditioned social practice, most frequently involving going out and spending free time outside home on Friday or Saturday nights. The fact that you can watch a film at home by using more advanced, perfect and technologically developed equipment does not mean that the practice of cinema-going will stop, just like the possibility of eating at home does not lead to mass restaurant bankruptcy. "Cinema-going" is a culture-determined social practice and an opportunity to get involved in other practices, which are deliberately chaotically listed by Charles Acland:

> Public movie performances are occasions for eating, for disregarding one's usual dietary strictures, for knowingly overpaying for too much food, for sneaking snacks and drinks, for both planned and impromptu socializing, for working, for flirting, for sexual play, for gossiping, for staking out territory in theatre seats, for threatening noisy spectators, for being threatened, for arguments, for reading, for talking about future movie going, for relaxing, for sharing in the experience of screening with other audience members, for fleeting glimpses at possible alliances and allegiances of taste, politics, and identity, for being to close to strangers, for being crowded in your winter clothes, for being frozen by overactive air-conditioning, for being bored, for sleeping, for disappointment, for joy, for arousal, for disgust, for slouching, for hand holding, for drug taking, for standing in lines, for making phone calls, for playing video games, for the evaluation of trailers, for discussions of what preceded the film and of

in the period 1996–2006. At the same time, the number of cinema screens on the Old Continent increased from 22,368 to 29,046 (cf. Newman-Baudais 2007, 8–9).

what will follow, and for both remembering and forgetting oneself (Acland 2003, 57–58).

The growth of multiplexes was a deliberate strategy that required huge investment outlays and aimed at "managing" the cinema audiences and shaping the "cinema-going" practice. However, public picture shows are also a place where globalization in the "macro" scale (involving the global Hollywood film industry, huge investments and profits, economic approach and market strategies) meets globalization in the "micro" scale, with its bottom-up effects, culture-determined social practices of individuals or small groups, shaping the practice of participating in cinema shows on one's own, by giving sense, negotiating meaning, familiarizing with it and using it for one's needs, such as a plethora of other secondary aims listed above by Acland.

On the "macro" level, the strategy of the whole Hollywood film industry, with a central role played by multiplexes, seems to be based on a network of interrelations where, according to Thomas Elsaesser who writes about contemporary cinema "everything connects". A picture show in the cinema is intertwined with media, goods and services, including television, the Internet, VHS and DVD, computer games, advertising, toys and merchandise, books and comic books, songs and video clips (in the dimension of cultural texts alone). On the other hand, there is another network of consumption of snacks and cold drinks accompanying the film screening, a network of restaurants and bars in megaplexes, shopping and architecture of malls of which multiplexes are part (in the dimension of surroundings that are broader than cultural texts alone). Instead of being perceived as something distinguished and belonging to the refined "high art" and simultaneously threatened by the new media and transformations in the postmodern society, cinema becomes one of many cultural texts (treated as inferior in the traditional cinematology discourse) and practices of the consumer society. The film text is then among a plethora of various paratexts. Symbiosis or synergy developed or was created instead of the "cannibalistic" or "paragon"-like vision of relations between the "old" and the "new" media. This harmonious inclusion in the mainstream of other products and practices may be described with the above mentioned simple formula by Thomas Elsaesser, i.e. *everything connects* in the reality of contemporary cinema. It can also be dubbed the *reprise of vaudeville bill* after Toby Miller, as quoted above (Miller et al. 2005, 42).

The "vaudeville" character of cinema at the early stage of its development involved a specific structure of picture shows. The film screening was accompanied by other attractions for the audience, such as performances of comics, stand-up comedians and music bands. Lotteries were organized among filmgoers with household appliances or clothes as prizes. The "vaudeville" character of cinema disappeared gradually alongside the cinema "refinement", mentioned at the beginning of this section, since the cinema wanted to attract the middle class and get rid of the nickelodeon odium and the association with undemanding entertainment for the working class. It disappeared quite efficiently because such performances or lotteries were something absolutely unthinkable in the modernism times, during shows of works by Antonioni, Fellini or Bergman. The film was perceived as a uniform and autonomous phenomenon, something clearly separated from other audiovisual forms during the film screening. Such uniformity, autonomy and separation determined the textual approach to films which dominated the university film studies since their very beginning.

Putting the multiplex-related processes aside, the "vaudeville" character of contemporary film means that the film is once again located among the whole range of related audiovisual forms of entertainment: multiple channel TV stations, VHS and DVD, rentals and discs attached to magazines, websites, computer games, comic books, commercials or urban billboards. There is a flow of themes and stylistic motifs among these forms and the film itself uses its proteusian potential. A given work transforms, multiplies, changes its shape in a Proteus-like manner, permeates various distribution channels and works within various media, thus becoming not so much a uniform phenomenon related to a given location and consumption model, but rather a shimmering and changeable multimedia form.

Television and the new media have long been perceived in Europe, especially by film experts, as antagonists of cinema responsible for decreasing the number of filmgoers. Meanwhile, the title of the tenth volume of *History of the American Cinema* written by Stephen Prince and devoted to the period of 1980–1989, is *A New Pot of Gold: Hollywood under the Electronic Rainbow*. Practice has shown that in the "global Hollywood" reality, a film works like a part of surroundings based on the new media and its relations with these surroundings are those of cooperation or a symbiosis that brings mutual benefits. The consumption of individual media products and cultural texts, as well as "cinema-going" and non-textual consumption forms intertwine and stimulate one another. The successful turnout in cinemas translates into huge profits from TV and DVD rights, and from sales of licensed toys and gadgets. On the other hand, television, the DVD market or the toy market frequently save budgets of individual films and bring financial stability to large studios. It is quite frequent that as much as 30–40% of revenues generated by multiplexes come from the sales of soft drinks and snacks, such as nachos and popcorn. Multiplexes also benefit from their location in shopping malls.[7] These, in turn, often finance the construction of a cinema or support an existing cinema financially because it is an additional factor that attracts clients.

Putting aside the aspects of cinema as a culture-determined social practice, it remains significant and alive on the "macro" level also because of its economic dimension. Thus, we can talk about the cinema as the "engine" or the "locomotive" of the audiovisual industry. It facilitates wide-ranging distribution on television and DVDs. Thus, it is a "preservative" that "prolongs" the lifecycle of perishable film products[8] and makes it possible for them to last in other distribution channels. Or, as Charles Acland claims, cinema remains a place where "young" film texts are born to attain "maturity" (understood as full profits) in other channels (Acland 2003, 146, 152). Current films have many lives, just like computer game characters.

It is thus difficult to defy an impression that transformations of the film culture determined by the appearance of multiplexes remain underappreciated in film studies. In this context, watching films in an art house or a traditional cinema on the one hand, and in a multiplex, on the other, are not usually perceived as different practices. However, it actually seems that they are essentially "something else" to an increasingly larger extent. They are situated in separate institutional and discourse contexts, they are related with separate types of reception expectations and gratification. They seem to be located in increasingly separate "cinematographic systems". Participation in film screenings in those systems becomes two different experiences that are still denoted by means of the same phrase, "cinema-going", but only due to some linguistic traditions.

Hence, it seems that we are dealing here with the "invisible infrastructure" effect. The infrastructure of an art house or a traditional cinema in a city centre and the infrastructure of a multiplex and megaplex do not remain culturally neutral. The construction of multiplexes in Western Europe in the early 1990s and in Central Eastern Europe in the

---

[7] The profits from sales of snacks and drinks in cinemas all over the world reached USD 4.5 billion. On the other hand, the global revenues from sales of cinema tickets in the same year were less than USD 20 billion (Miller et al. 2005, 307; Newman-Baudais 2007, 38).

[8] According to one Hollywood producer, cinema films are "products that potentially lasted only a few days, but were not cheap to make, unlike the similarly perishable fruit or vegetables" (Bakker 2003, 107–108; quoted in Miller et al. 2005, 295).

late 1990s was funded mainly with American capital. Americans also finance the building of modern cinemas in India and China.[9] At the same time, the multiplex with its paratexts remains an American invention. This model is later exported and applied to other continents, becoming a key element and visible architectural indicator of the rule and borders of "global Hollywood". American investors commenced the construction of multiplexes in Europe and on other continents in order to strengthen Hollywood's domination, which had already been visible in production and distribution. Since the mid 1980s, it once again has become actively involved in the sector of film shows. This enabled additional control, but first of all the transformation of the global film culture, the social perception of cinema and the cinema-going practice. In the long-term, it is the characteristics of a film screening venue that shape the audience, its behaviours and expectations as to the Tenth Muse.

The picture show was set in the context of consumption and entertainment, not the "high art". A film ceased to be associated with screenings in film clubs or respectable film libraries. It was no longer connected with erudite speeches before the screening and heated debates after it. It had nothing to do with young intellectuals disputing over coffee. "Reception practices" became combined with the shopping mall experience, where motion pictures were just one of many visual pleasures offered there, one of many elements of the chaos of changeable sensual impressions. They are an "architectural trailer" of some sort (according to Acland's statement). Its trailer precedes, adapts, fine-tunes and shapes the subsequent reception of a film.[10] Simultaneously, the watching of a film in the multiplex space does not have to be the most important, or even a necessary activity. The surroundings are designed to offer and reap profits from other consumption activities. Acland quotes Roger Harris,

---

[9] As early as in the late 1970s, American companies extended an interest-free loan amounting to 10 million rupees to India for the construction or refurbishment of cinemas. India, alongside China, is still treated by Hollywood as a market with great potential for future profits. Therefore, as mentioned earlier, Hollywood representatives are willing to help China in constructing "large film auditoria", i.e. multiplexes and their characteristic film consumption patterns (Miller et al. 2005, 317, 323).

[10] Using Paul Virillio's intuition about the dromologic nature of film, which emphasizes the closeness of a filmgoer's and car passenger's experience, we can identify another trailer, namely, the necessity to drive a car to reach megaplexes located usually in the suburbs of large cities. This necessity appears much more often in this case as compared to visits in traditional cinemas, usually located in city centres.

Vice-President for Marketing and Management in Famous Players, a Canadian chain of multiplexes:

> We want to change people's ways of thinking about movies, particularly at old tradition of arriving 10 minutes before the movie starts and running out the door as soon as it's over [...] We want them to hang around, come early, stay late. Conceivably you could come and have quite a good time without seeing a movie, although that's not what we have in mind (Roger Harris quoted in Acland 2003, 202).

The model multiplex filmgoer desired by the industry would thus be a contemporary *flâneur* wandering around the multiplex. It would be a *flâneur* who moves in the surroundings designed especially for him and frequently reaches into his pocket. This similarity between a multiplex and a shopping mall with this 19th century tradition has been pointed out by Anne Friedberg (1994). For her, a screen in a cinema located in a large shopping mall is a natural extension of shop windows. The only difference is that such a screen presents moving pictures.

Multiplexes as the Limes of "Global Hollywood"

Multiplexes and the above described transformation of the film culture are the "natural environment" for Hollywood blockbusters. They create a space into which these films can fit and with which they can harmonize. The space seems to be designed especially for them. If we can use the statistics from the last two decades to claim that "filmgoers are back to cinemas", or actually that "filmgoers are back to multiplex cinemas", we could specify that phrase even more and state that "filmgoers are back to multiplex cinemas to buy tickets for Hollywood blockbusters". As the "natural environment" for blockbusters, multiplexes are also rather an unnatural environment for other types of cinema. Modest *auteur* films or achievements of the European cinema other than super productions celebrating national myths seem to be "out of place" if screened in multiplexes. Shown among bars, restaurants, shops, game arcades, nachos, popcorn and soft drinks they generate the persistent impression of dissonance and strangeness. "Global Hollywood" productions, on the other hand, are seen as "naturalized" elements of film cultures of individual countries and are not considered "strange" or "exterior", at least in multiplexes. Just the opposite, there is a growing sense of "strangeness" of local, national films widely distributed in local multiplexes.

This difference leads to a conclusion about two cinema-going practices moving apart: one being the globally dominant multiplex-Hollywood practice with its economic, institutional and discourse aspects and the other being a niche, European-local-artistic practice with its own discourse, institutional and economic aspects (with symbolic economics dominating over economics in general). The fact that 75–90% of filmgoers in European countries visit multiplexes shows another shift. If the Tenth Muse, as it seems, has moved from film clubs to multiplexes, it is difficult to defy the impression that "national cinema" or "national artistic cinema" has largely moved out of cinema theatres and "moved into" television and festivals, or retrospectives.

We can see shifts of the cultural "map" of venues in which film has "lived" (both the film-commodity of the global industry and the film-product of local hand production) after 1980. Even if those two types of films seemingly exist in the same location (such as television) on this map, the location itself plays a slightly different role for each product. Thus, the film-commodity of "global Hollywood" is located in such venues on the "map" as cinemas, especially multiplexes (which are the "engine" still fuelling this model and determining profits from other sources) and television stations (a source of additional profits, these are usually private stations). It holds the central position on the DVD market and harmoniously permeates other territories on the "map", such as the market of advertising, merchandise and toys, popular literature, comic books, video clips. The film of the other type also "lives" on television, this time it is usually public television. It is frequently the main territory for this film model and constitutes the basic, and not an additional, source of financing production. It also serves as a niche that enables survival and, what is most important; it is the only place for screening a given title. The map of this model also includes festivals, retrospectives, art houses, libraries, museums, civic centers, schools and universities. Thus, two separate paratexts are created. They fit separate discourses and institutions.

One more shift can be identified if we were to use the map metaphor in a different way, by using a broader map of contemporary culture, not limited to films only, and shifts happening there. It seems that cinema once again moves in the culture space—this time from the centre to its peripheries, thus leaving the area of "high culture" traditionally occupied from the 1960s. This process is in line with the differentiation between high culture and low culture (folk culture) made by Pierre Bourdieu in *Distinction* (1984). While the former is related to the "clear perception", distance, cool and disinterested contemplation that helps to notice intellectual and formal values of an integral and separate work of art, the former combines with sensual and carnal pleasure, consumption and identification, blurred borders between the show and the reality, immersion that questions the cool distance of the person perceiving the work. The Tenth Muse emerges from nickelodeons and "common cinema", i.e. areas belonging to the low culture (folk culture). However, in its modernist period it is elevated and becomes an unquestionable part of high culture. The characteristics of multiplexes with their omnipresent consumption, including unlimited consumption of food, which is typical of feasts in folk culture, with their de-separation, dispersion of attention and fluctuations of sensual experiences are once again seen as close to the description of low culture (folk culture).

This might seem to be a return to the starting point, to the "birthplace" of cinema. The difference is that the status of high culture is less certain than at the beginning of the previous century and the thesis about consumption and entertainment being the peripheries of the culture space is disputable. Paradoxically, the alternative to multiplexes (art houses, festivals and reviews of *auteur* films) may be increasingly peripheral. The dichotomy of the Hollywood cinema (popular, commercial cinema) and artistic cinema has obviously always existed and has always been reflected in a different number of viewers. However, the domination of the former and the deep isolation of the latter have never been as visible as in the last two or three decades. The separation of these two types has never seemed so profound and the whole film culture has never been so strongly dominated and shaped by the first model, looking as if they are in excellent co-existence or even an organically integrated economic and cultural mechanism.

The appearance of multiplex cinemas has most frequently been considered as something negative in the film studies discourse. It has been perceived as a sign of the commercialization and decline of cinema. Still, it is worth remembering that the multiplex shift in the film industry has secured its survival and prospects for further, economic at least, expansion, which is evidenced by problems with parking cars in front of multi-screen cinemas every weekend and by their interiors that sometimes resemble lobbies of very crowded airports. However paradoxical it may seem, the European cinema owes its current existence to a certain extent to the Hollywood cinema. Over 70% share of Hollywood in the European market is generally viewed as a threat. However, it is difficult to predict that if Hollywood films disappeared from European screens for some unknown reason, millions of viewers would automatically want to watch European films in cinemas other than multiplexes. It is more probable that in such a situation the majority of filmgoers would simply choose other types of entertainment. Hence, it is the Hollywood blockbusters, the robust marketing machine of "global Hollywood", investments in the construction of multiplexes and the transformation of the whole film culture which leads to making it part of consumer culture, that keep the phenomenon known as "cinema" and the social practice known as "cinema-going" alive also on the European continent.

This does not change the fact that multiplexes and the related film culture model simultaneously weaken the position of the artistic cinema and the local national cinema. They create a cross-continental network where geographically separated audiences of various nationalities and cultures are connected in time and watch the same films (and frequently consume the same snacks and drinks) in almost similar venues and at the same time.[11] The French film experts, usually very critical towards

---

[11] In his book, Acland lists the following American chains of multiplexes operating outside the US in 2002—Loews Cineplex (owner: Sony): Austria, Canada, Hungary, Italy, Korea, Spain, Turkey; Cinemark: Argentina, Brazil, Canada, Chile, Columbia, Costa Rica, Ecuador, Salvador, Honduras, Nicaragua, Mexico, Peru, Taiwan; AMC: Canada, France, Hong Kong, Japan, Portugal, Spain, Sweden, UK; General Cinema: Argentina, Brazil, Chile, Mexico, Uruguay; Warner Bros. International (owner: AOL Time Warner): Australia, Italy, Japan, Portugal, Spain, Taiwan, UK; National Amusements (associated with Viacom): Argentina, Chile, UK; United Cinemas International (owners: Viacom and Vivendi Universal): Austria, Brazil, China, Germany, Ireland, Italy, Japan, Panama, Poland, Portugal, Spain and UK; United Cinemas International—Central Europe (associated with UCI): Czech Republic, Hungary, Slovakia, Turkey; Wallace Theaters (Marshall Islands, Micronesia, Guam, Mariana Islands); Caribbean Cinemas: Dominican Republic, Small Antilles; Cinemastar Luxury Theaters: Mexico; United Artists Theater Circuit (owner: Regal Entertainment Group): Hong Kong, India, Thailand (Acland 2003, 140–141).

Significant mergers have taken place in the sector between strong players on the American market in recent years. The result was the establishment of a powerful National CineMedia network (in 2002, AMC acquired General Cinema, it merged with Loews Cineplex in 2005 and a merger of AMC, Cinemark and Regal Entertainment Group took place in 2006).

It is worth noticing that owners of four studios out of the current Hollywood Big Six producers and distributors control also large international multiplex chains (Loews Cineplex is part of the same corporation as Columbia; National Amusements and United Cinema International belong to the same group and Paramount and earlier Universal before being acquired by General Electric; Warner Bros. International is obviously part of AOL Time Warner that also controls the studio itself). Simultaneously, these chains are also very strong market players in Europe (cf. Jäckel 2003, 125).

Although two French chains (UGC and Europalaces), Village Roadshow from Australia and Kinepolis from Belgium are also quite strong in Europe, they still follow the "universal" American model and the ownership structure does not

Hollywood-dominated film culture, once called multiplexes "the cruisers for American films". It seems that we can risk yet another simile. Multiplexes are the material and symbolic signs of the reign of "global Hollywood", setting its limes, similarly to the limes of the Empire set by the posts of Roman forces. In the material, organizational and economic dimension, what is beyond the borders of the powerful "global Hollywood" is just an exotic, insignificant and fragmented world of small and individual national cinematographies and the increasingly anachronistic and disappearing auteur model.[12]

References

Adamczak, Marcin. 2011. "Z DKF-u do multiplexu" In *Kino po kinie. Film w kulturze uczestnictwa*, edited by Andrzej Gwóźdź, 85–118. Warszawa: Oficyna Naukowa.

Acland, Charles R. 2003. *Screen Traffic: Movies, Multiplexes, and Global Culture.* Durham: Duke University Press.

Bakker, Gerben. 2003. "Building Knowledge about the Consumer: The Emergence of Market Research in the Motion Picture Industry." *Business History* 45 (1): 101–127.

Bourdieu, Pierre. 1984. *Distinction: A Social Critique of the Judgment of Taste.* Cambridge, MA: Harvard University Press.

Dale, Martin. 1997. *The Movie Game: The Film Business in Britain, Europe and America.* London: Cassell.

Elsaesser, Thomas. 2001. "The Blockbuster: Everything Connects, but not Everything Goes." In *The End of Cinema as We Know It: American Film in the Nineties*, edited by Jon Lewis, 11–22. New York: New York University Press.

Friedberg, Anne. 1994. *Window Shopping: Cinema and the Postmodern.* Berkeley: University of California Press.

Hozic, Aida A. 2001. *Hollyworld: Space, Power, and Fantasy in the American Economy.* Ithaca: Cornell University Press.

Jäckel, Anne. 2003. *European Film Industries.* London: British Film Institute.

---

prevent them from operating within "global Hollywood". They do not differ in terms of their architecture, interior decoration or repertoire.

[12] While collecting material for this article the author benefited from scholarship from Foundation for Polish Science. Parts of text were previously published in Polish (Adamczak 2011).

Lerner, Preston. 1999. "Shadow Force: Hundreds of Movies Have Been Reshaped as a Result of Work by Joseph Farrell's National Research Group." *Los Angeles Times*, November 18.
Lewis, Jon, ed. 2001. *The End of Cinema as We Know It: American Film in the Nineties.* New York: New York University Press.
Miller, Toby, Nitin Govil, John McMurria, Richard Maxwell, and Ting Wang. 2005. *Global Hollywood: No. 2.* London: British Film Institute.
Newman-Baudais, Susan, ed. 2007. *Focus 2007: World Film Market Trends.* Cannes: Marché du Film.
Prince, Stephen. 2002. *History of the American Cinema,* Volume 10: *A New Pot of Gold: Hollywood under the Electronic Rainbow, 1980–1989.* Berkeley: University of California Press.
Shiel, Mark. 2001. "Cinema and the City in History and Theory." In *Cinema and the City: Film and Urban Societies in a Global Context*, edited by Mark Shiel and Tony Fitzmaurice, 1–18. London: Wiley-Blackwell.
Vasconcelos, Antonio Pedro. 1994. *Report by the Think-tank on the Audiovisual Policy in the European Union.* Luxembourg: Office of Official Publications of the European Community.

PART II:

NEW PROSPECTS ON CONSUMER CULTURE RESEARCH

A Strategic Approach to Customer Orientation

Franz Liebl

Customer Orientation: Second Wave of Marketing Myopia?

It was in 1960 when Levitt argued in his famous article on "Marketing Myopia" that product orientation should give way to "customer orientation" in order to secure long-term business success. Since then, putting customers at the centre of marketing efforts has seen several revivals. In the late 1980s being "close to the customer" received increasing management awareness. And during the 1990s, particularly in a context of business process re-engineering and total quality management, customer satisfaction was regarded as a main performance indicator for optimizing the business system of a company. This was the reason why in that period a large portion of companies had undergone customer satisfaction surveys and organization-wide programs for increasing customer orientation.

According to this logic, customer orientation is expressed by two complementary streams of thinking:

First: ask customers what they want and then craft products and services according to these needs.

Second: ask customers how satisfied they are and then optimize business processes and the offering accordingly.

However, it turned out that there was only a relatively weak correspondence between customer satisfaction on the one hand and strategic success on the other hand (Reichheld 1993; Macdonald 1995; Herrmann, Huber and Braunstein 2000). Porter (1996) came to the conclusion that business process re-engineering had increased the level of customer satisfaction for all businesses without creating the specific competitive advantages the individual companies had in mind. As a consequence, if we look at customer orientation from a strategic point of view, we need a different approach.

The problem gets worse because of individualization. According to sociologists (e.g. Beck, Maffesoli, Hitzler, Gross, Bauman) individualization means a de-standardization of biographies and a pluralisation of lifestyles. Beck and Beck-Gernsheim (2002) point out that individualization is not only an urban phenomenon but that in rural areas phenomena of individualization and hybridization exist as well. The authors refer to an essay by the German writer Hans Magnus Enzensberger, who already 20 years ago summarized “the average exoticism of everyday life”:

> Into the shoes of the village idiots and the oddballs, of the eccentrics and the queer fish, has stepped the average deviationist, who no longer stands out at all from millions like him (Enzensberger 1992, 179).

This is also reflected in buying and consumption patterns, not least driven by the availability of countless buying options in the market (Gross 1994), and has led, according to Gabriel and Lang (1995), to *The Unmanageable Consumer*. While the term had been only a vague speculation when their book appeared in 1995, the authors recently have pointed out that today this diagnosis is more valid than ever before (2009). The unmanageability includes some well-known phenomena (Liebl 2010): “brand stress”, “style wars”, “hybrid buying behaviour”, and deviant forms of usage (e.g. “bricolage”, *détournement*, “fandalism” and various forms of “hacking” products; see Düllo and Liebl 2005 and Liebl 2008). Because these phenomena are not addressed by the conventional techniques of researching customer wants and measuring customer satisfaction, customer orientation—conceptualized as being oriented towards customers as described above—runs the danger of becoming a new form of marketing myopia (Brown 2001). In this paper, the notion of customer orientation will be discussed from a strategic point of view. We are going to use several case studies in order to, firstly, rethink and reformulate the concept of customer orientation and to, secondly, extend and radicalize the concept in various directions.

Case Study 1: Service Stations

The starting point of this meta-research were the results of a large qualitative study (n = 60) in the service-station market. The original aim of this study was an analysis of the main brands in this consumer market, with an emphasis on the market leader, Aral (for details see Liebl et al. 2005). In this study customers of service stations were asked about their relationships to the brands in the market. Besides applying conventional association techniques in order to find out about the “core” or “essence” of the brands, the study was particularly focusing on how the brands were related to the lifeworlds of the consumers by using storylistening techniques (Liebl and Rughase 2002). The general associations about the brands led to very surprising results. The consensual core of the strongest brand in the market, Aral, was (just) "blue", i.e. the colour of their corporate design. Astonishingly, this result sets the company Aral far apart from its competition, because consumers were not able to correctly identify the colours of the other brands. This is even more true for claims or other artefacts of the brands. In other words, the core of a brand tends to be trivial or even non-existent. And even when it may exist, as in the case of the market leader Aral, it tends to be strategically insignificant, as this "essence" marks no difference between customers and non-customers.

With respect to methodology this implies that association techniques did not lead to strategically useful results—in contrast to the storylistening technique which allowed us to detect distinct patterns in these stories, thereby providing new criteria for customer segmentation (for further details, see Liebl et al. 2005). In particular, we detected two fundamentally different reasons why people are willingly using one and the same service station: firstly, because of personal relationships and, secondly, because they feel oriented by the business system. What does this imply for strategic brand management? The brand is not very important for those with personal relationships, because in that case people matter. The strength of the brand matters most in the other case, which represents the majority of customers. For them the corporate design is not just an aesthetic experience, it represents above all optimized ergonomics, both mentally and physically. Here the brand design is more or less tantamount to the business system; the brand can be regarded as a physical and mental orientation system. This is substantiated by the stories customers tell:

> It's my personality, I need order around me. Everything must be in order, must be clean. And this specific Aral station that I have in mind is really big and not packed. The shop layout is dominated by straight lines; it has clearly defined rack areas. The outside area is well structured, it's a huge space. Everything is in its place like it had been planned: the pressure control for tyres stands exactly at a 90 degree angle to the driving lane. This is totally different compared to these little rural stations built around a small house. In this order I feel very comfortable.

There were even customers who could describe the layout of a shop in cinematographic detail. One customer summarizes:

> I like the outfit very much. Particularly the blue, it is more modern, perhaps even more aggressive, but very attractive. The design seems very clear to me, and I care much about the visual design.

The following artwork by German artist Ralf Peters (Fig. 5-1) nicely illustrates what the core of the brand, the colour blue, really means when we link the stories of the customers to the general associations. "Blue" does not refer to general cultural codes, like blue as the colour of money or similar symbolizations; it rather stands for the orientation the business system provides to customers. In this photograph, the artist deleted all letters and writings and verbal expressions of the brand. However, if Aral customers arrived at this particular service station, they would have no problem using this station and orienting themselves at this station.

From this study we learnt that customer orientation, from a strategic perspective, is not so much about companies being oriented towards the customer, but about customers being oriented by the brand and its offerings. The storylistening part of the study revealed the following strategic issues based on orientation:

– What are the orientations of customers towards the brand and the offering?

– How do customers orient themselves in a business system?

– Are there specific needs for orientation?

– Which offerings can a company create in order to provide orientation?

– Can customers be segmented with respect to their orientation(s) or with respect to their need(s) for orientation?

The fact that orientation is a fundamental strategic issue for businesses was substantiated by a number of storylistening studies in very different contexts, i.e. in different industries and in both business-to-business and business-to-consumer settings. Two examples shall illustrate the analogies:

(1) A storylistening study revealed that orientation was a major problem for chain bookstores when they turned into megastores of several thousands of square meters. The reaction of buyers was like this: "Since the bookstore has become bigger, I buy less because I cannot find the books I want."

(2) A storylistening study in the wholesale market for paper found out that the distributor's customers (i.e. printing companies) could be segmented by their orientation towards the future of their business. One segment expected price wars and ruinous competition which presumably would cause extreme price and time pressure for their suppliers; whereas the other segment was oriented towards a future based on differentiation

and high technology which in contrast will require particularly competent and technologically sophisticated suppliers (Liebl and Rughase 2002).

From these examples it is easy to conclude that the issues of orientation are particularly important in order to:

– create new markets by innovative products and services and
– develop a business strategically.

From Orientation to (Painful) Education

There is only a small step between orienting people and educating them. In the second part of this paper the notion of orientation is expanded and radicalized; examples are shown that there is an increasing need for being educated which can be successfully met by companies and their offerings. But what could radicalization mean in this particular context? Let us take the idea of customer satisfaction seriously. Let us ask: what is it that really satisfies the customer? There must be many unsatisfied needs like masochistic tendencies, bad and querulous moods, the joy of tinkering and improvisation or the thrill of potential failure (Liebl 1999). They can be served and provide wonderful experiences. Perhaps these deviant but ubiquitous tendencies are compatible with the needs of companies to serve customers in a low-cost manner. It would be ideal if an insulting minimum service made customers feel divine. This balance of domination and submission—this symbiosis of masochism and sadism—in a customer relationship is important (Mehrabian and Russell 1974; Fournier 1998), but not very well understood in marketing theory.

In his *Harvard Business Review* article "Torment Your Customers (They'll Love It)" Brown (2001) argues that customers do not at all want to always get what they wish and do not at all want to be permanently pampered by Total Customer Care:

> Don't get me wrong: I have nothing against customers. Some of my best friends are customers. Customers are a good thing, by and large, provided they're kept well downwind. My problem is with the concept of—and I shudder to write the term—"customer centricity". Everyone in business today seems to take it as a God-given truth that companies were put on this earth for one purpose alone: to pander to customers. Marketers spend all their time slavishly tracking the needs of buyers, then meticulously crafting products and pitches to satisfy them. If companies were Dickens characters, marketing would be Uriah Heep: unctuous, ubiquitous, and unbearable. The truth is, customers don't know what they want. They never have. They never will be. The wretches don't even know what they don't want, as the success of countless rejected-by-focus-groups products, from the Chrysler minivan to the Sony Walkman, readily attests. A

Fig. 5-1: Ralf Peters: *Tankstelle - blau*, 1998. Courtesy: Bernhard Knaus Fine Art, Frankfurt am Main, Germany

Fig. 5-2: Komar & Melamid: *America's Most Wanted Painting*, 1997. Reprinted from Wypijewski 1997

> mindless devotion to customers means me-too products, copycat advertising campaigns, and marketplace stagnation (Brown 2001, 83).

This line of thinking is substantiated by cultural theorists—"The DJ doesn't know what she wants until she hears it" (Eshun 1998)—and entrepreneurs whose business models capitalize on the problems created by an abundance of choice: "The average consumer does not know what he wants, as he is overwhelmed by this challenge" (Soethof 2010). From the standpoint of strategic marketing, it is too simplistic to fulfil customer wants instead of creating genuine innovations. A particularly striking example is presented by Russian artists Komar and Melamid. They made surveys using a comprehensive standardized questionnaire about what people want to see on paintings and what they do not want to see. What they regard as beautiful and as ugly. Which colours they prefer. Whether they prefer abstract art or landscapes; and which objects or persons should be represented on the painting (Wypijewski 1997). According to their market research, the most popular painting of the USA would roughly look like the one in Fig. 5-2. Where we end up, when art listens to customer wants, is obvious: in customer-oriented kitsch.

Brown's and Komar/Melamid's ideas and statements support our aim of extending orientation in a direction of educating customers. It also conforms to recent conclusions by Ullrich (2010) who advocates an aesthetic education of consumers. Although Brown's arguments seem striking, he does not elaborate what it means today to educate and torment customers successfully. This is the question that is going to be addressed in the remainder of this paper. Two case studies are presented in order to document business models based on customer education and domination/submission.

Case Study 2: Ikea

When we deal with education, we are always dealing with domination and submission and sadomasochistic rituals between master and apprentice. Düllo (2006) shows that (painful) education is also a major part of IKEA's successful business design. The author, a cultural theorist with a background in pedagogy, has interviewed many consumers concerning their relationships to IKEA and has been regularly observing people in IKEA stores. Düllo (2000) regards the influence of IKEA as so pervasive that he even speaks of an "IKEAization of German households". The three most important aspects of customer education identified by Düllo can be summarized as follows: By experimenting with cheap accessories and affordable furniture, people who do not know very much about design can develop their tastes and their styling competences. But this has a price for the consumers, because the process is not painless: IKEA is a most difficult test bed for couples and their relationships.

> Many decisions and impressions are compressed down to a few hours. And particularly on Saturdays, the store is packed with people, which still increases the stress level. […] The expectations produced by the catalogue are higher than what is met by the actual supply. When couples exit with empty hands, their arguing lasts while driving back home (Düllo 2006).

This means that those who are not buying will be punished; but also, that those who buy are going to be punished too, because at home they have to put together the pieces of furniture. This may take hours and hours and not only 20 minutes as advertised in the catalogue (Fig. 5-3). The cultural analyst explains why customers are willing to do this:

> We are living in an age of indirectness. Things are pre-fabricated. The experience of DIY is missing today. The attractive side of DIY is the experience of immediateness. The masculine feeling of working on a part of the world causes satisfaction (Düllo 2006; Fig. 5-4).

However, and this is another interesting feature of IKEA's educational program, clients will not get this satisfaction easily. At least, it seems so. Apparently there is almost always one screw missing in the IKEA toolbox (Fig. 5-5). The cultural analyst regards this as a myth:

> The myth of the missing screw is a very tricky fake. The same is true for the myth of the seemingly complicated instruction manuals. These are challenges that people want to meet (ibid.).

Now we have outlined the educational mechanisms of IKEA's business design. Summing it up, we can say that IKEA provides to awkward consumers a space for experiments and simulations with educational value. These simulations are targeting specific deficits of both genders. Women can develop their tastes in a trial-and-error manner without ruining their household financially. And men are practising their masculinity by meeting fake challenges and solving simulated problems. In short, IKEA provides domestication in the twofold sense of the word. The result is a well-tempered mixture of pleasure and pain, which may be the reason for its mass-compatibility.

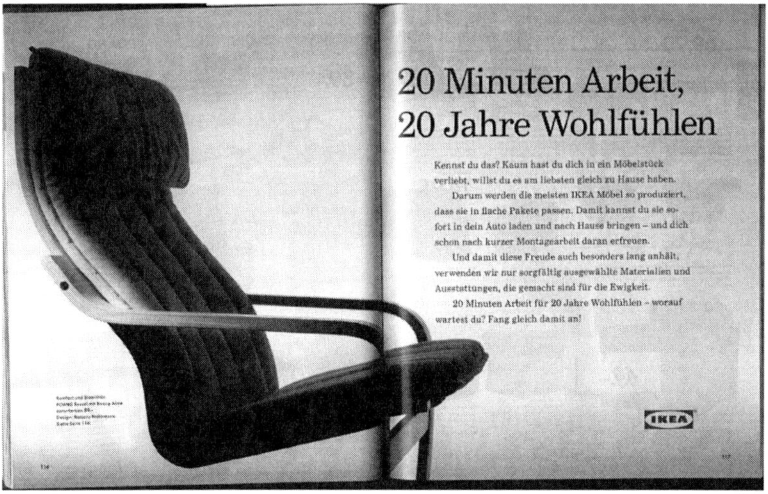

Fig. 5-3: IKEA Catalogue: “20 Minutes of Work. 20 Years of Homeliness”

Fig. 5-4: IKEA Catalogue: “Work as You Like it”

Fig. 5-5: IKEA Catalogue: “We Save This. You Save That.”

Case Study 3: Witten/Herdecke University

Domination and submission are common subjects in advertising. German journalist Holger Liebs (2002) wrote:

> Pornography is the fashion tool of the moment. The times of cold and noble, lady-like eroticism as in the case of Peter Lindbergh and Helmut Newton are gone. Bestiality and sadomasochism, masturbation and all sorts of fetishism are now en vogue.

However, in the context of strategic customer orientation the symbolisms of a “porno chic” are not as relevant as the material phenomena of the offering. Nevertheless, the following advertising campaign is particularly interesting, because it represents a proper reflection of the offering and the business system.

The example refers to a campaign for the (private) University of Witten/Herdecke. During more than a decade there had been repeated attempts to launch an advertising campaign for the university. But there was never a satisfactory proposition and there was never a design that fitted with the feelings and images that faculty and students had of themselves. Things suddenly changed when German weekly newspaper *Die Zeit* (Hartung 2004) asked some advertising agencies to create fictitious campaigns for selected German universities. The newspaper people had done this on their own behalf without asking these universities. The result, a creation by advertising agency Springer & Jacoby, is shown in Fig. 5-6.

Fig. 5-6: Campaign for Witten/Herdecke University: "Germany's Hardcore School of Thinking"

The claim can be roughly translated as "Germany's hardcore school of thinking". This design was a stunning success in the organization. "Yes, it's exactly like this!" was the spontaneous and consensual reaction—not only of the faculty staff but particularly of the students. It was more than a nice idea of creating a trashy image in order to communicate it to the people outside; it was a valid description of what was going on inside, creating a high amount of identification and pride within the organization itself. Students at Witten/Herdecke University pay considerable tuition fees for being challenged and for being required to continually test their own limits. This is not comfortable at all, and sometimes it even hurts. But this is exactly the thrill for those who expose themselves to such an offering, in order to finally cope with it. "If it won't kill me, it will make me stronger": This is the reason why Witten/Herdecke University is always ranked among the top universities with respect to student satisfaction.

Conclusions

The case studies reveal that customers' dispositions are complex, counter-intuitive and paradoxical. Customers want to meet challenges, test their own limits, build communities of suffering and address deficits in competences. A contemporary way of customer orientation does not mean being *oriented towards* the customer but *orienting the* customer. Education and training is part of this orientation process which may even include "blood, sweat and tears". This insight is going to spread gradually. A recent issue of *GDI Impuls* (GDI 2009), a trend journal edited by the Zurich-based Gottlieb Duttweiler Institute, was dedicated to the subject of "un-". Under the label "un-convenience" the following conclusion was drawn: "if you want to increase the wellness factor of your offering, you will have to make consumption more inconvenient." This represents an approach that has been reflected in design for more than one decade. Japanese designer Naoto Fukasawa (2007) spoke of "The good of not being too convenient" when introducing his concept of a toaster for just one slice of bread. Similarly, British design theorist Anthony Dunne (1999) refers to "user-unfriendliness" as a gentle form of provocation which characterises the post-optimal object. According to Dunne, this (constructive) concept should not be confused with user-hostility and is derived from poetry where being convenient and obvious is not the ultimate aim.

If we look at products with a so-called "cult quality", we will very often find that they carefully handle a delicate balance between domination and submission or pleasure and pain. This is increasingly supported by techniques like limiting product availability or merciless selection of clients. Louis Vuitton is one of the companies that show particular virtuosity in this respect; they have recently restricted access to their stores, limited the number of items sold to a single client, and reduced opening times before Christmas.

Therefore, customer orientation is not about arbitrarily breaking *some* rules of the marketplace; it is about understanding and using paradoxical dispositions of customers which shape their uses and production of meanings. The issue behind the notion of "customer orientation" is the following: What is the idea of man in marketing? It is apparent that in marketing the underlying concept is a little simplistic and dominated by a logic of "happy go lucky". Thus there is little wonder that this human being called customer is so rarely satisfied. In the final analysis, it is still true what Patrick LeQuement, former head of design at Renault, had said about strategic marketing and customer orientation: it is not about asking people what they want and then crafting products according to their answers. It is about creating products that people could not imagine, but about which they say in hindsight, that they had always wanted them (Büschemann 1999).

References

Beck, Ulrich, and Elisabeth Beck-Gernsheim. 2002. *Individualization: Institutionalized Individualism and its Social and Political Consequences.* London: Sage.

Brown, Stephen. 2001. "Torment Your Customers (They'll Love It)." *Harvard Business Review* 79 (6): 82–88.

Büschemann, Karl-Heinz. 1999. "Dem Zeitgeist auf der Spur: Was der Kunde nicht will, aber immer wollte – Designer Patrick Le Quement verhilft Renault zu erfolgreichen Autos und einem modernen Image." *Süddeutsche Zeitung*, December 20.

Düllo, Thomas. 2000. "'Ikeaisierung' der Wohnwelt: Wie uns ein Wohnkonzept zu Dauerjugendlichen macht." In *ZimmerWelten: Wie junge Menschen heute wohnen*, edited by Jan Carstensen, Thomas Düllo, and Claudia Richartz-Sasse, 92–99. Essen: Klartext.

—. 2006. "Erfahren von Direktheit." Interview by Andreas Grosse-Halbür. Wirtschaftswoche, May 12. http://www.wiwo.de/unternehmen-maerkte /erfahren-von-direktheit-140546.

Düllo, Thomas, and Franz Liebl, eds. 2005. *Cultural Hacking: Kunst des Strategischen Handelns.* Wien, New York: Springer.

Dunne, Anthony. 1999. *Hertzian Tales: Electronic Products, Aesthetic Experience and Critical Design.* London: RCA CRD Research.

Enzensberger, Hans-Magnus. 1992. *Mediocrity and Delusion: Collected Diversions.* London: Verso Books.

Eshun, Kodwo. 1998. *More Brilliant than the Sun: Adventures in Sonic Fiction.* London: Quartet.

Fournier, Susan. 1998. "Consumers and Their Brands: Developing Relationship Theory in Consumer Research." *Journal of Consumer Research* 24 (3): 343–373.

Fukasawa, Naoto. 2007. *Naoto Fukasawa.* London: Phaidon Press.

Gabriel, Yiannis, and Tim Lang. 1995. *The Unmanageable Consumer: Contemporary Consumption and Its Fragmentation.* London: Sage.

—. 2009. "New Faces and New Masks of Today's Consumer." *Journal of Consumer Culture* 3: 312–341.

GDI (Gottlieb Duttweiler Institute). 2009. *GDI Impuls*, no. 4. Zürich: Gottlieb Duttweiler Institute.

Gross, Peter. 1994. *Die Multioptionsgesellschaft.* Frankfurt: Suhrkamp.

Hartung, Manuel J. 2004. "Studier bei mir.“ *Zeit Online*, September 30. http://www.zeit.de/2004/41/C-werbung.

Herrmann, Andreas, Frank Huber, and Christine Braunstein. 2000. "Kundenzufriedenheit garantiert nicht immer mehr Gewinn." *Harvard Business Manager* 22 (1): 45–55.

Levitt, Theodore. 1960. "Marketing Myopia." *Harvard Business Review* 38 (4): 45–56.

Liebl, Franz. 1999. "Der Roberto-Blanco-Faktor." *Brand eins* 1 (3): 112–113.

—. 2008. "Konsuminnovationen durch Cultural Hacking: Das Beispiel Ikea-Hacking.“ In *Konsumguerilla: Widerstand gegen Massenkultur?*, edited by Birgit Richard, and Alexander Ruhl, 33–54. Frankfurt am Main: Campus.

—. 2010. "'Bricolo-Chic': Der Bastler als Schnittstelle von Marketing, Trendforschung und Cultural Studies (updated version)." In *Populäre Kultur als repräsentative Kultur: Die Herausforderung der Cultural Studies*, edited by Udo Göttlich, Winfried Gebhardt, and Clemens Albrecht, 261–289. Köln: Halem.

Liebl, Franz, Claudia Mennicken, Thorsten Voigt, and Tim Wesener. 2005. "'Ja, mit einem guten Gefühl auf jeden Fall.' Die Markenbilder von Aral und BP in den Köpfen der Kunden." In *Markenfusion: Strategie und Gestaltung – Warum Aral kommt und BP bleibt*, edited by Bernd Vangerow, Uwe Franke, Bettina Lehmann, Franz Liebl, and Claudia Mennicken, 79–87. Basel: Birkhäuser.

Liebl, Franz, and Olaf G. Rughase. 2002. "Storylistening." *GDI Impuls* 20 (2): 34–39.

Liebs, Holger. 2002. "Größer als das Leben – Orgien, Orgien, wir wollen Orgien: Wie die Modefotografie die Kunstwelt erobert." *Süddeutsche Zeitung*, April 25.

Macdonald, Stuart. 1995. "Too Close for Comfort? The Strategic Implications of Getting Close to the Customer." *California Management Review* 37 (4): 8–27.

Mehrabian, Albert, and James A. Russell. 1974. *An Approach to Environmental Psychology.* Cambridge, MA: MIT Press.

Porter, Michael E. 1996. "What Is Strategy?" *Harvard Business Review* 74 (6): 61–78.
Reichheld, Frederick F. 1993. "Loyalty-Based Management." *Harvard Business Review* 71 (2): 64–73.
Soethof, Fabian. 2010. "Verbraucher wissen nicht, was sie wollen." *Zitty Berlin* 26: 44–45.
Ullrich, Wolfgang. 2010. "On the Aesthetic Education of Consumer." Paper presented at the conference *Consumer Culture: Between Aesthetics, Social Distinction and Ecological Activism*, Palacký University Olomouc, Olomouc, October 7–9.
Wypijewski, JoAnn, ed. 1997. *Painting by Numbers: Komar and Melamid's Scientific Guide to Art*, New York: Farrar Straus Giroux, 1997.

MASS INTELLIGENCE AND THE COMMODITIZED READER

IVANA USPENSKI

The rise of the Internet and the overwhelming dependency of all of humankind on it since it was introduced to mass users in the last decade of the 20th century, as well as human kind's ever growing dependency on mechanical, prosthetic mediation in sizing up the world in the age of new media cultures have brought about significant changes in the ways humans in general tend to interact with and see the world around themselves. One of the fields which may have suffered the most significant changes in this shift from the traditional anthropocentric model of culture to the cyborg one is the field of reception, of extracting meaning from the interactions one makes with the world and the meanings one extracts from these interactions. In this sense it is the very process of reading that needs to be readdressed and reconceptualized. The very process of reading, understood very loosely and structuralistically as the process of extraction and consumption of meaning or affects, is no longer activity done and produced solely by an anthropomorphic entity, but we need to bear in mind the fact that nowadays the reading is often being done (and if I may add ever more so) by machines, computers. In everyday life we tend to talk about the computers *reading* data, the computers *reading* algorithms or software *reading* the inputs, but we don't actually think very much of it. Well, we should. Before I address this issue in a more detailed way, let me just point out how the position of *reader* has developed over history, which can give us more precise inputs in defining the role of this agent today.

If one looks back and tries to establish the key milestones in the development of the reader as a concept and its respective reading strategies, one could argue that there were actually three very important cultural settings which gave birth to their respective reading agents. One is the bourgeois society of the 18th century and onwards that Sartres writes about in his groundbreaking work *What Is Literature?*. It is the society characterized by its overarching quest for individual expression of thought and expressing individual taste which has in its turn led to a deeply individual attitude towards literature consumption and reading in general. This basically means that the reading process, which in earlier times was the process which had been engaging peers and families around folk tales or myths read out loud by the "head" of the family, with the invention of the printing press and wide dissemination of books, has now changed completely and turned into a very individual and intimate experience. The bourgeois reader, when confronted with a novel or a poem literally plunged into it looking for hidden meanings and moral teachings planted into the words by the author. The reader tried to interpret the actions, words and doings of the book's heroes in accordance with her or his own age, social, historical, or cultural contexts. The pleasure one extracted from such a process was a deeply individual and emotional one. The reading process of the bourgeois society was thus a sort of quest for meaning undertaken by a reader going through fiction and making individual cognitive and affective efforts, which when finished awarded the reader with the ultimate satisfaction of closure. Even though envisioning of the bourgeois reader thus has the risk of romanticizing the entire concept, one of the indicators proving such a state was of course the dominant position of the novel as the most popular fiction literary genre of the age. This is quite understandable considering the fact that it was the only genre able to give a sense of linearity and purpose to the reader through its cause and effect structure anchored in its narrativity.

The second milestone in re-inventing the reader as a concept and its role in the production and consumption of cultural artefacts was the rise of mass media, the electronic ones, with television and cinema leading the way. The mid-20th century witnessed masses of people consuming the same media content disseminated via their TV or radio sets or in their movie theatres at the same time. When theory tried to address this new found phenomenon it logically reached for the terminology found in theatrical and other performing arts which had of old been addressing multiple spectatorships. Therefore, mass media contents gave birth to mass spectatorship, multiplying the multiple spectatorship of old times tens- or even hundreds-fold. So, mass media stories gave birth to mass media readers which in their own terms were now addressed as audiences. The concept of audience is a very complex and wide one, but in plain words it sums up the reading strategies and experiences of individuals to common conclusions and presentations about meanings they extract from the respective mass media content, thus presenting the audience as a holistic entity with its common characteristics determined by the cultural, historical, economical, age and other contexts of the individuals forming this audience. Therefore, it is safe to say that the reading process in the era of mass media has already been set as a less intimate and less individual experience, than the one of the bourgeois society, executed and delivered by audiences which are defined according to the similar traits of the individuals composing them with regards to their social status, age, race or sex, whereas their differences remain set aside. The audience of the 20th century was thus a construct of the industry of entertainment producing mass media texts for global cultural consumption (as defined already by one of the pioneers of media reception studies, Robert Escaprit).

To sum up, the reading agent of the bourgeois society was just that, a reader as an individual entity experiencing reading as a deeply personal process. Starting from the mid-20th century mass media gave rise to the new concept of mass media audience as a dominant reading agent shifting the status of a reading process from a lone quest to the one of common consumption. But what about new media texts and new media cultures? How have new media interfaces and new media screens influenced the development of this agent further? I would argue that we can no longer talk about the reader in the bourgeois sense of the word, nor about the audiences in the media studies sense of the word, but about intelligences. I propose to introduce the term "intelligence" instead of "reader" or "audience" in order to grasp just this most significant characteristic of the new media meaning (or affect) extraction processes and that is that it is being done by two ontologically different agents: by biological minds (humans) on the one hand, and by synthesized electronic minds (machines) on the other hand.

When using the term "intelligence" here I am using it in its full scope. This means that I am not addressing only the noospheric level of the term, but also the other level specifically developed in Western world terminology, covering the level of data and knowledge, as well as the overall intellectual ability to grasp them. In this paper, apart from the ontological, ground difference between the electronic and biological intelligences, as those of a machine and a human, I will try to make further differentiation between two important concepts of new media reading intelligences and those are the concepts of collective intelligence on one hand and the mass intelligence, on the other and especially when referring to Internet text.

The term "collective intelligence" was introduced to media theory by French philosopher Pierre Lévy in 1994. With this term Lévy has tried to mark the specific phenomenon which arises in the age of new media as a result of the specific influence the Internet as a global network has on the production of cultural artefacts and the consumption of knowledge. The question Lévy actually tries to answer when proposing this term is how the connectivity brought about by the Internet and the process of networking in general can help individuals, when connected, act collectively and thus make them express a higher degree of intelligence than any individual, group or computer on their own could ever have. By pinpointing this phenomenon Lévy expressed his conviction that the Internet and mass connectivity between people and respective technologies would finally result in radical civilization-wide changes. He prophetically stresses the following: "I foretell the coming of one planet-wide civilization based on the practice of collective intelligence in cyberspace" (Lévy 2001). According to his standpoint the dominant moving force of the new civilization is nested in collective imagination, which is to trigger, initiate and produce all the levels of reality to come. This basically means that the concept of ontological reality as it was traditionally accepted as a set of conventions of physical space and time within which a human bodily entity operates nowadays gets enriched by a series of new categories disseminated from digital platforms most commonly referred to today as virtual realities. The actions, responsibilities and production strategies performed by a human entity in a digitized world amount to the same significance and significant consequences as the actions she or he performs within the boundaries of the physical reality their body belongs to, as Lévy has sharply put it "We are responsible for the world which we create together through our thoughts, words and deeds" (ibid.).

What is additionally important is that Lévy is certain that collective intelligence as a new media phenomenon cannot be analyzed or talked about separately from the processes of reading and interpretation specifically taking place on the Internet. In order to encapsulate the specific nature of the process of reading with regards to Internet texts Lévy coined a new term for it, naming Internet reading a "profound vision", further stating that the reality and the meaning are not given by themselves, but on the contrary are only potential and can only be discovered through the process of reading as free understanding. Still, we should bear in mind the fact that the concept of freedom in the term "free understanding" is by no means arbitrary. It relies on choosing amongst a set of predefined choices, a set of predetermined paths. The sum of all thus made and possible choices which is what forms a collective intelligence, bears the responsibility for the actual inscription and manifestation of the digital world at any particular moment, as well as for the implications this world is projecting to material, bodily reality. The main question which therefore arises when one thinks about the new processes of reading and interpretation is which reality out of the sums of all potential realities these processes shall invoke? James Surowiecki, the author of the groundbreaking work in this field *The Wisdom of Crowds* would argue that it would be at the same time the most probable and optimal out of all potential realities, simply because "the crowd is holding a nearly complete picture of the world in its collective brain" (Surowiecki 2005, 11). The concept of the collective brain introduced here by Surowiecki, which clearly evokes the concept of the World Brain presented by H. G. Welles decades ago is crucial here, because in collective intelligences we are not talking about diversified sums of individual intellects, but rather we are taking it as a holistic, ontological entity. A collective intelligence does not equal any of the individual knowledge growing strategies, but rather is represented as a qualitative sum of all of them which can be treated only as one, singular but heterogeneous entity.

As it is commonly referred to, the Internet is based on an open and global exchange of data. In a surrounding thus set the overall human experience, imagination, intelligence, arts and knowledge become mobile, potent and disseminable to the extreme. The knowledge is no longer a set of confirmed and fixed facts, but rather a project which is in a constant condition of taking place and execution, an online project conducted by collective intelligences. The problematization of collective intelligences is just picking up pace, so there is no one clear insight, or one widely accepted definition of the term, on which we can rely. Still, this is the term with which contemporary theory tries to describe in a more exact manner the problems of accumulation and update of human knowledge. Up to recently those were the processes which took decades, even centuries to evolve and be noticed, but which now take place in "real-time", actually witnessed by the individuals and collectives who directly take part in this accumulation and update. Therefore, collective intelligence is not only a very rapid, almost instantaneous gathering and mastering of the existing information and concepts on the Internet, but rather its fundamental mark is in what Jane McGonigal has recognized as "work with the collected facts and viewpoints to actively author, discover and invent new, computer-fuelled ways of thinking, strategizing and coordinating" (McGonigal 2007). Therefore, the starting thesis planted by Lévy that no one knows everything, but everyone knows something has ground rooted the differential knowledge as a key category of power online. This means that the power-rate of an individual in a collective intelligence is directly proportional to the rate of positive differential knowledge this individual contributes to the collective intelligence in question. The bigger the scope of new, previously uncollected, unmarked and unaccumulated knowledge an individual brings to the collective intelligence, the bigger will be the influence and the authority this individual will receive back from the collective intelligence, whereas the collective intelligence is defined in accordance with Jenkins' envisioning of the term as the "ability of virtual communities to leverage the combined expertise of their members" (Jenkins 2006, 26–27).

To illustrate the above mentioned I should like to introduce an example which will clearly demonstrate how the collective intelligences operate, and that is Wikipedia. Wikipedia is an Internet project run online. It is an encyclopaedia of all around knowledge written directly by the Internet users in the Wiki software. Wikipedia is already the biggest encyclopaedia of human knowledge ever written. It is composed of texts written by Internet users and verified by their peers, meaning other Internet users. This basically means that in order to be posted in Wikipedia an article as an encyclopaedic unit proposed by its writer/user needs to have a relevant number of references proving its authenticity and veracity. Still, even when the article is supported by a relevant number of references and factual statements it is by no means fixed or unchangeable. On the contrary, each collective intelligence project, and thus even Wikipedia, leaves open the possibility for its contents to be altered, changed, questioned by other users and other authors who, if enough evidence and reliable reference material is provided can replace the article with a new one, a more precise one written by themselves. Besides the fact that collective intelligence lies on the presupposition that all knowledge is simply a platform which can be challenged, altered and updated, its other important marking is the velocity of its development, which has now come very close to being instantaneous. As Manuel Castelles has put it, up to the 20th century new technologies were mastered through the processes of usage and doing. This process has picked up pace so violently in the 21st century, that we are now in the era when usage is learnt and mastered already through the very process of new technology production.

It is important to note, though, that when we are talking about "collective intelligences", we are not referring only to the cumulative noetic mass of individuals being part of a certain knowledge community. This term also engathers all the documents, information, conclusions and knowledge shared and stored within this community, or "collective", which is the term I would rather use instead of "community" as John Seely Brown and Douglas Thomas use this term.[1] It also encapsulates all the

[1] In an interview with Henry Jenkins these authors of *A New Culture of Learning: Cultivating the Imagination for a World of Constant Change* have implied that instead of using global accepted term "community", they rather refer to collectives,

potential individual capacity of knowledge the members of the collective in question have, and in a sense referring to its absolute positive capacity (meaning that it excludes all the falsities, repetitions and duplications, accounting only for positive differential knowledge enabling constant evolution of a collective intelligence), even if in a certain Internet text this capacity is not specifically manifested or textualized.

But what about all those duplications? The same readings which take place thousands of times or the readings which bring about wrong conclusions and errors? Are they not to be treated as reading processes, regardless of whether done by humans or machines? Of course they are to be treated as readings, but with different specifics even more relevant for the consumerism theories and scholarships. The term I propose for these manifestations is "mass intelligence". There is no clear notion in contemporary literature of the difference between collective and mass intelligence. "Mass intelligence" is actually a term I am taking from Internet business economy, where it is defined as a "process by which the mental acumen of individuals is successfully combined in some way that the noise does not drown the signal of truth" (Wikinomics 2010). But the term thus defined is of no real relevance for the phenomenon of the commoditized reader I'm trying to associate it with, so in this paper I will try to propose an alternative definition of the term, specific for the new media studies discourse, which will hopefully as opposed to the term "collective intelligence" enable us to have a clearer insight into the characteristics of the commoditized reader online.

The first time I came across the term "mass intelligence" was when reading a very inspiring article named "The Age of Mass Intelligence", written by John Parker and published in the December 2008 issue of the *Intelligent Life* magazine. Even though Parker doesn't actually define this term and he uses it rather arbitrarily, giving it various generic meanings, this very article has key significance in presenting several interesting findings and pointing towards new conclusions in the question of knowledge capacity and the noematic evolution of humankind. The opinion of the general public regarding human intelligence is usually that humankind is becoming more and more dependent on computers and machines in doing everyday tasks, so that instead of evolving and developing its intellectual capacity further, it is actually degrading and becoming less efficient and less effective in dealing with everyday issues and problems. Parker tries to prove the contrary or that actually as we have

---

which they define as "collections of people who form around a central platform [...] [They] are actually institutions that enable and enhance individual agency" (Jenkins 2011).

become more exposed to superficial communication flows or even less involved in executing intellectual tasks on our own, there is a significant and crucial tendency towards intellectual self-improvement and knowledge widening present. As Parker sees it, it is especially notable with regards to the greater interest individuals demonstrate today for "high art" artefacts as well as increasing demand for continuing education programs and the growth of number of people holding master's of PhD degrees. As Parker has put it "people want more intellectually demanding things to see and hear, not fewer. Surely both things are happening at once: part of the population is dumbing down, part is wising up" (Parker 2008). So, as Parker sees it, "mass intelligence" is the term covering the general issues of humankind's intellect and its urge to be exposed to higher levels of intellectual stimuli. He does not, on the other hand, make clear distinctions between the terms "collective intelligence" and "mass intelligence" and even uses them as synonyms.

Still, in order to fully grasp the notion of the role of the new media reader and its commoditization online, the difference between collective and mass intelligence cannot be stressed strongly enough. Let us just take the examples of popular and mass culture and try to point out the differences between them. The parallel in this distinction can then be drawn to the problems of mass and collective intelligence as well. John Fiske, one of the key theoreticians of popular culture and culture in general, defines popular culture according to the role it has in the overall process of circulation of power, and that is its active role in resisting the hegemonic power of dominant ideologies. According to Fiske, popular culture opposes the ideology of consumerism. It cannot by any means be defined in relation to consumption, but rather as an active process of creation and evocation of meanings which arises when popular culture as a force meets artefacts of mass production within the boundaries set by a certain social system. Popular culture is in its core a productive force, a "bottom-up" process, which means that the direction of its development and embodiment goes from the audience, reader, user acting upon and intervening on contents or texts offered by the industry of mass entertainment or mass production. As opposed to popular culture, mass culture is represented by a "top-bottom" process of mass consumption of cultural artefacts produced by this very same industry and offered to the wide audiences and consumers. The main difference lies in the fact that not only can the products of mass culture be consumed, but they can also be labelled, priced and offered as commodities on markets, being at the same time imprinted with collective desires externally imposed by mass media and advertising systems. On the other hand, the artefacts of popular culture cannot be commoditized predominantly due to the fact that they are determined by their semantic significance, rather than their actual industrial production and numeric value. They are thus determined by the discourses arising around the objects of mass culture when meaning-making strategies of popular culture agents act upon those objects extracting them from their roles as products for mass consumption and turning them into completely new discursivc popular culture artefacts. As Henry Jenkins has put it:

> Popular culture is what happens to the materials of mass culture when they get into the hands of consumers, when a song played on the radio becomes so associated with a particularly romantic evening that the two young lovers decide to call it "our song" (Jenkins 2006, 136).

Fiske nevertheless believes that mass culture is all about believing in dominant ideologies and their hegemonic position, which is grounded in the belief that commodities produced and offered by mass-production industries can be artificially imposed to consumers in such a manner that they override the differences in needs amongst individual members of the audiences or consumers, offering them uniform products and thus forcing them to waive their rights to individuality and personalization. To sum up, mass culture is all about industrial mass production of artefacts designed to be consumed, whereas popular culture is all about extracting customized meanings out of mass-produced artefacts aimed towards overall individualization and customization.

Mass culture doesn't recognize exceptions, alternative readings or alternative uses; there is no possibility for an individual to critically relate to its artefacts within the boundaries of mass culture. Its artefacts are mass-produced, quantifiable and one can only talk about their number and market value, they can only be taken as plain sums of individual elements in their quantity and price. In order for mass culture as part of consumer society to survive, the language of its artefacts needs to be radically simplified, so that it can override all the diversified social idiolects and appeal only to the common ones making it comprehensible for the widest possible audiences and number of consumers.

So, if we relate popular culture to collective intelligence, as a productive and evolutionary force, mass culture is then to be related to mass intelligence in such a manner that they both represented mass-produced quantifiable elements which can be labelled, priced and sold. But what is then the actual mass-intelligence product which gets commoditized? It is the mass intelligence itself. Each time an individual visits a page, clicks on a "like" button or posts a comment she or he invests a little of her or his own intelligence online. By doing so they are actually producing certain values. These traces of their online activities can be counted and valorised, expressed by numbers, quantified and thus priced, offered as commodities and sold. Mass intelligence is a simple, arbitrary sum of all of those traces, read and collected by a machine (a synthetic algorithm), quantified, packed as commodity and sold as a number of clicks, likes, displays, impressions etc. It doesn't deal with content or with meaning as collective intelligences do. It doesn't care for the duplications or false data or its quality in general, the amount of data is all that is of significance for a mass intelligence. It is very close to the concept of the audience as defined within the advertising industry, counting only the sums of ratings, and not accounting for the meaning extraction strategies which lay behind these ratings. Within mass intelligence, the content is relevant only insomuch as it is the means to quantify its activities and work invested, whereas in collective intelligences the content is relevant as a means for extracting meanings for further collective intelligence development. Mass intelligence is a commodity, collective intelligence is a force.

As is the case with mass culture, in order to survive in the new-media economy mass intelligence needs to be based on the oversimplification of its vocabulary. All the distortions brought about by the differences in individual usage and activities online need to be avoided and packed in templates so that a specific algorithm can process the data statistically in order to commoditize it. Just consider Facebook. People and their relations are extremely complicated, but on Facebook, in order to compose a profile one is forced to choose amongst a set of predefined categories ("in a relationship", "married", "male", "age 25", etc.). All those fine and delicate differences between our human actions which mark us as unique individuals are set aside and we get labelled and sorted and processed and read. So, the agent who actually does the reading in the case of mass intelligence is the computer, a machine reading the traces of our work invested online behind ourselves, collecting them and commoditizing them, turning the actual human reading agents into a commodity. It would be safe to state that mass intelligence thus is a simple sum of all the information a certain online community deposes of during its activities conducted online and this information includes duplications, falsities, errors or unreliable data. Like mass culture, neither is mass intelligence based on semantic production or alternative readings of contents imposed by industry. Mass intelligence is therefore, just like artefacts of mass culture, commoditized and it can be traded for money or other goods and it is most often offered to the advertising industry. The elementary unit of mass intelligence is a numeric one; it is a number (of clicks, impressions, likes). The elementary unit of collective intelligence is differentiated content. Mass intelligence, like the mass commoditized reader is actually a construct, a product of computer-based software reading strategies.

Let us again present an example. Google with all its subpages and subservices is an ultimate reading machine and dominant mass intelligence agent. In fact, all search engines are, but the PageRank algorithm Google is based on is as close as an algorithm can get to processing and identifying the authority and relevance of an information pack based on the human work and time invested in searching and interacting with it. (Aarseth uses the term "ergon" to mark this significant working activity an individual invests when browsing the Internet). In blunt and highly simplified words the PageRank algorithm is programmed to define the significance of a web page and its hierarchy in relation to all the search results outputted by the search engine responding to a set of strings as a search input. For each and every web page "PageRank is an objective measure of its citation importance that corresponds well with people's subjective idea of importance" (Brin and Page 1998). Simply put the relevance and consequently value of an Internet page is defined by the number and quality of links which refer to it.

The radical change which Google has introduced to the world of the Internet is based on the absolute automation of the process of data gathering and indexation. Old search engines like AltaVista or even Yahoo at its pioneer stage were initially based on manual data organization and indexation, heavily determined by the human factor, thus basically inheriting all the stereotypes and canons of traditional media archiving processes. They were guided by an encyclopaedic hierarchy of superimposed structures and predefined slots, structures fairly resembling those of heavily branched trees, which made them slow and rigid. The automation of the processes of indexation and sorting based on the number of clicks and their respective quality has significantly increased the relevance and reliability of the results thus outputted. The quality and the relevance I am referring to here are, on the other hand, supported by the amount and relevance of the actual human work invested through perception, inspection and action on any given hyperlinked page, meaning that it is actually supported by the quality and intensity of human ergodic activity. This actually means that the Google PageRank algorithm at the core of its automation process uses human perceptive and intellectual ergodic energy invested freely online as algorithmic input and then transforms it and outputs it as statistical, numerical data, or mass intelligence which can be quantified and therefore also commoditized.

Human attention, intelligence and insights in this manner are labelled with their respective economic value and offered to the market as a commodity.

Another example is the news.google.com website, delivering news from very diverse areas, collected all over the Internet and presented according to their popularity and searches done for them through the Google search engine. To make it clear, this site by no means represents collective intelligence, as its content is not generated by users. Rather, it is based on gathering and presenting news which have delivered the best quantifiable results. Thus, the news items which finally get presented are actually the ones which are based on the highest absolute common denominator of mass-readers' interests which is acquired through numerically counting the algorithm parameters, and with the logical presumption that this is exactly the kind of content which will further attract the biggest possible number of readers, resulting in biggest invested ergon through clicks, displays, likes, links, etc. So, the actual content and semantic significance of the actual news presented on this site are of no relevance. The only thing that is of relevance is the amount of traffic which this content can attract and produce, and which in turn can be packed, labelled, commoditized and sold to the advertising industry. As John Markoff has put it: "Google's software systematically exploits human knowledge and decisions about what is significant" (Markoff 2006; quoted in Carr 2008, 219). Whenever we click on a link or load a web page, Google becomes smarter for just this piece of information, and the Google shareholders become richer. In contrast to the human mind which has a selective and limited capacity for storing data, and no capacity whatsoever of storing conflicting data with equal objective cognitive distance, computers as reading machines have the unlimited ability of storing and never forgetting tons of information packs, even when they are confronting each other. This means that in the human mind a certain piece of information can be either correct or false. In a computer algorithm it can change its states depending on the actual software running and reading this piece of information. The basic difference between collective and mass intelligence lies in the fact that collective intelligences are set to choose one piece of information as correct, based on the presumption that it is the one most likely to contribute to the advancement of knowledge, so the act of selection is what matters, whereas in mass intelligences all the information bits exist on the same level, and the act of simple arbitrary collecting is what takes place. If a descriptive definition needs to be formulated, then mass intelligence would be the non-critical and arbitrary global gathering and accumulation of human knowledge, offering readers mass-interest texts which they can read, to which they can react, on which they can comment or to which they can hyperlink with the sole purpose of making these readers' ergodic activities quantifiable goods to which material value can be added in the form of price. Mass intelligence in the age of new media actually represents the commoditized work of new media readers.

As a conclusion I would like to underline that when considering the terms "collective intelligence" and "mass intelligence" a value judgement shouldn't be made in favour of either of the two. It is not possible to state that mass intelligence is not of the same usefulness and value as collective intelligence due to the fact that the former is not a productive force, whereas the latter is. Both terms are equally important and simply represent actual categories in new media culture as we find it today. Even though it is stated that mass intelligence is not a productive force, we shouldn't go so far as to state that it is not a useful one. We should just consider the examples Surowiecki gives, when stating that, even though mass intelligence brings with it a lot of unreliable data and errors, statistically, taken as a whole its average quality is almost always closer to truth and accuracy than any individual would come to by oneself. In the Google News example, the news items which are presented are the ones which have numerically triggered the highest number of individuals to read them, but consequently it is very probable that the content presented thus is relevant as well. The only point made here is that we should recognize the difference between the two and their respective strategies and use them accordingly. Should we need the fastest possible guess about how many pieces of popcorn fit in a super-sized popcorn bag we might just rely on the mass-intelligence data, but collective intelligence is the type we should turn to if we are trying to find the answer to the meaning of life.

References

Brin, Sergey, and Lawrence Page. 1998. "The Anatomy of a Large Scale Hypertextual Web Search Engine." Paper presented at the *Seventh International World-Wide Web Conference* (WWW 7), Brisbane, Australia, April 14–18. http://infolab.stanford.edu/~backrub/google.html.

Carr, Nicholas. 2008. *The Big Switch: Rewiring the World from Edison to Google.* New York, London: W. W. Norton.

Jenkins, Henry. 2006. *Convergence Culture: Where Old and New Media Collide.* New York, London: New York University Press.

—. 2011. "A New Culture of Learning: An Interview with John Seely Brown and Douglas Thomas (Part Two)." *Confessions of an Aca-Fan: The Official Weblog of Henry Jenkins*, January 21. http://henryjenkins.org/2011/01/a_new_culture_of_learning_an_i_1.html.

Lévy, Pierre. 2001. "Collective Intelligence: A Civilization." *Crossings: eJournal of Art and Technology* 1 (1). http://crossings.tcd.ie/issues/1.1/Levy/.

Markoff, John. 2006. "Entrepreneurs See a Web Guided by Common Sense." *New York Times*, November 12.

McGonigal, Jane. 2007. "Why I Love Bees: A Case Study in Collective Intelligence Gaming." http://www.avantgame.com/McGonigal_WhyILoveBees_Feb2007.pdf.

Parker, John. 2008. "The Age of Mass Intelligence." *The Economist: Intelligent Life Magazine* (Winter). http://www.moreintelligentlife.com/story/age-mass-intelligence.

Surowiecki, James. 2005. *The Wisdom of Crowds.* New York: Anchor Books. Kindle edition.

Wikinomics. 2010. "Mass Intelligence." Contributed March 10. http://www.socialtext.net/wikinomics/index.cgi?mass_intelligence.

GREY IS GORGEOUS: ON DOVE'S CAMPAIGN FOR REAL BEAUTY TARGETING OLDER CONSUMERS

KARIN LÖVGREN

Introduction

What do you think? Wrinkled or wonderful? The woman smiling back from the ad is attractive, her smile is warm and friendly, and her head is slightly tilted as her eyes meet the onlooker. Her skin is wrinkled and she is wonderful, truly beautiful. She is Irene, 96 years old at the time and she was a model for one of several ads portraying women with different appearances, inviting the observer to participate and cast a vote on whether the models' looks are a deviation from narrow beauty ideals or whether the concept of beauty can include a diversity of looks and appearances. Was the model fat or fit, flawed or flawless, can you be considered beautiful with small breasts, with grey hair, or past a certain age? These were the questions asked through the visual representations (Fig. 7-1).

The ads, appearing both interactively on the Internet and in more traditional media formats, such as print ads and on billboards, were part of Dove's launching of the "Campaign for Real Beauty", as it was dubbed. The Unilever company Dove claimed they wanted to change women's conceptions of beauty and strive for more diversity in norms and ideals regarding appearances. How can this campaign be understood in terms of gender and age? How is ageing represented?

Previous research on advertising using older models has focused on age stereotypes, representation in terms of number, roles of the older person, values ascribed to the older person and for what products the older person is used as a model (for an overview see Zhang et al. 2006). When discussing potential impact on perception and attitudes towards older people there has been a tacit understanding that media representations impact how the elderly are seen and valued. The results are discussed in cautious terms: cultural values may be influenced by the portraits presented in advertisements. The relationship between media material and its impact on cultural beliefs is too complex to answer in terms of cause and effect. Mediated messages cannot be demarcated from other media discourses or for that matter other forms of communication. Current research emphasizes the role of the viewer in interpreting the image, acknowledging the flexible ways in which the representation works (Featherstone and Hepworth 2007; Rose 2001). The former, however, underscores that images of old age can be understood as key resources in making sense of ageing (Featherstone and Hepworth 2007, 735).

Fig. 7-1: The outdoor advert titled "Wrinkled? Wonderful?" done by Ogilvy & Mather advertising agency for Dove skincare products in United Kingdom (released in December 2004)

Hence this article cannot assess and evaluate Dove's campaign in terms of the impact of representations of ageing. I will analyse adverts for anti-ageing products, comment on how middle aged women readers of popular press talked about advertisements addressing them, and in what can be termed an "ideology critical approach" analyse Dove's campaign especially in terms of its representations of ageing. I consider the changes in visual representation shown in Dove's Pro-age advertisements using older women as models in relation to age, ageing and gender. This is a close reading, using methods from visual analysis to discuss their messages about ageing, in comparison to much of the previous research on adverts using older models, which has been quantitative. In the article's conclusion I will come back to issues of the impact and meaning of advertisements in terms of ageism.

Material and Method

The present article draws on several forms of empirical material.[1] Fourteen interviews were carried out with women in the age range 45–63 years. The sampling strategy used here was to find different kinds of readers, from the devoted reader subscribing to the magazines, to the single copy buyer, but also including the reluctant or critical reader. The interviews were loosely structured, using a check list or interview guide to cover different topics, but letting the conversation steer the interview, the intent being to, in an ethnographic tradition, capture the wordings and expressions used by the informants. I looked at magazines and advertisements together with the interviewees. The concrete examples were used as a starting point to talk about the popular press and specifically about how ageing was represented. The interviews were transcribed verbatim. Analysis of the interviews was also carried out in an ethnographic manner, searching for patterns, recurring themes, and discrepancies in the narratives.

The main focus in this article is an analysis of Dove's marketing campaign, in terms of gender and age. I have thus used both text and visual analysis. For the text analysis I have asked questions regarding how age, and specifically ageing, is written about: what words or phrases are recurring, what rhetorical devices are used. How the readers are being addressed by advertisements has also been a focus. The slogans used in advertisements are usually short, often witty, with a catch phrase that gets the reader's attention. These texts have been analysed together with the visuals. For the visual analysis, a bricolage of methods from the cultural studies tradition was used to analyse the advertisements and the popular magazines in which they were featured (Sturken and Cartwright 2001; Rose 2001; O'Barr 1994). The primary purpose of the analyses is to describe, understand and problematize what the visual imagery conveys with regard to age and ageing. It can thus be described as an ideology critical approach. Here the cultural contexts of production and consumption of the visual are of relevance, as well as the power relations in which the image is encompassed. There are no simple truths to the meaning of the visual; instead meaning is created in the use and interpretation of the images (Sturken and Cartwright 2001). Visual literacy and interpretative skills are acquired; we learn how to interpret icons,

[1] The study is part of a larger research project (Lövgren 2009) where advertisers, marketers and journalists were also interviewed. In the present article, the angle of Dove's advertising has been further developed.

symbols, different visual genres and how to communicate through visual means.

I have started with a close reading of a sample of adverts: the ones frequently published in magazines targeting older women, with age as a unique selling point. The women interviewed also pointed out adverts that they found representative of adverts in this genre of popular press. Roughly they divided them into two categories. One was mainstream adverts that they said never really caught their attention. They demonstrated how they browsed past them and instead pointed out feature articles that interested them. The other category consisted of advertisements that got their attention by being striking or different. Advertisements from both categories have been included in my sample. I started by analysing the advertisements' denotations—what is being depicted and how. I then analysed the cultural associations, the connotations of the adverts. Different symbols or icons, different visual rhetorics, are used in shorthand communications with the readers. Meaning is created in signs that are culturally relevant and valid (Rose 2001, 69–99). Many adverts follow the same visual rhetoric. Included in the genre is a promise of change and transformation, but also a message that there is a problem that must be solved. The advertisement must have dimensions of realism, credibility and reliability in order to convince the consumer that the product is worth purchasing.

It is women's bodies that are represented as being in need of beauty and appearance work (Bordo 2004; Macdonald 1995). The increasing interest in the body can be related to the consumption society, where consumption is seen as part of people's identity work and where both hedonistic indulgence and body ideals of thin, slim, fit and youthful are emphasized (Bordo 2004; Featherstone and Hepworth 2007).

Too Old to Be in an Anti-ageing Ad

A characteristic of Dove's campaign was its hybridity. The company worked with several media channels and in different media formats. Dove presented a series of research reports on what women think of beauty parallel to their launching of new product lines and new advertisements (Etcoff et al. 2004; Etcoff et al. 2006; Butler et al. 2006). The campaign had an impact not only in paid-for advertisements, but also in editorials. In a commercially overloaded everyday life, getting journalistic coverage is considered the best advertising (Gill 2007).

Another large channel for the campaign was the Internet, with different websites and hyperlinks to product information, offers of samples, articles, blogs, or videos.

There are similarities between the visual imagery used in the advertising for Dove's product line, Pro-age, and other mainstream advertising targeting women with beauty products, and there are also differences. The Pro-age ads, just like mainstream ads, are visually constructed with a woman as eye catcher and a catch phrase, in this case "too old to be in an anti-ageing ad". The text refers to the fact that the depicted women are older than the established norm in advertising.

One characteristic of the Dove Pro-age advertisements that marks them as different from other advertising images is that the women portrayed are naked. How can this be interpreted?

Nakedness has connotations of revealing, of having nothing to hide, showing the whole truth, and thus of honesty. This gives the advertisements an aura of authenticity, thereby strengthening the ads' claim that the products do what they promise to do; the products' claim of reliability is visually asserted through the nudity. The nudity enhances the daring of the campaign: here are advertisements to be noticed, boldly asserting their difference.

The nudity distinguishes this part of the campaign from previous advertisements for Dove products, with visual imagery of younger women, of different sizes and shapes, depicted in white cotton underwear, connoting innocence and wholesomeness. One way to construe this difference is that the younger women's bodies are more charged with sexuality and therefore need to have their genitals and breasts covered in order not to convey an eroticized or sexualized reading of the advertisements, whereas older women can more safely be represented nude, with less risk of misinterpretation and without a sexualized reception of the ads. This difference of display then latches on to conceptions of age norms and a cultural bond between youth and sexuality.

The nudity, together with the way the models were posed, places the ads in an art tradition: the women sit in sculptural poses, covering both their breasts and their genitals representing the bodies as art objects. With the exception of some jewellery, which enhances the cultural dimensions of the ads, the women are in the nude. The nudity also underscores the fact that it is women's bodies that are displayed, women's bodies that are the objects of the onlooker's gaze and women's bodies that are compelled to change or in this case kept from changing. The advertisements' message is still that there is a problem that needs to be addressed through consumption. The text, "Beauty has no age limit" alludes to a best-before date, after which women are considered too old to be visual eye catchers, displayed in the nude. In spite of the claim that beauty has no age limit, we are reminded that there is a best-before date for visual representations.

A distinctive feature of the ads in the Pro-age series is that the women are older than is usually the case in advertising. Several of the models have grey hair, which in visual representations often is used as a symbol to connote higher age. In advertising, the norm for who is represented has been a young person. The fact that models in advertising are generally very young has been interpreted as reflecting the conflation between youth and beauty in Western beauty ideals (Bordo 2004). Youth equals health, fertility and beauty. Young models have also been used when the aim is to reach older consumer groups. The explanation for this has been that a youthful image appeals to both old and young audiences; that youthfulness has connotations of being modern, new, hip, evolving; positive values that brands want to be associated with. Another reason for using young models may be that women are alleged to have a subjective age approximately ten years younger than their chronological age to which marketers should appeal (Carrigan and Szmigin 2000; Gunter 1998; Lövgren 2009).

Dove's campaign stands out against the backdrop of the mainstream, formulaic advertisements. The audaciousness Dove showed in using older models must be interpreted in relation to norms in advertising regarding who is portrayed. This can be described in terms of the unmarked versus marked category, where the unmarked or primary category is the silent, self-evident norm, while the marked category is the opposite (Sturken and Cartwright 2001). The norm equals youth and beauty. The older women in the Pro-age ads can thus be interpreted as representing the exception to the rule, with old being the marked category. The majority of the models used are white women. As the unmarked category or the norm, the viewer does not notice the colour of their skin; instead the black model becomes the marked category. Race has been used to give products an exotic feeling and to an increasing extent to show social awareness and sophistication (ibid.). Correspondingly, Dove's campaign can be interpreted as showing social awareness by visually representing women in an age category other than the norm in advertising for skin lotions.

The ads all represent the models as beautiful, thus adhering to an established norm in advertising that can be understood to latch onto the idea that recognition of the beauty of the model leads to positive associations for the product as well (Söderlund 2006). What is new in Dove's campaigns is the emphasis on the idea that the women are "real", not professional models, and with appearances that slightly alter the conventions of what is included in definitions of beauty. The extent to which the advertisements portray "real beauty" can be discussed. The company has been careful to represent the women in a glamorous way.

In many senses, the women's bodies are representative of a Western beauty ideal: slim, thin, taught skin and even facial features. Despite the real beauty slogan of the campaign, the advertisements' visual representation is not one of realism, but of staged glamour. The norm of the importance of looking young risks being further reinforced when the visual imagery actually focuses on glamorous ideals instead of on more realistic representations of real bodies. This has to be interpreted in relation to the tacit assumptions behind advertising. The model used in the interactive campaign on beauty ideal whom viewers could rate as wrinkled or wonderful, that I refer to in the opening of this article, was reported to be 96 at the time; thus she could safely have her wrinkles emphasized. At this stage of life wrinkles are no longer a threat, whereas they are represented as something that should be combated for middle aged women in a transition period to old age.

A common denominator for these ads—and for almost all in this genre—is the use of photography. Photography is thought to render a reflection of reality, thus giving an impression of truth and accuracy, which lends credibility to the advertisements' promise of what the product will accomplish (Rose 2001).

Using photographer Annie Leibovitz to take the photos in the Pro-age campaign indicates that this was a serious undertaking by Dove. The photographer's name is rarely given in commercial shoots, one famous exception being Benetton's campaigns with Toscani as the photographer. Using a renowned and established photographer, known for her photographs of celebrities for magazine covers, gives status and thus credibility to the campaign. Patrick Dangin, well known for his skills in photo retouching, also worked on Dove's campaigns. He was interviewed for an article in The New Yorker (Collins 2008) and was quoted saying:

> "Do you know how much retouching was on that?" he asked. "But it was great to do, a challenge, to keep everyone's skin and faces showing the mileage but not looking unattractive" (Collins 2008).

A heated debate followed: Had the Pro-age campaign been retouched and how much? Dove answered that no retouching had been done on Annie Leibovitz's photographs, merely a removal of dust, but no digital manipulation. The controversy around this indicates how issues of credibility were at stake here. It was important that the pictures appeared authentic, and that they could be interpreted as displaying exactly what

Dove's campaign promised: a more accurate representation of real women in the targeted age category. If Dove were to have credibility in their claims of wanting to contribute to a change in conceptions of beauty, it was important that they come across as sincere and honest in their own use of visual images.

Pro-Age Products

The products in the Pro-age series are all in designed packaging, the colouring is a deep burgundy, interestingly a colour associated with older women (Twigg 2007), and the font is of a somewhat larger size, probably meant to be easier to read for a person whose eyesight has weakened due to age. But what are the products for? The company's presentation of them reads:

With advancing age skin can lose essential moisture revealing age spots, wrinkles and dullness. Dove Pro-age day moisturizer (Fig. 7-2) is specially designed to give your skin immediate luminosity and minimize the appearance of age spots and wrinkles with light-diffusing optics (Dove 2010).

Fig. 7-2: Dove Pro-age beauty body lotion

In many respects, these products can be described as "age accurate", to use a phrase from the Dove reports, but also as repeating an established, ageist cultural message: beauty and looks diminish with age. This, as the cultural imperative states, has to be fought; signs of ageing have to be delayed, even with the help of light-diffusing optics. It is rhetorically impressive to be able to launch products that are as anti-ageing as anything currently on the market and admonish women to work on their appearances, while claiming that these products are in fact something new and different.

The large cohort of baby boomers has grown up as accomplished consumers and is considered to have growing power. Here is an advertising campaign designed to appeal to and flatter these specific prospective consumers. How better to acknowledge them than by targeting them with products that help hide the visual evidence of ageing and by celebrating them in the adverts as beautiful and attractive, if still in need of certain products to remain so. They are made visible and appealed to as older consumers and at the same time ageing is denied by saying they are still young, as a matter of fact too young to be old, which is one of the conclusions of the company's research reports.

By the linking of a corporate social message that Dove wanted to liberate women from stifling beauty norms and endorse more diverse ideals, the company appealed to consumers. They came across as feminist and emancipatory, while at the same time selling products. As far as the Pro-age line is concerned, Dove both celebrated older women by representing them as glamorous and sold them products intended to delay the visual signs of ageing.

Informants' Discussion of the Adverts

During the interviews, my informants voiced critical, distancing opinions about advertisements, dissecting them in an analytical fashion. They would quickly scan the advertisement, suggesting it was "pretty", "fresh looking", "uninteresting", or just browse past the ad, letting their eyes roam the pages, instead pointing out a spread of purses or shoes that caught their attention. Generally the women were critical in their assessments of the advertisements, using words like "photo shopped" or "retouched", "looks unreal", "like a painting". They claimed to know that the celebrity endorser in the advertisement uses Botox, and they pointed out the incongruousness in advertisements with young looking women depicted with grey hair to symbolise older age, or merely wrinkles at the eyes, indicating laughter rather than worry lines. They all showed awareness of how advertisements are produced.

> There are no creams that take away wrinkles, they come from inside. I can't really accept that they cheat people like this. I know that normal ageing can never be stopped. Perhaps you can help nature some, but you can never erase the fact that the skin starts sagging with age. You can still look good, be fresh-looking. (Quote from an interview with a woman in her late fifties.)

> I don't understand this ad. Is she supposed to be older? I don't get her age. Is she supposed to be an older woman but be this fresh-looking? I don't get it. Does she have grey hair? I don't understand this concept of anti-age treatment; they have so many different terms for that. And what wrinkles? No, I skip that one, you can't do that, you can't catch up with yourself. [...] It is very hard to tell her age. It is incredibly difficult because one can't recognize how much they photo shop the images. You can deduce that her hair makes her look older, but she is not really old. (Quote from an interview with a woman in her late forties.)

Regardless of the critical, penetrating attitude when talking of advertisements, the informants all claimed that they thought advertising works. The reason given for this conclusion was that advertising exists. All these millions and millions invested in advertising are evidence that it works, they concurred. Perhaps it works on a sub-conscious level, some said. Others proposed that advertising works, but mainly on others, especially younger, more gullible consumers.

> You can't escape this subliminal influence, regardless of age it is there all the time. If something is reinforced enough we are influenced. But with increasing age we dare question more what it is we let ourselves consciously be influenced by…

> You are more critical.

> You don't swallow 100% that this is the best. (Quote from a group interview with women in their late forties to early fifties.)

Advertising was taken for granted, naturalised and invisible, part of contemporary society.

The women I interviewed all focused on an ad from Dove's Pro-age advertising: the photograph of a black, slightly more well-rounded woman, naked, curled together with a beaming warm smile, velvety black skin enhanced by the contrast to her white teeth and the white pearl earrings and necklace, which are the only things she is wearing (Fig. 7-3). Most talked about how radiant she looked, about how she looked content, confident, at ease with herself, in her skin, in her body. It is a beautiful photograph. She was described as gorgeous. The black model portrayed catches the attention of those who see the advertisement. But it is also worth noting that she represents a double othering in many respects, being the marked category that emphasizes the norm of slim, young, and white in mainstream visual imagery. I understand the informants' statements to show an appreciation of the campaign that was running at the time the interviews took place. I also interpret the women's comments about her appeal as indicating that they found her a liberating image. She was described as radiating self-esteem, regardless of her size or age. Because she also represented something different in terms of her skin colour, the women did not compare themselves with her. Her body did not remind them of their own or evoke comparisons. She was not an endorser the women identified with, nor was she interpreted in aspirational terms. Instead, with the distancing made possible by her skin colour, she safely represented older age and higher weight; she carried the weight and the years, so to speak. The advertisement and the message that beauty has no age limit were appreciated and noticed precisely because of the otherness that made the woman stand out from the mainstream visual image.

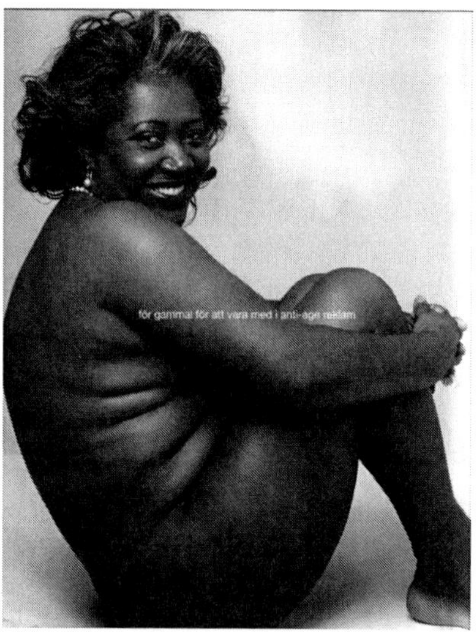

Fig. 7-3: Dove print advert titled "Beauty Has No Age Limit" done by Ogilvy & Mather advertising agency (released in June 2007)

In my view, the informants' ambivalent and sometimes contradictory discourses on advertisements and on the popular press have to do in part with methodological issues. Interviews, even those with an open conversational style, are more likely to capture commonly held discourses that reflect awareness of how one should think or of what one should say. Especially difficult when interviewing on silent reception processes is the fact that probing for answers forces the respondent to put into words thoughts and feelings that may not be explicitly formulated for the respondent herself. The reading process—whether of an image or a text—can take place at different levels and either go with the grain of the text, accepting its premises, or be more critical, raising questions and objections (see Hall 1980 on different forms of reception and readings: preferred, negotiated or oppositional). My interviews with readers of popular press indicate that most readings and reception processes are in fact negotiated, in that the interviewee can take different stances during the interview and thus illuminate different forms of reception. The process of interviewing invites more critical interpretations, a more distanced form of reading than the one described when informants are asked to define the pleasure of reading, or when they talk about leisure reading. With regard to asking questions about the reception of an ad, I believe the interview process invites answers that present the respondent as critical and aware of how commercial forces attempt to lure the consumer. Thus the answers reflect the stance of an aware consumer.

My informants also talked about consumption and their thoughts about anti-ageing products. Supposedly, women want what Dove calls age accurate products. The interviews I conducted with women in this age category were too few and the comments on choice of beauty products were also too few to allow any conclusions to be drawn concerning how the interviewees preferred to be addressed, but there was a tendency to want to be excluded from the older age category, and thus not addressed as a member of it. One woman who explicitly talked about Dove's campaign as stunning, celebrating diversity, showing how attractive middle-aged women are, also spoke of how insulted she felt when she was given one of the products as a gift. The gift implied, according to her interpretation, that she needed to look younger, that she appeared to be old, and that she should do something about it. This might also be interpreted as reflecting not only how insulting it can be to be taken as older, just as it is considered a compliment to be taken as younger, but also as an indication of the imperative to show that one has not let go of one's appearance. This implies a broader neglect and lack of caring. None of the other interviewees had bought the products in the series, even though they all talked of the ad campaign as daring and emancipatory. Based on this one could wonder if the campaign was successful from a commercial point of view, but such conclusions cannot be drawn from the interviews. Firstly advertising works by familiarising consumers with the brand so that even if a purchase is not undertaken in conjunction with seeing the advert, it can still influence the consumer on future occasions. Secondly people in interviews might adhere to cultural scripts and convey that they are critical consumers, not listening to the lure of advertisements, rather than acknowledge the influence of commercial messages. Judging not least from Dove's own reports, the campaign has been successful in terms of sales and in terms of its impact on debate, thus establishing the trade mark of the company.

The interviewed women said they either chose cosmetics based on price (buying a new brand if it was on sale when they had run out of their current product) or that they selected them with the help of a professional, buying their products from a beauty parlour or at a specialized retailer.

Age and Gender in Marketing Addressing Older Women

Women are culturally constructed as more physical than men are, more as bodies. Their appearance is linked to issues of self-esteem. It is communicated to women that their looks matter and that their self-worth depends on them, whereas men's self-esteem is connected to achieving and doing. This basic, underlying cultural conception is not challenged by Dove's campaign. In many respects, the campaign instead reinforces the notion that women's bodies matter and the belief that women have low self-esteem. The problem is to be found in the women themselves. It is either the young girl herself who despite her courting cavalier is unable to accept herself, as in the viral movie *Amy*, or it is her mother who has failed to "inoculate" her daughter with enough self-esteem (Etcoff et al. 2006, 8). The upholding of gendered norms regarding bodies and appearances is further reinforced by another Unilever company, Axe, which uses visual images of women in their advertising when targeting men. Thus women's bodies are both fraught with problems that require work or consumption and serve as objects of visual pleasure for men. The media are questioned, but the resistance to how women are represented in ads and popular media is, according to Dove, a matter for the family. Thus responsibility is individualised. Societal issues such as how values and norms are spread, and might gradually change, are not included in the analysis.

Age and gender are used as demographic factors to distinguish between and create target groups, ensuring an outlet for the continuous production of goods and merchandise. This differentiation continues with regard to age, launching different beauty products for women of various ages or magazines for women of a certain age. Market researchers segment the market into different age-related categories: tweens, teens, young adults. The older consumer is differentiated into finer segments: the thrifty elderly, children of the Second World War, the generation of the first teenagers, the protest generation and the flower power generation is one example (Sifo 2008) while "happy boomers", "the liberated", "the peaceful" and "the very elderly" is another.[2] This is related to the market's need to stimulate consumption, resulting in a need to construct new target groups (Brembeck 2001; Katz 2005). Every segment is presented as different from the others, with different needs and consumption patterns that in turn require interpretation if they are to be understood and properly addressed. Difference is constructed using class, gender, age, sexuality, ethnicity, and lifestyle. Some of these categories, like class and ethnicity, have been more difficult to use in marketing, while others, mainly gender and age, have been perceived as legitimate cultures to construct and exploit (Astroff 1997; Brembeck 2001).

Is age less problematic than class or ethnicity? What supports such an interpretation is the abundance of age-related categorizations used when discussing target groups. At the same time, it appears that addressing a person as "old", or as ageing, is more problematic. Here euphemisms or circumlocutions are often used: there is talk of "+-ers", using an age and a plus sign to reach and include many potential consumers. The epithets are many times witty and often nostalgic, with allusions to popular culture as symbols for a generation or with allusions to the *Zeitgeist*. These categories are fluid, with definitions overlapping and contradicting one another. Many times the target groups are in fact circumlocutions for money and spending power. Here the relevance of age is reinforced through its sheer use. The more the market diversifies, the more pertinent chronology becomes (Blaikie 1999, 74).

Related to the use of age as a targeting factor is the concept of "the young of all ages". Youth is declared to be a question of attitude rather than chronology. Others talk of uni-age, claiming we live in a post-chronological era, where age norms and time tables for an appropriate life course are not as valid as they once were. The notion that a youthful lifestyle—with little difference in clothing styles, music preferences, consumption habits, etc.—spread over the course of life is taken as an argument for the latter theory. In contrast to this, there are also claims asserting that age is being given increasing relevance. There is also

[2] http://www.senioragency.com.

a dimension of age denial in the idea of "young in mind", demonstrating a dislike of being included in the older age category, and testifying to the value attributed to youth and the comparable potential status loss associated with being considered old.

The market uses age segmentation as one viable way to define and construe target groups, thus reinforcing the relevance of age, while at the same time addressing consumers with the promise of uni-age, a life of eternal youth. In Dove's campaign they are both using age-segmented marketing, with specific products for an older consumer category, and labelling them as uni-age, or as they say: "too young to be old".

Impact: Consumerism and Ageism

Media are used as resources for people in making sense of the world, in communication with others and in presenting the self to others. Discourses are drawn upon as tools in coming across as culturally understandable beings. But media are not the only source for discourses, informal conversations or institutions also communicate cultural meanings that are in turn negotiated and interpreted. Media reflect and reshape cultural meanings that are also found in other interactions. It would be reductive to claim that media are the culprits in conveying ageist messages that influence and perpetuate ageism and sexism. The relationship is one of a complex interflow and not one of imposition by the sender through text to receiver. However this is not to be understood as an indication that media are merely reflecting and not shaping or contributing to cultural meaning making: mediated messages matter.

Firstly there is a question of who is represented. Media researcher Gaye Tuchman (1978/1981) found that women were symbolically annihilated by media. This is comparable to how old people have been represented in media. The old are underrepresented in terms of their number. Secondly they are also underrepresented in how they are written about or depicted. As far as advertising goes the norm has been showing young consumers, thereby appealing to consumers of all ages, since no one self-identifies as older (Lövgren 2009). When older models have been used this has been for a restricted range of products, mainly related to health, thus contributing to and reinforcing an association between old age and sickness, frailty and dependence (Zhang et al. 2006). That Dove shows older women and thus avoids rendering women over 50 invisible is a good dimension of the advertising campaign, just as the magazines addressing women over 50 are a good thing when they make women of this age category visible. Showing older women as beautiful and glamorous represents a change in contrast to the more commonly used models in their twenties. As I have shown in this article however what this difference entails and how it can be understood needs further analysis.

The Pro-age ads are examples of how the media industry has adapted to feminism. The phrase "media feminism" has been coined to capture the media's flirtation with a social movement, and adoption of issues of girl power or equality, whilst at the same time working within the established heterosexual gender order and never in reality challenging structural issues of inequality. With the concept they also capture a broader ideology of consumerism in contemporary society, where consumption is not only a means of showing identity and searching for social approval, but also a means of expressing ethical principles and seeking pleasure. Thus Dove can be understood to use an appeal to feminism and consumption. Using the term "feminist consumerism", Johnston and Taylor (2008) stress how effective this is as a marketing tool, in that it both acknowledges emancipatory ideals and channels resistance into commodity purchases.

Diversity in beauty standards is a good thing, but one of the results of the campaign is also a strengthening of the bond between issues of appearance and women, which demands living up to a concern about how one appears in the eyes of others. Dove uses its advertising with social corporate responsibility as an exemption warrant not to reflexively question the bond between women, appearances and consumption. These advertisements never truly challenge society's gender contract. This, of course, is a logical consequence of the commercial logic the company operates within. The representation of glamorous role models, albeit of older chronological age, but still young looking, together with the sale of products to delay signs of ageing, enforces the message that ageing should be hidden and that it is taboo to look one's chronological age.

References

Astroff, Roberta. 1997. "Capital's Cultural Study: Marketing Popular Ethnography of US Latino culture." In *Buy This Book: Studies in Advertising and Consumption*, edited by Mica Nava, Andrew Blake, Iain MacRury, and Barry Richards, 120–136. London: Routledge.

Blaikie, Andrew. 1999. *Ageing and Popular Culture.* Cambridge: Cambridge University Press.

Bordo, Susan. 2004. *Unbearable Weight: Feminism, Western Culture, and the Body.* Berkeley, CA: University of California Press.

Brembeck, Helene, Viveka Berggren Torell, Marie Falkström, and Barbro Johansson, eds. 2001. *Det konsumerande barnet: representationer av barn och konsumtion i svensk dags- och veckopress under 1900-talet med utgångspunkt i reklamannonser.* Göteborg: Etnologiska föreningen i Västsverige.

Brønn, Peggy Simcic, and Albana Belliu Vrioni. 2001. "Corporate Social Responsibility and Cause-related Marketing: An Overview." *International Journal of Advertising* 20 (2): 207–222.

Butler, Robert, Nancy Etcoff, Susie Orbach, and Heidi D'Agostino. 2006. *Beauty Comes of Age. Findings of the 2006 Dove Global Study on Aging, Beauty and Well-Being.* http://www.beperkthoudbaar.info/upload/documents/dove/Dove_2006_Global_Report__Beauty_Comes_of_Age.pdf.

Carrigan, Marylyn, and Isabelle Szmigin. 2000. "Advertising in an Ageing Society." *Ageing and Society* 20 (2): 217–233.

Collins, Lauren. 2003. "Ageist Ideology and Discourses of Control in Skincare Product Marketing." In *Discourse, the Body, and Identity*, edited by Justine Coupland, and Richard Gwyn, 127–150. Basingstoke: Palgrave Macmillan.

—. 2008. "Pixel Perfect. Pascal Dangin's Virtual Reality." *The New Yorker*, May 12.

Coupland, Justine. 2007. "Gendered Discourses on the 'Problem' of Ageing: Consumerized Solutions." *Discourse & Communication* 1 (1): 37–61.

Dove. 2010. "The Real Beauty Debate." Accessed October 7. http://www.dove.co.uk/cfrb/the-real-beauty-debate.html;jsessionid=4982D3D92FF2DB95C481F619C389C688.

Etcoff, Nancy, Susie Orbach, Jennifer Scott, and Heidi D'Agostino. 2004. *The Real Truth about Beauty: A Global Report. Findings of the Global Study on Women, Beauty and Well-Being.* http://www.strategyone.com/documents/dove_white_paper_final.pdf.

—. 2006. *Beyond Stereotypes: Rebuilding the Foundation of Beauty Beliefs. Findings of the 2005 Dove Global Study.* http://www.vawpreventionscotland.org.uk/sites/default/files/Dove%20Beyond%20Stereotypes%20White%20Paper.pdf.

Featherstone, Mike, and Mike Hepworth. 2007. "Images of Aging." In *Encyclopedia of Gerontology: Age, Aging, and the Aged*, 1, A–K, edited by James E. Birren, 735–742. San Diego: Academic Press.

Gill, Rosalind. 2007. *Gender and the Media.* Cambridge: Polity.

Gunter, Barrie. 1998. *Understanding the Older Consumer: The Grey Market.* London: Routledge.

Hall, Stuart. 1980. "Encoding/decoding." In *Culture, Media, Language: Working Papers in Cultural Studies, 1972–79*, edited by Stuart Hall, 128–138. London: Hutchinson.

Johnston, Josée, and Judith Taylor. 2008. "Feminist Consumerism and Fat Activists: A Comparative Study of Grassroots Activism and the Dove Real Beauty Campaign." *Signs: Journal of Women in Culture and Society* 33 (4): 941–966.

Katz, Stephen. 2005. *Cultural Aging: Life Course, Lifestyle, and Senior Worlds.* Peterborough, ON: Broadview Press.

Lövgren, Karin. 2009. "Se lika ung ut som du känner dig': kulturella föreställningar om ålder och åldrande i populärpress för kvinnor över 40." PhD diss., Linköpings universitet.

Macdonald, Myra. 1995. *Representing Women: Myths of Femininity in the Popular Media.* London: Arnold.

O'Barr, William M. 1994. *Culture and the Ad: Exploring Otherness in the World of Advertising.* Boulder: Westview Press.

Rose, Gillian. 2001. *Visual Methodologies: An Introduction to the Interpretation of Visual Materials.* London: Sage.

Sifo research international. 2008. "Mogna människor." http://www.sifo.se/Public/News/NewsArchive.aspx?ArticleId=2f003621-6766-4269-84e3-29ca9212951f>/Nyheter/Nyhetsrkiv/2008-03-13.

Sturken, Marita, and Lisa Cartwright. 2001. *Practices of Looking: An Introduction to Visual Culture.* Oxford: Oxford University Press.

Söderlund, Magnus. 2006. "I huvudet på konsumenten." *Forskning och Framsteg* 8: 36–39.

Tuchman, Gaye. 1978/1981. "The Symbolic Annihilation of Women by the Mass Media." In *The Manufacture of News: Social Problems, Deviance and the Mass Media*, edited by Stanley Cohen, and Jock Young, 169–185. London: Constable.

Twigg, Julia. 2007. "Clothing, Age and the Body: A Critical Review." *Ageing and Society* 27 (2): 285–305.

Zhang, Yan Bing, Jake Harwood, Angie Williams, Virpi Ylänne-McEwen, Paul Mark Wadleigh, and Caja Thimm. 2006. "The Portrayal of Older Adults in Advertising." *Journal of Language and Social Psychology* 25 (3): 264–282.

LIFE SATISFACTION: IMPULSIVE BUYING BEHAVIOUR AND GENDER

SAMUEL LINCOLN BEZERRA LINS

Impulse buying has been a widely researched area (Da Costa 2002). Although it is true that these studies have been carried out in various countries (Verplanken and Herabadi 2001; Verplanken et al. 2005; Da Costa and Larán 2006), it is worth highlighting that very few studies in this area have been done in Brazil.

According to a POPAI[1] survey (2006), 21% of purchases of Brazilian consumers were driven by impulse. Brazil is also the country with the highest percentage of purchase decisions made at the Point of Sales, at 85%, followed by the Netherlands (80.4%), France (76%), Great Britain (75.5%), USA (72 %), Australia (70%), and Belgium (69.6%), (POPAI, 1998). Furthermore, a survey carried out by Sense Envirosell (Camargo and Corrêa, 2007) estimates that 15% of all purchases done in supermarkets in Brazil are impulse driven. These data allow us to conclude that impulse buying is a part of the everyday lives of Brazilian consumers and a topic worth studying.

Life Satisfaction

Life Satisfaction has been recognized to be an important indicator of subjective well-being (Diener 2000). It represents a cognitive evaluation process in which the individual perception of one's general aspects of life and is used as its only evaluation criterion (Pavot and Diener 2008).

Shin and Johnson (1978) define life satisfaction as a person's global evaluation of his/her own quality of life according to individually established criteria. This assessment of one's current state is based on the comparison between individual standards and the perceived reality of diverse areas of life seen as important by each person.

---

[1] The Global Association for Marketing at Retail from Brazil.

Research on life satisfaction has found multiple important factors contributing to it (e.g. work satisfaction, family). Consequently, it is appropriate to propose a comprehensive life satisfaction measurement standard, since combining factors of multiple and specific competences does not always allow for comparison (Pavot and Diener 2008).

In this sense, the Satisfaction With Life Scale (SWLS) (Diener et al. 1985) was developed for measuring the personal cognitive evaluation referring to the general aspects of life, disregarding constructs such as positive and negative affections. This instrument is amongst the most commonly used to measure subjective well-being, and has shown good psychometric properties, including high internal consistency and reliability (ibid.).

Impulse Buying

Impulse buying relates, primarily, to unplanned purchases (Rook 1987). Impulse buying behaviour is expressed through an immediate desire to purchase, provoked by the presence of the object that one intends to buy, and is frequently followed by feelings of excitement and pleasure, in addition to a craving for buying something. Thus:

> [I]mpulse buying occurs when a consumer experiences a sudden, often powerful and persistent urge to buy something immediately. The impulse to buy is hedonically complex and may stimulate emotional conflict. Also, impulse buying is prone to occur with diminished regard for its consequences (Rook 1987, 191).

According to Rook (ibid.), impulse buying is a compound of five aspects.

Spontaneity: An unexpected urge to take action, motivating the consumer to purchase promptly. This urgent appeal for shopping is generally activated by promotional actions or direct visual stimulus at the point of sale.

Sense of psychological instability: The intensity of the immediate buying behaviour somewhat influences consumer's cognitive valuations on what decision to make (advantages and disadvantages, or the expectations for the intangible reward brought about by the purchase), thus leading to a state of lack of control over one's actions.

Psychological conflict: The consumer goes through a state of internal conflict in which the immediate reward obtained from the impulse-driven purchase is evaluated, considering the negative outcomes that it may cause; that is to say, impulse buying leads to a conflict between the benefits and risks that arise from this action.

Reduction of cognitive capacity to make valuations: Once the consumer gets involved in impulse buying, an extrapolation of his/her emotional states, which leads to low cognitive control over the decision made, takes place. This occurs like an automatic action activated by psychological impulses in which the valuation of alternatives is set aside.

Consequence discredit due to the anxiety resultant from purchase impulsivity: The potentially negative consequences are ignored, with no further judgment of possibilities. The consequences can range from regretting the purchase to developing pathological behaviour, such as compulsive buying.

Moreover, impulse buying is made up of two psychological processes: the affective and the cognitive. It is evident that these two processes occur simultaneously to the consumer decision making process. Comprehending how these processes combine and influence impulsivity or self-control is an important step towards understanding the process of impulse buying (Coley 2002).

In spite of this, unplanned and impulse purchases should not necessarily be considered a pathological phenomenon. Instead, they should be treated as a contemporary consumption habit, specifically in the retail environment (Wood 1998). Consequently, impulse buying differs from compulsive buying. Compulsive buying is characterized by a constant desire to buy something, as the main means of compensating for intense anxiety. This type of behaviour is chronic and cyclical. Thus, the main difference between these two purchasing patterns is that the former refers to the product purchased, whereas the latter regards the purchasing behaviour (Karsaklian 2004).

Various factors are thought to influence impulse buying: the store environment (Da Costa and Larán 2006), self-esteem (Fernandes and Veiga 2006), emotional states (Hausman 2000), values (Fitzmaurice 2008), social influence (Rook and Fisher 1995) and humour (Beatty and Ferrell 1998). In this sense, Silvera, Lavack and Kropp (2008) emphasize the importance of associating this purchasing behaviour to other psychological constructs, in the case of this article, life satisfaction.

The persistence of this type of behaviour is a possible threat and potentially self-destructive for the individual, since it can be considered a breakout resulting from the negative emotional state of a person with low self-esteem or with a predisposition for negative affects (Verplanken et al. 2005). This "dark" side of impulse buying makes it a peculiarly interesting phenomenon for scientific research (Hirschman 1991).

Verplanken et al. (2005) proposes a theoretical model indicating that negative psychological states are the dominant force that lead to impulse buying. Nevertheless, Verplanken et al. (ibid.) describe their model as preliminary and still in need of additional validation. The observation that individuals with lower self-esteem and life satisfaction act more impulsively, both in the physical and virtual environments, highlights the important roles that emotional and cognitive factors play in the impulsive buying behaviour (Hausman 2000). In summary, individuals with a more prominent impulsive buying behaviour show psycho-sociological and contextual characteristics that distinguish them from more reflexive and controlled characters (Wells and Prensky 1996).

Gender

Research on consumption patterns has demonstrated great differences between purchasing behaviours of the different genders (Grewal et al. 2003), and the differences between the purchasing behaviours of men and women has been an object of study for decades.

Recently, changes in the behaviour of men and women when it comes to their roles in purchasing have been becoming even more evident. Men have been buying cosmetic lotions and depilatory waxes whereas women have been deciding on the purchase of automobiles (Bacellar, Gouveia and Miranda 2006).

In Brazil, data from IBGE (2000) show that 35% of men assist women in household chores and that 25% are single parents, that is to say, play the roles of father and mother to their children. And, as to purchasing decisions, how does the male consumer behave? The IBGE survey defined at least five distinct types of behaviour adopted when deciding what to put into the shopping cart. Many men have suffered from stress, depression and other illnesses due to social pressure (from media, family, professional environment, and other men), although the awareness of the possibility of change is a great step towards incorporating the new masculine characteristics.

It is possible to affirm that the tendency for impulse buying is more evident amongst women (Woodruff 1997). In a study carried out by Silvera, Lavack and Kropp (2008), results pointed out that an impulsive buying behaviour tends to be more common amongst women than it is amongst men, substantiating other studies with similar results (Wood 1998).

According to Gąsiorowska (2008), gender moderates the relations between individual differences and the tendency for impulse buying, so these purchases would definitely have different backgrounds for men and women, thus pointing out the necessity to perform more studies on this matter in order to better understand these differences.

Gender differences in impulse buying can partially reflect on the fact that the buying habits of men and women are different, essentially because they purchase different types of products. Men traditionally tend to purchase durable goods, such as cars, computers, technological devices, while women buy objects of decoration, kitchenware and beauty and cosmetic products (Rook and Hoch 1985).

The literature points out several other differences between men and women, in respect to: intentions, values, decision-making processes when buying, information processing, types of items purchased, motives and reasons for buying, influences when deciding what to purchase, feelings and emotions when buying, attitudes towards consumption and time spent shopping (Coley 2002).

Comprehending the importance of these processes eases the understanding of how they relate to impulse buying and how men and women interpret internal and external stimuli as a whole. Lastly, becoming aware of how and why emotional and cognitive processes occur will result in great benefits to our understanding of the subject of impulse buying.

Methodology

This research aims to verify the relation between impulse buying and life satisfaction; to test male and female differences in impulse buying and life satisfaction; and to distinguish gender differences in cognitive and affective processes and their relationships to impulse buying.

Sample and Procedure

The increasing and widespread use of the Internet has aroused interest in researchers to perform studies collecting data through participants in the virtual environment (Birnbaum 2000). Moreover, the correspondence between conventional and online research has been evidenced in correlational studies (Wachelke and De Andrade 2009).

A questionnaire containing all the measures used in the present study was administered via web surveying 214 Brazilian undergraduates from the Federal University of Paraiba, Brazil (103 male and 111 female; with mean age of 22 years SD = 2.2; min = 16; max = 36).

Instruments

Life Satisfaction was measured using the five-item Satisfaction With Life Scale (SWLS) (Diener et al. 1985). The SWLS is one-dimensional ($\alpha = 0.85$) and contains items measuring a person's cognitive assessment of global life satisfaction (e.g. "The conditions of my life are excellent"). Responses on all items are given using seven-point Likert scales, higher values corresponding to a higher degree of life satisfaction.

The consumer buying impulsivity scale developed by Youn (2000) was translated and validated for its usage within the Brazilian context by Da Costa (2002). It is a compound of 24 items grouped in five factors and two psychological process components: (a) the affective process (irresistible urge to buy, positive buying emotion, mood management); (b) the cognitive process (cognitive deliberation [the items in this factor have been inverted], disregard for the future). The sum of the five dimensions makes up the impulsivity factor. Each item was evaluated through a seven-point Likert Scale (1 = strongly disagree and 7 = strongly agree). The 5-dimensions demonstrated adequate internal consistency (Cronbach's alphas ranging from 0.72 to 0.90).

Results

At the outset, a Pearson's R correlation between the five factors of the CBIS and the impulsivity factor was conducted. Only the cognitive deliberation factor presented a negative correlation ($r = -0.202$; $p<0.01$), a result partially according to what Verplanken et al. (2005) proposed, which suggests the negative relation between impulse buying and life satisfaction, the factor that emerged was that referring to the lack of evaluation of the consequences, so those who don't consider thoroughly the results of their buying actions, a typical characteristic of the impulsive buyer (lowering cognitive capacity to make valuations and consequence discredit) tends to be unsatisfied with life.

This is possibly due to the fact that people are unable to clearly evaluate their current state of life, have a hard time establishing clear standards and goals for their lives, thus not knowing whether they are "near or far" of reaching what they need and desire in order to satisfy their necessities, being people who undergo a constant state of dissatisfaction and have a low capacity for making valuations. Furthermore, these results differ from those obtained by Fernandes and Veiga (2006) where all factors but "cognitive deliberation" and "positive buying emotion" presented correlation (Table 8-1).

Table 8-1: Correlation between Impulse Buying and Life Satisfaction

Consumer Buying Impulsivity Scale (CBIS)	Satisfaction With the Life Scale (SWLS)			
	Brazil			Portugal (Fernandes and Veiga 2006)
	Men and Women	Men	Women	Men and Women
Irresistible urge to buy	-0.045	-0.032	-0.075	-0.166**
Positive buying emotion	0.044	0.034	-0.013	-0.105
Mood management	0.033	-0.065	0.009	-0.170**
Cognitive deliberation	-0.202**	-0.232*	-0.176	-0.091
Disregard for the future	-0.041	-0.029	-0.106	-0.154*
Impulsivity	0.041	-0.074	-0.081	-0.183**

* Correlation is significant at the 0.05 level (2-tailed)
** Correlation is significant at the 0.01 level (2-tailed)

When comparing men and women, once again the "cognitive deliberation" factor was the only one to present a weak correlation (r = -0.232; $p<0.05$); in women, no factors emerged. Therefore, it is possible to observe that this relation between life satisfaction and low cognitive investment in buying can only be verified within the male sample. When making buying decisions, men tend to be more cautious than women, so they are not so "cognitively deliberate", a more common behaviour amongst women, so those who invest the least time and cognitive attention in choosing a product tend to be more dissatisfied with life.

Finally, a possible explanatory reason for the presence of this relation are the characteristics of the Satisfaction with Life Scale (SWLS), which do not take the affective aspects into account, since its objective is solely to evaluate a person's global cognitive perception referring to their life satisfaction. Thus, the results showed exactly this cognitive relationship between the cognitive dimensions. In the correlations between the impulsivity psychological process components and the satisfaction with life, the cognitive process was the only one to present a negative correlation ($r = 0.14$; $p<0.05$), very similar findings to those obtained by Silvera, Lavack and Kropp (2008), at a very low correlation, though. (Table 8-2)

Table 8-2: Correlation between Impulsivity Psychological Process Components and Life Satisfaction

Impulse Process	Satisfaction With the Life Scale (SWLS)	
	Brazil	U.S.A. (Silvera, Lavack and Kropp 2008)
Affective	0.017	-0.08
Cognitive	-0.14*	-0.15*

* Correlation is significant at the 0.05 level (2-tailed)

Subsequently, a comparison of means of the impulsivity and life satisfaction scale was done to verify which gender is the most satisfied with life and which is more likely to buy driven by impulse. Results demonstrate that women are more satisfied with life than men [t(212 = 2.19; p<0.030]. Nevertheless, researches relating gender to life satisfaction are incongruous, considering that there are studies which have not reported significant effects of gender in life satisfaction (Paolini, Yanez and Kelly 2006), others that point out men as being more satisfied (Geis and Klein 1990), and lastly, others that substantiate the results of this research (Dorahy et al. 1996). These diverging results can be attributed to characteristics typical to the sample studied that are influenced by specific factors (education, faith, age, income, marital status etc.) which interfere in life satisfaction.

Results have also shown that women are more likely to buy on impulse [t(212) = 3.26; p< 0.001)], accordingly to results of other studies that also point out women as being more likely to do so (Rook and Hoch 1985; Wood 1998; Jalees 2009). .

Table 8-3: Comparison of means of Satisfaction with Life and Impulsivity Constructs

Variables	Gender		T	df	sig
	Men	Women			
Satisfaction with life	4.89	5.25	2.19	212	0.030
Impulsivity	2.46	2.91	3.26	212	0.001

Comparing means of the five factors of impulsivity between genders, it is found that women present more positive mood states that lead to impulse buying (positive buying emotion t(212) = 3.46; p< 0.001 and mood management t(212) = 5.88; p< 0.001), and are more neglectful of future consequences caused by their buying actions (disregard for the future $t(212) = 2.37$; $p < 0.002$) than men (Table 8-4).

A considerable difference between genders regarding the psychological process components involved in buying impulsivity was also noticed. Women employ affective [$t(212) = 3.91$; $p < 0.001$)] and cognitive [$t(212) = 2.5$; $p < 0.010$)] processes more often than men when buying. These results demonstrate that women are more likely to buy under the influence of affective processes than men. These results show that women have a higher propensity to value the emotional and the symbolic, whilst men are more instrumental and functional (Coley 2002).

Table 8-4: Comparison of means of the five impulsivity factors

Variables	Gender		t	Df	Sig
	Men	Women			
Irresistible urge to buy	2.30	2.43	0.827	212	0.409
Positive buying emotion	2.41	3.09	3.46	212	0.001
Mood management	2.46	3.53	5.88	3.53	0.001
Cognitive deliberation	2.66	2.63	0.253	212	0.800
Disregard for the future	2.46	2.86	2.37	212	0.002

Regarding the overall cognitive processes, results show that, when shopping for something, women tend to think more than men. In general, women are more patient and questioning than men concerning purchasing decisions. They calculate the positive and negative aspects of each product, seeking to make the best selection and be proud of their ability to choose the perfect item (Underhill 1999). In contrast, men see shopping as a waste of time, which explains to some extent the reasons why they do not invest a lot of cognitive effort when purchasing a product. Typically, men go in a store with a clear choice of a product in their minds and, without wasting any extra time, pick the item they intend to buy and leave the store as soon as they possibly can (Rook and Hoch 1985) (Table 8-5).

Table 8-5: Comparison of means of the Psychological Process Components

	BRAZIL					USA (Coley 2002)				
Process	Gender		t	df	sig	Gender		T	df	sig
	Men	Wo-men				Men	Wo-men			
Affec-tive	2.39	3.01	3.91	212	.000	2.67	2.95	5.28	275	.000
Cogni-tive	2.56	2.74	1.37	212	.171	2.58	2.74	2.36	275	.019

Discussions and Implications

Nowadays, the widespread desire to be a "trend setter" leads people to adopt consumption behaviours consistent with that in search of recognition, approval and inclusion (Bauman 2007). Nonetheless, in order to increase their purchasing capacity, consumers do not rest; on the contrary, they are always awake and alert, frequently exposed to the latest temptations, in a permanent state of excitement (Bauman 1998). Within this context, studies on consumer behaviour have developed to be increasingly relevant and important, given that they not only are applied studies but also deal with a theme that has been attracting interest due to cultural changes on the dynamics of the modus vivendi in today's globalized society.

A vast number of studies have been carried out aiming to understand compulsive buying (Wood 1998; Karsaklian 2004). However, impulse buying is still the subject of very few publications in Brazilian scientific literature.

The theoretical limitations of this research should be highlighted, considering that the buying behaviour is very complex and influenced by other variables that were not considered in this study, such as social influence (Yang, He and Lee 2007), the store environment (Da Costa and Larán 2006) and personality traits (Kassarjian 1971).

The consumer is not the measure of all things, so researchers of consumer behaviour must be aware of this so as not to focus their studies solely on individual consumer characteristics. Understanding that they should also consider the strong influence of cultural and environmental factors to which consumers are subject is a premise for performing studies in that area, since the understanding of the consumption phenomenon should also take into account variables of socio-cultural and economic natures.

In fact, it is possible that both men and women are likely to buy on impulse, and are also subject to the same influences, but considering that women buy more than men, it becomes easier and more evident to observe these impulsive traits in them. It is common that, when responding to the questionnaire, respondents may not consider the products that they themselves purchase, so men will always be seen as less impulsive and survey results will validate that, since they will not have thought of certain typical masculine products nor will they have thought about their favourite products, and will most likely have thought about buying in general, attributing this thought to the a feminine stereotype of buying and spending more when shopping for something.

This study aimed to relate an ordinary buying behaviour (impulse buying) to a construct related to subjective well-being (life satisfaction), but for what reason? It is known that we live in a consumptive society characterized by immediacy which is fast-paced, fuelled by intense dissatisfaction and results in a constant desire to buy, perpetuated through disposal and substitution of products. Society is filled with ruptures and discontinuities, a fact which leaves most individuals to spend most of their time protecting themselves from unwanted information and searching for a new identity through consumption (Bauman 2007).

This search for the construction of a personal and group identity has been mediated by consumption. In other words, through the purchase of products and use of services, people will many times feel better and happier, as they are likely to be better accepted by their group and fulfil their own needs, thus achieving happiness. It this sense, the search for personal happiness develops into a socially legitimate reason to do anything desired. Everything becomes acceptable in the search for happiness.

The achieving of this very happiness starts to be symbolized by objects and titles (e.g. a job, a house, clothes of a certain brand, a new car). "To buy or not to buy" is now the question to be asked, and buying makes all of "my efforts" worthwhile. So, happiness becomes a consequence of purchasing something, rather than a feeling of stability and well-being. Having is now much stronger than being. You are what you have and the abstract (thing) turns into the concrete (thing) through a trade in values. Nevertheless, this quest for full satisfaction provokes a series of behaviours and habits typical of our current society, manifested through consumer behaviours.

"What's wrong with happiness?" was a question posed by Michael Rustin (2007) and reflected by Bauman (2008) which takes us to a reflection on our current society. Why is it that it is increasingly richer but still far from reaching ideal happiness? Consumption has intensified more and more, but this growth has not been followed by an improvement in emotional well-being. On the contrary, the consumption of antidepressants and numbers of unhappy and psychologically unbalanced people have gone up dramatically. So, has this consumptive society been truly successful in promoting happiness?

References

Bacellar, Fátima C. T., Tânia M. O. A. Gouveia, and Liliana C. Miranda. 2006. "Homens Vão Às Compras no Supermercado: Atitudes, Opiniões e Hábitos." IX SEMEAD Seminários em Administração São Paulo 2006. Acessed December 11, 2010. http://www.ead.fea.usp.br/semead/9semead/resultado_semead/trabalhosPDF/171.pdf.

Bauman, Zygmunt. 1998. *Globalization: The Human Consequences.* New York: Columbia University Press.

—. 2007. *Consuming Life.* Cambridge: Polity.

—. 2008. *The Art of Life.* Cambridge: Polity.

Beatty, Sharon E., and Elizabeth M. Ferrell. 1998. "Impulse Buying: Modeling Its Precursors." *Journal of Retailing* 74 (2): 169–191.

Birnbaum, Michael H., ed. 2000. *Psychological Experiments on the Internet.* San Diego: Academic Press.

Camargo, Leoleli, and Rafael Corrêa. 2007. "O cérebro, esse perdulário." *Revista Veja Edition 1993*, January 31. http://veja.abril.com.br/310107/p_070.html.

Coley, Amanda L. 2002. "Affective and Cognitive Processes Involved in Impulse Buying." PhD diss., The University Of Georgia.

Da Costa, Filipe C. X. 2002. "Influências Ambientais e o Comportamento de Compra por Impulso: Um Estudo em Lojas Físicas e Virtuais." PhD diss., FAE-USP São Paulo.

Da Costa, Filipe C. X., and Juliano A. Larán. 2006. "Influências do ambiente de loja e o comportamento de compra por impulso: a visão dos clientes de lojas virtuais." *R.Adm.* 41 (1): 96–106.

Diener, Ed. 2000. "Subjective Well-being: The Science of Happiness, and a Proposal for a National Index." *American Psychologist* 55 (1): 34–43.

Diener, Ed, Robert A. Emmons, Randy J. Larsen, and Sharon Griffin. 1985. "The Satisfaction with Life Scale." *Journal of Personality Assessment* 49 (1): 71–75.

Dorahy, Martin J., John F. Schumaker, Paul L. Simpson, and C. G. Deshpande. 1996. "Depressive Symptoms and Life Satisfaction in

Indian and Australian University Students." *Journal of Personality and Clinical Studies* 12: 1–10.

Fernandes, Paulo M., and Feliciano H. Veiga. 2006. "Impulsividade do consumidor na compra." In *Activação do Desenvolvimento Psicológico: Actas do Simpósio Internacional*, edited by José Tavares, A. Pereira, C. Fernandes, and S. Monteiro, 201–207. Aveiro: University of Aveiro.

Fitzmaurice, Julie. 2008. "Splurge Purchases and Materialism." *Journal of Consumer Marketing* 25 (6): 332– 338.

Gąsiorowska, Agata. 2008. "Gender as Moderator of Temperamental Background of Impulse Buying Tendency." Paper presented at the IAREP/SABE 2008 World Meeting at Rome, Luiss Guido Carli, Roma September 3–6. www.luiss.it/iarep2008/programme/papers/273.pdf.

Geis, Julie A., and Helen A. Klein. 1990. "The Relationship of Life Satisfaction to Life Change among the Elderly." *The Journal of Genetic Psychology* 151 (2): 269–271.

Hausman, Angela. 2000. "A Multi-method Investigation of Consumer Motivations in Impulse Buying Behavior." *Journal of Consumer Marketing* 17 (5): 403–426.

Hirschman, Elizabeth C. 1991. "Secular Morality and the Dark Side of Consumer Behavior." In *Advances in Consumer Research* 18, edited by Rebecca H. Holman, and Michael R. Solomon, 1–4. Provo, UT: Association for Consumer Research.

IBGE. 2000. "Censo 2000." http://www.ibge.gov.br/censo/default.php.

Karsaklian, Eliane. 2004. *Comportamento Do Consumidor.* São Paulo: Atlas.

Kassarjian, Harold H. 1971. "Personality and Consumer Behavior: A Review." *Journal of Marketing Research* 8 (4): 409–418.

Kim, Kwangok, and Dennis T. Lowry. 2005. "Television Commercials as a Lagging Social Indicator: Gender Role Stereotypes in Korean Television Advertising." *Sex Roles* 53 (11–12): 901–910.

Mokhlis, Safiek, and Hayatul S. Salleh. 2009. "Consumer Decision-Making Styles in Malaysia: An Exploratory Study of Gender Differences." *European Journal of Social Sciences* 10 (4): 574–584.

Paolini, Lisa, Alejandro Yanez, and William Kelly. 2006. "An Examination of Worry and Life Satisfaction among College Students." *Individual Differences Research* 4 (5): 331–339.

Pavot William and Ed Diener. 2008. "The Satisfaction With Life Scale and the Emerging Construct of Life Satisfaction." *Journal of Positive Psychology* 3 (2): 137–152.

Point of Purchase Advertising Institute (POPAI). 1998. *Estudos sobre o Comportamento do consumidor no Ponto-de-Venda.* Brasil: POPAI.

—. 2006. *Estudos sobre o Comportamento do consumidor no Ponto-de-Venda.* Brasil: POPAI.

Rook, Dennis W. 1987. "The Buying Impulse." *Journal of Consumer Research* 14 (2): 189–199.

Rook, Dennis W., and Stephen J. Hoch. 1985. "Consuming Impulses". In *Advances in Consumer Research* 12, edited by Elizabeth C. Hirschman, and Moris B. Holbrook, 23–27. Provo, UT: Association for Consumer Research.

Rook, Dennis W., and Robert J. Fisher. 1995. "Normative Influences on Impulsive Buying Behavior." *Journal of Consumer Research* 22 (3): 305–313.

Rustin, Michael. 2007. "What's Wrong with Happiness?" *Soundings* 36 (Summer): 67–84.

Shin, Doh C., and Daniel M. Johnson. 1978. "Avowed Happiness as an Overall Assessment of the Quality of Life." *Social Indicators Research* 5 (1–4): 475–492.

Silvera, David H., Anne M. Lavack, and Fredric Kropp. 2008. "Impulse Buying: The Role of Affect, Social Influence, and Subjective Wellbeing." *Journal of Consumer Marketing* 25 (1): 23–33.

Underhill, Paco. 1999. *Vamos às compras: a ciência do consumo.* São Paulo: Campus.

Verplanken, Bas, and Astrid G. Herabadi. 2001. "Individual Differences in Impulse Buying Tendency: Feeling and No Thinking." *European Journal of Personality* 15 (1): 71–83.

Verplanken, Bas, Astrid G. Herabadi, Judith A. Perry, and David H. Silvera. 2005. "Consumer Style and Health: The Role of Impulsive Buying in Unhealthy Eating." *Psychology and Health* 20 (4): 429–441.

Wachelke, João F. R., and Alexsandro L. de Andrade. 2009. "Influência de recrutamento de participantes em sítios temáticos e comunidades virtuais nos resultados de medidas psicológicas aplicadas pela internet." *Psicologia: Teoria e Pesquisa* 25 (3): 357–367.

Wells, William D., and David Prensky. 1996. *Consumer Behavior.* New York: John Wiley & Sons.

Wood, Michael. 1998. "Socio-Economic Status, Delay of Gratification, and Impulse Buying." *Journal of Economic Psychology* 19 (3): 295–320.

Woodruff, Robert B. 1997. "Customer Value: The Next Source for Competitive Advantage." *Journal of the Academy of Marketing Science* 25 (2): 139–153.

Yang, Jiagin, Xihao He, and Huei Lee. 2007. "Social Reference Group Influence on Mobile Phone Purchasing Behaviour: A Cross-nation Comparative Study." *International Journal of Mobile Communications* 5 (3): 319–338.

Youn, Seounmi. 2000. "The Dimensional Structure of Consumer Buying Impulsivity: Measurement and Validation." PhD diss., University of Minnessota, Minnessota, USA.

PART III:

CRITIQUE OF CONSUMER CULTURE

BEYOND CONSUMERISM: THE CRITIQUE OF CONSUMPTION, DEMOCRACY, AND THE POLITICS OF PROSPERITY

KATE SOPER

Introduction

The market driven "consumerist" lifestyle has long been defended and promoted as an agent of "freedom and democracy" and the advancement of generally progressive agendas on race, gender and sexuality. But it is also widely condemned for its social exploitation, and now increasingly for its environmental destruction and unsustainability. Affluent societies are thus entering upon a cultural moment of unprecedented disquiet about unchecked consumption. The upshot is the emergence of consumer culture as a site of new forms of democratic concern, political engagement, and cultural representation.

The paper will argue that in addition to the environmental and ethical reasons for this new concern, there is the evidence of growing disaffection over the negative legacy of the "consumerist" lifestyle for consumers themselves. The "alternative hedonism" implicit in these forms of consumer ambivalence will be analysed with a view to disentangling its outlook on human needs and fulfilment from both earlier leftwing critiques of commodification and from postmodernist celebrations of consumer culture as a resource of "identity politics" and self-styling. "Alternative hedonism" is presented in this context as the impulse behind a new "political imaginary" that could help us to move towards a fairer, environmentally sustainable and more enjoyable future. How, the paper will ask, can this new outlook on the "politics of prosperity" be best promoted and represented; and how might consumption now come to function as a pressure point for the relay of political changes needed to secure a sustainable economy.

Consumption Criticism

Until recently, few have questioned the model of prosperity associated with the market-driven "consumerist" way of living. Many indeed have viewed it as both the sole means to a "high" standard of living, and the only reliable vehicle of "freedom and democracy". But today, Western society is entering upon a more troubled relationship to unchecked consumption, and the problems of "over-development" and sustainability are moving centre-stage. Consumption, in short, is now emerging as an area of political contention, and a site where new forms of democratic concern, political engagement and cultural representation might begin to have significant impact.

Alarms over what is now widely recognised to be anthropogenic global warming have, of course, played the major role in this. But there have been a number of other factors at work, many of them fuelled by the latest financial crisis. There is the anger and anxiety many now feel about living in a world that has so plainly favoured the greed and ever more conspicuous, and environmentally vandalising, consumption of the already very wealthy, and allowed the gap between richest and poorest to grow to inflammatory proportions. The yawning inequalities of income between the poorest countries and the developed economies have also created what Mike Davis, in his recent book, *Planet of Slums*, terms a 21st economic regime of "informal survivalism" centred on ever expanding urban slums where billions of people scratch a bare existence in the most reduced of living conditions. Davis tells us that, at the current rate, by 2020 half the world's urban population will live in poverty, most in the slum areas of these new mega- and hyper-cities (Davis 2006).

In this context, moral revulsion against the suffering and injustice resulting from neo-liberal economic policies is combining with a growing sense of exposure to their potentially explosive political consequences. And to this we may add the evidence, to which I shall return shortly, of a growing disquiet over the negative legacy of the consumerist lifestyle for consumers themselves.

Yet despite this new climate of concern, mainstream thinking has given little consideration to other economic models or conceptions of prosperity. Despite their concern about global warming, governments and corporate elites believe or hope that new technologies will solve the problem, thus ensuring continued economic expansion with little alteration in lifestyle. Their common presumption is that the consumerist model of the "good life" is the one we want to hold on to as far as we can, and that any curb on that will necessarily prove unwelcome. We hear hardly anything of what might be gained by pursuing a less work driven and acquisitive way of life.

There is an obvious reason for this. Since the immediate mission of the global market is not human or environmental well-being but the multiplication and diversification of "satisfiers" that can realise profit, counter-consumerism would prove very bad for business. Companies, therefore, ever fearful of what they call "need saturation", spend huge sums on encouraging new consumer whims. The infiltration of the child's world by branding gurus and marketing experts is particularly blatant (Williams 2008; Schor 2004). In fact, the ingenuity that goes into "grooming" children for a life of consuming would be regarded as sinisterly totalitarian were it to occur in any other context but that of the market. Dependent as it is on the revenue from commercials, the media has done little to stem the flow of this advertising activity. For more than a decade, the anti-consumerist campaigning group, Adbusters, has been trying to buy airtime for its social marketing TV spots, often called "un-commercials" and have been regularly rejected by the major networks around the world. All this has meant a more or less total, and undemocratic, veto on other representations of need, desire and pleasure.

Yet despite this virtual repression of alternatives, there are signs that the contradictions between capitalist and ecological pressures, and between what the economy demands and what is humanly most valued, will not be contained indefinitely. Today at least some consumers, the ethical shoppers, are beginning to adopt a more "citizenly" and considered approach to what they buy. Ethical shopping, it is true, is not an affordable option for everyone, and it can readily figure as "greenwash" for producers and retailers, sometimes functioning as little more than a fashion gimmick. Being associated with dutiful buying rather than self-interest, it does little to invite us to revise conceptions of our own well-being and the role of consumption in securing it. Nonetheless ethical purchase and investment reflects a more globally accountable way of thinking about one's supposedly wholly "private" interests, and as such challenges the conventional (rational choice theory) view of the consumer as obedient only to narrow self-interest and hence incapable of bringing the reflexivity and democratic concern associated with citizenship to this aspect of life (Daunton and Hilton 2001; Ginsborg 2005; Soper 2007; Soper and Trentmann 2008). Many political theorists and sociologists of consumption now acknowledge the growing significance of the more reflexive and self-consciously political constituencies associated with "virtuous shopping" (Lang and Yiannis 1995; Friedman 1999; Klein 2000; Scammell 2000; Micheletti 2003; Micheletti and Peretti 2003; Barnett et al. 2005; Harrison,

Newholm and Shaw 2005; Littler 2005; Sassatelli 2007, 2009; Binkley and Littler 2008). In the argument of Daniel Miller, one of the more influential:

> On the one hand, consumption appears as the key contemporary "problem" responsible for massive suffering and inequality. At the same time it is the locus of any future "solution" as a progressive movement in the world, by making the alimentary institutions of trade and government finally responsible to humanity for the consequences of their actions. [...] From the legacy of Ralph Nader in the United States, through consumer movements in Malaysia, to the consumer cooperatives of Japan, to the green movements of Western Europe, the politicized form of consumption concern has become increasingly fundamental to the formation of many branches of alternative politics [...] (Miller 1995, 31, cf. 40–41).

And the green movement, he goes on to suggest, has now tempered its mystical relationship to a reified notion of nature with a more rationalistic concern with the defetishisation of goods, and is showing increasing awareness of the consequence of goods for peoples as well as for the planet's natural resources. These arguments chime with those voiced in Michele Micheletti's study of recent consumer campaigns, which show, she argues, "that there is a political connection between our daily consumer choices and important global issues of environmentalism, labour rights, human rights, and sustainable development. There is, in other words, a politics of consumer products, which for growing numbers of people implies the need to think politically privately" (Micheletti 2003, 47; cf. Miller 2001a, 111–148).

Ethical shopping, then, is one aspect of the more "citizenly" approach to consumption in our time. But another is associated with disenchantment with the consumer lifestyle itself, both in the sense that other conceptions of the "good life" are gaining more of a hold among some, and in the sense that affluence is now more commonly seen as compromised by the stress, time-scarcity, air pollution, traffic congestion, obesity and general ill health that go together with it (Levett 2003; Bunting 2004; Shah 2005; Soper et al. 2009). In other words, consumerism is today being questioned not only because of its ethical and environmental consequences, but because of its negative impact on people themselves, and the ways it distrains on both sensual pleasure and more spiritual forms of well-being. We can take note in this connection of the many laments in affluent societies for what has gone missing from our lives under the relentless pressure from neo-liberal economic policies, and the frequently expressed interests in intangible goods such as more free time, more personal contacts, and a slower pace of life. The voicings of discontent are still low-key, diffuse, and politically unfocussed. They are the frustrated murmurings of those who are aware of their impotence to take on the corporate giants, and have little coherent idea of what to put in place of the existing order. But the regrets and disquiet are real enough, and they feed into a now quite widely felt sense of the opportunities that have been squandered in recent decades for enjoying more relaxed and less narrowly reductive ways of living.

This is reflected, too, in the concerns of policy makers with the economic and social effects of the high-stress, fast-food lifestyle, and in the recent studies that have indicated that buying more does not bring greater happiness, and that economic growth has no direct correlation with improved levels of well-being.[1] As the UK government's independent watchdog on sustainable development sums it up in its recent report on "Redefining Prosperity" ever since the ground-breaking work of Abraham Maslow and Manfred Max Neef, psychologists and alternative economists have set out to demonstrate that, far from there being any automatic increase in well-being for every increase in levels of consumption, much of our current consumption is turning out to be a very inadequate surrogate for meeting human needs in a more satisfying, durable way (Sustainable Development Commission 2003).

There is now, moreover, a body of research indicating that as people have woken up to the "inadequate surrogacy" of their consumerist lifestyle, and opted for less materialistic values, so they have gained in happiness and well-being. Work-related stress and ill health is on the increase around the world, and even in areas where job satisfaction in the past has to some extent compensated for relative lack of earnings, stress and insecurity have now begun to take their toll (Durning 1992; Easterlin 2001; Levett 2003; Brown and Kasser 2005; Kasser 2002; 2008).

These developments are indicative of the paradox at the heart of the growth economy, an economic system that can only flourish if people keep spending, which means that they must keep working, which means that they have less time to do things for themselves, which means they have to buy more goods and services to make up for the time deficit. This is a dynamic that tends to the elimination of straightforward and inexpensive

---

[1] The NEF "Happy Planet Index" was begun in 2006. A second Index was provided in June 2009. It measures a combination of life expectancy, life satisfaction and ecological footprint, nation by nation, and arrives at a score that relates use of resources to longevity and well-being. No nation is yet achieving sustainability (living within the one planet, although those at the top, headed currently by Costa Rica, are getting close) the Czech Republic is currently 92nd; Norway 88th.

forms of gratification, only then for companies to profit further through the provision of more expensive compensatory modes of consumption for those who can afford them. The leisure and tourist industry has increasingly tailored its offerings to the overworked, with holiday breaks that promise to make good the loss in "quality" time. This is from the brochure for one such provider:

> For those of us with huge overdrafts at the Bank of Hours-in-the-Day, the real luxury is time. Time with the kids, phone switched off. Or time for yourself, to read and relax in peace. Luxury is a long lunch recovering the person you love, or a gourmet dinner with friends, cooked to order and served by your own private pool. It's me-time. Family time. The elusive holy grail of modern life (Coastline holidays at: www.coastline.co.uk).

Then there are the speed dating and Wife Selecting agencies that promise to make up for your loss of the arts of loving and relating; the extreme sports that promise to take you "back to nature"; or the multiplication of gyms to which people drive in order to do treadmill running in cities where, because there are so many cars on the street, they no longer find it pleasant or safe to walk or run. (In Los Angeles, as dusk falls, the multi-storey gyms are packed, the streets ominously empty).

The consumer society, one may therefore argue, is now becoming increasingly dependent for its continued flourishing on our collective preparedness to spend the money we earn by working too hard and too long on the goods which help to satisfy the goods we have increasingly sacrificed through over-work and over-production.

Alternative Hedonism

It is in this context that I have been pressing for what I have termed the "alternative hedonist" approach to winning support for sustainable lifestyles and for forms of governance promoting them. This responds to the current situation not only as a crisis, and by no means only as presaging future gloom and doom, but as offering an opportunity to advance beyond a mode of life that is not just environmentally disastrous but also in many respects unpleasurable and self-denying. Alternative hedonism is premised, in fact, on the idea that even if the consumerist lifestyle were indefinitely sustainable it would not enhance human happiness and well-being (or not beyond a certain point that has already past). And it claims that it is new forms of desire rather than fears of ecological disaster that are likely to have most impact in any move towards more sustainable modes of consuming. The seductive depiction of alternatives to resource-intensive, polluting and unhealthy consumerist lifestyles is therefore critical not only to meeting commitments on climate change but also to building any more substantial opposition in the future to the economic governance of our times. In sum, a counter-consumerist ethic and politics should appeal, not only to altruistic compassion and environmental concern, but also to the self-regarding gratifications of consuming differently.

Clearly my argument is calling for a redefinition of prosperity and this chimes with the growing demands for a the GNP measure of productivity to yield to others—such as the UNDP Human Development Index (HDI) and the Index of Sustainable Economic Welfare (ISEW) that are more reflective of real levels of well-being rather than purely quantitative economic growth. And there is now good evidence, too, on the links between greater equality of income and improved happiness, and on the role that could be played in enhancing general human well-being by shifting to a low or no growth economy (Wilkinson and Pickett 2009; Jackson 2004; 2009). It also offers a theoretical framework for reflecting on the reasons behind the formation of the growing number of campaigning networks linking those who have opted for "downshifting", reduced working hours and more sustainable lifestyles.[2] But it is not issuing jeremiads against consumption, nor calling for deprivation. On the contrary, it deplores the brutalising, unpleasurable, and puritanical aspects of the "consumerist" lifestyle rather than its hedonist decadence. It argues that the consumerist way of living offers too little in the way of sensual joy and fulfilment rather than too much.

There are, indeed, key aspects of my argument that differentiate its position from other critiques of consumption. The first is the emphasis on pleasure rather than austerity and ascetism. This is not a critique in the tradition of those, and here we go back to Plato and Aristotle, who have condemned luxury and commerce as a corruption of manly virtue, and praised the "simple" and ascetic lifestyle, a tradition that still has echoes today in some religious teachings and certain sects that reject contemporary materialism (Sekora 1977; Berry 1994; the Voluntary Simplicity Movement, www.simpleliving.net).

The second major point of divergence from earlier critiques lies in its resistance to the kinds of cognitive claim about "real" needs that have characterised Marxist critiques of consumer culture (cf. Miller 2001b, 225–243). It seeks legitimation for its claims not in some supposedly objective knowledge of "true" needs (that only an elite of intellectuals

[2] See for example Slow Food, www.slowfood.com; Slow City, www.cittaslow.net; the Center for the New American Dream, www.newdream.org.

have access to) but in the embryonic forms of ambivalence about consumer culture that consumers themselves are now beginning to experience.

The concern is not to prove that consumers "really" need something quite other than what they profess to need (or want), a procedure which is paternalistic and undemocratic, but to reflect on the hedonist aspirations prompting changes in experienced or imagined need, and their implications for the development of a new electoral mandate for the forms of self-policing essential to sustainable living.

"Alternative hedonism", then, is not a theory about what ought to be needed, or desired, or actually consumed, but a theory about what some consumers are themselves beginning to discover about the "anti" or "counter" consumerist aspects of their own needs and preferences.[3] This both respects the actual experience of people, and credits them with a degree of autonomy.[4] And its main interest is thus in the hedonic aspirations prompting changes at the level of actual experience, or, to invoke Raymond Williams's concept, in an emerging "structure of feeling" that is both troubled by what was previously taken much more for granted, and aware, if only dimly, of former pleasures that are going missing, or other possible gratifications that are unlikely now to become available (Williams 1977, 132, cf. 128–136). The argument thus moves

[3] Those espousing the ecological cause are in general pretty good at diagnosing what has gone wrong and informing us of what is needed in order to put it right. In *The Limits to Growth* (Meadows et al. 1972) we are told, for example, that: "People don't need enormous cars; they need respect. They don't need closetfuls of clothes; they need to feel attractive and they need excitement and variety and beauty. People don't need electronic entertainment; they need something worthwhile to do with their lives. And so forth." But it is one thing to claim knowledge of what is "really" needed. It is quite another thing to reveal in what sense, if any, these are indeed the "needs" of consumers; and another again to show by what agencies and transitional means they might be more universally acknowledged and acted upon.

[4] Left has often in the past been rather evasive about that issue. This is because it has been anxious to claim both that its critique of the "falsity" of consumerism (together with its implied knowledge of what people "really" need) is democratically representative, and to explain the mismatch at any point in time between what consumers actually demand and what it is claimed they really want, by reference to their unfreedom, in other words, their ideological manipulation. But it seems no more convincing to view shopping enthusiasts as merely the unfortunate and unaccountable dupes of the consumer society, than to view them as fully autonomous and self-knowing beneficiaries of it. There is, in short, a tension around the issue of consumer needs and desires that it would be more honest to admit and openly discuss, rather than seek to suppress.

from an experienced ambivalence regarding existing patterns of consumption towards the alternative structure of satisfactions that are arguably latent within it, rather than presupposing the "unconscious" needs for this alternative and then casting around in a theoretical void for some consumers who might come to experience them.

In contrast to this, the emphasis of the critique of commodification associated with Marxism and Frankfurt School Critical Theory was always on the construction or manipulation of consumer "needs" and wants (Adorno 1974, 1991; Marcuse 1964, 1972; Leiss 1978; Haug 1986, 2006; Lodziak 1995; Gorz 1989; Jameson 1990, 1994; Bauman 1988; 1991; 1998) and not on the critical reflexivity of consumers; and production alone was seen as the site of potential mobilisation against the capitalist order, through the agency of worker militancy. The market society, on this view, had protracted its domination by subverting the will to resist it, or to enjoy any system of pleasures other than the one it provided. Resistance was thus theorised as prompted solely by the exploitations of the workplace, while consumption, viewed as essentially determined and controlled by production, was regarded as exercising a placating influence, and as tending to reconcile consumers to the existing order rather than firing them to oppose it. This politics, moreover, in its most orthodox form, was directed primarily at transforming the relationships of ownership and control over industrial production rather than at the quality and methods of production as such; it was about equalising access to consumption, rather than revolutionising its culture. In this situation, labour militancy and trade union activity in the West became confined to protection of income and employees' rights within the existing structures of globalised capital, and did little to challenge, let alone transform, the "work and spend" dynamic of affluent cultures. Comparably, in Eastern Europe during the Soviet regime, the aspiration was to "catch up and overtake" the form of industrial development associated with capitalism rather than to revolutionise the goals of prosperity itself.

The alternative hedonist argument also invites a rather more civically oriented conception of consumer needs/desires than is captured in the prevailing spectrum of theoretical perspectives. For whether consumers are viewed as manipulated and constructed by trans-individual systemic market pressures (Adorno 1974; 1991; Marcuse 1964; 1972; Haug 1986; 2006; Lodziak 1995) and signifying codes (Bourdieu 1984; Veblen 1994; Barthes 1973; 1990; Baudrillard 1990; 1996; 1998; cf. Bauman 1993; Clarke 2003) or as existentially authentic and heroically self-creating (Campbell 1995; 2002; cf. 1987, 60–86; Featherstone 1991; Willis 1990; Fiske 1989). In other words, whether consumers are viewed as "unfree" puppets of the system or as "freely" self-styling, they are not theorised in their being or aspect as consumers as reflecting and responsible agents who can come to assume accountability to the world beyond their immediate personal concerns. What is missing is the more complex and nuanced theoretical understanding required to accommodate the troubled and equivocal forms of reaction to the consumer society with which I am concerned here, and which, I would argue, complicate or transgress the "consumer-citizen" divide as currently conceived.

We might note in this context that both liberal and Marxist positions[5] invite discourses on needs and the legitimacy of ascribing them that are problematic in their implications and licence undemocratic and patronising attitudes on the part of policy makers to those they represent. Where the pro-market position regards needs as subjectively experienced and therefore most typically and reliably revealed in the exercise of purchasing power, leftwing theory points to the vast range of needs that remain unmet precisely for lack of effective demand, and in general affirms that needs indeed exist even where they are not consciously felt and acted upon. The former fails to accommodate the possibility of inexperienced or latent needs: needs that can be ascribed to individuals whether or not there is purchasing power to act on them, and sometimes even in the absence of any expression or articulation of them (the abused child's need for love, for example, the anorexic's need for food, the depressive's need for joyful experience). The limitation with the left approach is almost the reverse, namely, its over-readiness to ascribe needs even where these are expressly denied, and its resistance to accepting actual professions of need and patterns of consumption as evidence of authentic needing. The uncritical neo-liberal endorsement is undemocratic in its resistance to accepting properly representative evidence of the existence of need which is always more complex and contradictory than it acknowledges. The left position is undemocratic because it overlooks the important distinction between needs that can legitimately be ascribed to individuals whether or not they ever come to be felt (some psychological and medical needs, for example, are of this order) and the more properly political type of need which can only legitimately be said to exist insofar as there is some experience and acknowledgement of it (Doyal and Gough 1991, chap. 2, 3; Soper 1993, 69–81; Doyal 1993, 270–273). It thus tacitly lends support to a

[5] Postmodern theories (eg. Foucaultians) may be ambivalently positioned in terms of this political opposition, being more pro-market in their celebration of consumption as allowing for self-styling, diversity, pluralism, etc., but more left-leaning when they present existing regimes of power and discourse as a form of discipline upon selves who would otherwise be freer of its cultural tyranny.

"dictatorship over need" (Fehér, Heller and Márkus 1984). In contrast to both these positions on need, the "alternative hedonist" critique offers an immanent and dialectical counter generated within consumerist society itself.

To this let me add that counter to some anti-consumerist critiques, I do not presume that the "excesses" of modern consumption can be corrected through a return to a supposedly more "natural" "modus vivendi". However consumer society is analysed, and whatever normative position is adopted towards its "insatiability", whether it is thought to heighten our pleasures or frustrate them, it is clear that it plays upon aspects of selfhood that are neither readily gratified nor "natural", if by that is meant shared with or explicable by reference to the behaviour of other species. Non-human animals may emulate each other, and they are certainly observant of their pecking orders, but they do not consume for display or symbolic reasons; they may be deceived in their quests for satisfaction, but they do not pursue fantastical pleasures; and they are not interested in dissatisfaction as itself a condition of enjoyment. The critique associated with "alternative hedonism" does not deny the complexity of human desires, nor the need to accommodate the distinctively human quests for novelty, excitement, distraction, self-expression and the gratifications of *amour-propre*. It can even allow that the gratification of what Rousseau termed the *fureur de se distinguer*, the zeal for self-distinction which he associated with *amour-propre*, is most easily supplied through material acquisition (at least if you have the money for it.). But what comes more easily, of course, is not necessarily the most rewarding or fulfilling, and the "alternative hedonist" case is that in deflecting more "spiritual" demands on to materialist forms of display and competition, consumerism offers a too reductive, limited and partial rein to desire.[6] It offers contentment rather than ecstasy, reconciliation rather than transcendence. To invoke Adorno's metaphor, it offers a society in which "everyone lives in aeroplanes" but remains obedient to the edict: "Thou shalt not fly" (Adorno 1967, 95–117).

---

[6] For it is a tendency of consumer culture today to seek to accommodate all the more irreducibly symbolic and affective dimensions of human needing, whether for the more sensual or the more cerebral satisfactions, by treating them on the model of physiological need: as if they were, indeed, mere extensions or complications of material need, and could be met, for the most part, through the provision of tangible objects.

"Alternative Hedonism": A New Political Imaginary?

Consumerist culture is nowhere more hedonistically repressive in its commitments to a productivity and work ethic that are unfriendly to both human beings and the environment. It is dependent on the ceaseless making and retailing of resource hungry and ecologically damaging commodities, and it is resistant to the life-enhancing expansion of free time that might otherwise be realised. And dramatic illustration, for example, of this "Puritanism" in the US has been given by Juliet Schor, who has argued that if Americans had settled for a 1948 standard of living (measured in terms of marketed goods and services), every worker in the United States could now be taking every other year off from work, with pay. Instead, free time fell by nearly 40% post-1973 so although the average American by 1990 owned and consumed more than twice as much as he or she did in 1948, they also had considerably less leisure (Schor 1991; de Graaf 2003).

If we were to shift to a less work-intensive economy, it would reduce the rate at which people, goods and information had to be delivered or transmitted, and the impact on resource attrition and carbon emissions would be matched by huge benefits for ourselves. People would reclaim time for personal and family life. They would commute less and enjoy healthier modes of travelling such as walking, cycling and boating. Supermarket shopping would cede to a resurgence in high street retailing, thus avoiding the "clone town" syndrome and boosting local communities in ways that could reduce crime and foster new forms of conviviality and inter-generational exchange. All this would transform urban and rural living, especially for children, and provide more tranquil space for reflection, and opportunities for sensual experience denied by harried and insulated travel and work routines. And the costs would be negligible relative to those incurred by current provision, especially if one factors in the medical expenses to be saved through better public health and fewer accidents. Human ingenuity would surely also contrive a range of more eco-friendly excitements to make up for the loss of high-speed thrills. (One might here, for example, consider the popularity of the new "sublime" experiences provided by public art and sculpture, and the ways in which these have lent themselves, perhaps most notably Anish Kapoor's extraordinary urban and rural mirrors, to new forms of eco-friendly, non-consumerist idling, loitering, sky-gazing and conviviality. (One would like to think that such experiences capture the spirit of the future much more than does Virgin Galactic's promises of space tourism.)

And on this note, let me add that we need a cultural politics designed to encourage a shift in aesthetic perception as well as ethical response, and art has a definite role to play in this. I have compared this to the "consciousness raising" brought about through Western feminism and its gradual but profound impact on our way of life. As individuals became alerted to the role of gender in their being, and to its social construction and hence mutability, so they entered into complex, and often painful, processes of self-change. Such "reconstructions" can involve dramatic changes in affective response: changes whereby the attractions and repulsions of the world of lived experience undergo a kind of Gestalt Switch. A cultural renaissance working upon consumer sensibilities over coming years would result in some similar revisioning of self-interest and aesthetic response. The result would be that a lifestyle once seen as compelling comes to seem confining, and previously sought after commodities come to be viewed as cumbersome and ugly through association with unsustainable resource use, noise, toxicity or their legacy of un-recyclable waste (Soper 2008).

It would also mean a break with current orthodoxy about the role and purposes of education. Insofar as education is now increasingly subject to purely vocational policy frameworks, it inhibits the development of precisely those more varied cultural interests that would help to promote satisfaction and self-realisation in a less work-driven society (Ryle and Soper 2002, 181–187). Education would instead have to be seen as an intrinsically valuable preparation for life rather than as an adjunct of industry. And state pastoral care of the body would need to be matched by a concern about what goes into the mind, and its cultural well-being.

These ideas are utopian. But I have tried to show that they may now have some anchorage in the emergent "structure of feeling" of those who are troubled by the undesirable by-products of their own formerly less questioned sources of gratification. And there are other reasons, too, for resisting critics who dismiss the whole idea as fanciful. In the first place, its outlook is in many ways entirely consistent with the professed objectives of government itself to energy saving, reduction in greenhouse emissions, and better public health.[7] "Alternative hedonism" might also figure as a galvanising idea for new forms of inter-generational dialogue and social solidarity. It could also provide some spiritual meeting ground across the denominational and religious versus secular divides of a multicultural society.

---

[7] The level of concern in the UK is reflected in the recently established Forsight project on obesity (www.forsight.gov.uk/Obesity) and the work of scholars associated with it. See also the NCC proposals to Ofcom (www.ncc.org.uk).

The encouragement of "alternative hedonist" conceptions of the good life is also rational and realistic in more global terms if affluent nations are to be pressured into assuming proper responsibility for promoting sustainable development and global stability. Since alleviation of poverty and fairer distribution of resources are preconditions of progress in these directions, redressing some of the current imbalance in wealth and access to resources is both a moral and a pragmatic imperative: not only a demand of social justice, but a prerequisite of any long-term global ecological well-being and security.[8] Yet the international agencies and institutions committed to this agenda are likely to remain relatively powerless, and very little pressure will be applied on national governments to cooperate in promoting it, unless and until their electorates come to perceive that as in their own interests.[9]

I have argued here that "alternative hedonist" frameworks of thinking about the good life might alter conceptions of self-interest among affluent consumers, and thus help to set off this relay of political pressures for a fairer global distribution of resources. An alternative and ecologically sustainable conception of the good life can not only win the support of consumers within the richer nations, but also figure as an ideal through which less developed countries can consider critically the conventions and goals of "development" itself, and thereby better understand the worst consequences of north-west "over-development" and how to avoid them.[10]

Conclusion

And finally, lest I appear rather Luddite in all this, let me emphasise that greener technologies will be an essential part of the solution, and we

[8] It is true, of course, that a concern for pollution and resource attrition does not in itself imply a commitment to furthering global equality and justice, and that in the shorter term even quite severe ecological damage and depletion can be accommodated within the present extremely inegalitarian structure of distribution. But the longer we continue along that path, the more acute the competition for resources will be likely to become, and the more uncivil the methods to which the societies of affluence may have recourse in defending their advantage.

[9] The blame here lies as much with electorates who are reluctant to be policed on their most ecological damaging forms of consumption, as with their governments, who view themselves as accountable to their voters in the last analysis, and are equally loathe to jeopardise their re-election.

[10] Ernst U. von Weizsäcker has written. "In order to bring the developing countries back to health, not only is it necessary to correct unfair trade structures but also to wean them from their vision of the North's throwaway society" (Weizsäcker 1994; cf. Goodland and Daly 1992).

cannot begin to counter global warming without them. But the implementation of alternatives to the growth economy has at the same time to become a more central concern of governance, rather than ignored or dismissed as utopian fantasy. And in a climate of financial turmoil and extensive cynicism about government commitments on global warming, more honesty about this might well win greater cooperation and respect on the part of the electorate—especially if it were accompanied, as suggested, by imaginative representation of the fulfilments of living in a sustainable society.[11]

The commitment to low-growth sustainability can be seen in this sense as a continuation of the Enlightenment project. If we have a cosmopolitan care for the well-being of the more deprived people of the world, and a concern about the quality of life of future generations, then we need to campaign for a dramatic change of attitudes to work, consumption, pleasure and self-realisation in the more affluent communities. And such a revolution will surely be comparable in the forms of social transformation and personal epiphany it will demand to those brought about through the feminist, anti-racist and anti-colonialist movements of recent history.

Making headway with any alternative will undeniably be hugely difficult. Almost certainly, in the short-term we shall have a return to "business as usual", with a few big "green" infrastructure projects planned as a means of pump-priming our way out of recession and back into the promised land of growth, full employment and consumer spending. Yet the banking crisis has made the going harder for the advocates and representatives of greed, speculative cunning and profit-driven turbo-capitalism. It has strengthened the hand of interventionist, social-democratic government. Talk of a "Green New Deal" has been heard outside the red/green circles where the phrase originated;[12] EU leaders have been speaking, in early November 2008, of the need to re-engineer international financial institutions in ways that would help combat climate change and keep world food prices down.

And since, we all know really, that it is unrealistic to suppose that we can continue with current rates of expansion of production, work and material consumption over coming decades let alone into the next century,

---

[11] And results from a simulation model of the Canadian economy suggest that it is possible to have full employment, eradicate poverty, reduce greenhouse gas emissions and maintain fiscal balance without economic growth. For further details, see the "low grow model" advocated by Peter Victor (2008) and the papers from the Sustainable Development Commission.

[12] See www.neweconomics.org.

anything that contributes to a less hackneyed way of thinking about economic health and is more inventive about the quality of human well-being is surely to be welcomed.

References

Adorno, Theodor W. 1967. *Prisms.* Cambridge, MA: MIT Press.

—. 1974. *Minima Moralia: Reflections from Damaged Life.* London: New Left Books.

—. 1991. *The Culture Industry: Selected Essays on Mass Culture.* Edited by Jay M. Bernstein. London: Routledge.

Barnett, Clive, Paul Cloke, Nick Clarke, and Alice Malpass. 2005. "Consuming Ethics: Articulating the Subjects and Spaces of Ethical Consumption."*Antipode* 37 (1): 23–45.

Barthes, Roland. 1973. *Mythologies.* London: Paladin.

—. 1990. *The Fashion System.* Berkeley: University of California Press.

Baudrillard, Jean. 1990. *Seduction.* London: Palgrave Macmillan.

—. 1996. *The System of Objects.* London: Verso.

—. 1998. *The Consumer Society: Myths and Structures.* London: Sage.

Bauman, Zygmunt. 1988. *Freedom.* Milton Keynes: Open University Press.

—. 1991. *Modernity and Ambivalence.* Cambridge: Polity.

—. 1993. "The Sweet Scent of Decomposition." In *Forget Baudrillard?*, edited by Chris Rojek, and Bryan S. Turner, 22–46. London: Routledge.

—. 1998. *Work, Consumerism and the New Poor.* Milton Keynes: Open University Press.

Berry, Christopher J. 1994. *The Idea of Luxury: A Conceptual and Historical Investigation.* Cambridge: Cambridge University Press.

Binkley, Sam, and Jo Littler, eds. 2008. *Cultural Studies and Anti-Consumerism: A Critical Encounter*, special guest edited issue of *Cultural Studies* 22 (5).

Bourdieu, Pierre. 1984. *Distinction: A Social Critique of the Judgement of Taste.* London: Routledge.

Brown, Kirk W., and Tim Kasser. 2005. "Are Psychological and Ecological Well-being Compatible? The Role of Values, Mindfulness, and Lifestyle." *Social Indicators Research* 74 (2): 349–368.

Bunting, Madeleine. 2004. *Willing Slaves: How the Overwork Culture Is Ruling Our Lives.* London: HarperCollins.

Campbell, Colin. 1987. *The Romantic Ethic and the Spirit of Modern Consumerism.* Oxford: Blackwell.

—. 1995. "The Sociology of Consumption." In *Acknowledging Consumption: A Review of New Studies*, edited by Daniel Miller, 96–126. London, New York: Routledge.
—. 2002. "I Shop, Therefore I Know That I Am: The Metaphysical Basis of Modern Consumerism." In *Elusive Consumption*, edited by Karin M. Ekström, and Helene Brembeck, 27–44. London, New York: Berg.
Clarke, David B. 2003. *The Consumer Society and the Postmodern City.* London: Routledge.
Daunton, Martin, and Matthew Hilton, eds. 2001. *The Politics of Consumption: Material Culture and Citizenship in Europe and America.* Oxford, New York: Berg.
Davis, Mike. 2006. *Planet of Slums.* New York: Verso.
De Graaf, John, ed. 2003. *Take Back Your Time: Fighting Overwork and Time Poverty in America.* San Francisco: Berrett-Koehler.
Doyal, Len. 1993. "Reply to Kate Soper." In *New Approaches to Welfare Theory*, edited by Glenn Drover, and Patrick Kerans, 270–273. Aldershot: Edward Elgar.
Doyal, Len, and Ian Gough. 1991. *A Theory of Human Need.* London: Palgrave Macmillan.
Durning, Alan T. 1992. *How Much Is Enough? The Consumer Society and the Future of the Earth.* London: Earthscan.
Easterlin, Richard A. 2001. "Income and Happiness: Towards a Unified Theory." *Economic Journal* 111 (473): 465–484.
Fehér, Ferenc, Ágnes Heller, and György Márkus. 1984. *Dictatorship over Needs: Analysis of Soviet Societies.* Oxford: Blackwell.
Friedman, Monroe. 1999. *Consumer Boycotts: Effecting Change through the Marketplace and the Media.* London, New York: Routledge.
Featherstone, Mike. 1991. *Consumer Culture and Postmodernism.* London: Sage.
Fiske, John. 1989. *Reading the Popular.* Boston, MA: Unwin Hyman.
Ginsborg, Paul. 2005. *The Politics of Everyday Life: Making Choices, Changing Lives.* Harvard: Yale University Press.
Goodland, Robert, and Herman E. Daly. 1992. *Ten Reasons Why Northern Income Growth Is not the Solution to Southern Poverty.* Washington DC: Environment Department, World Bank.
Gorz, André. 1989. *Critique of Economic Reason.* London: Verso.
Haug, Wolfgang F. 1986. *Critique of Commodity Aesthetics.* Cambridge: Polity.
—. 2006. "Commodity Aesthetics Revisited: Exchange Relations as the Source of Antagonistic Aesthetization." *Radical Philosophy* 135: 18–24.

Harrison, Rob, Terry Newholm, and Deirdre Shaw, eds. 2005. *The Ethical Consumer.* London: Sage.
Jackson, Tim. 2004. *Chasing Progress: Beyond Measuring Economic Growth.* London: New Economics Foundation.
—. 2009. *Prosperity Without Growth: Economics for a Finite Planet.* London: Earthscan.
Jameson, Fredric. 1990. *Late Marxism: Adorno or the Persistence of the Dialectic.* London: Verso.
—. 1994. *The Seeds of Time.* New York: Columbia University Press.
Kasser, Tim. 2002. *The High Price of Materialism.* Cambridge, MA: MIT Press.
—. 2008. "Values and Prosperity." Paper to the SDC seminar on Visions of Prosperity, November 26, 2007. http://www.sd-commission.org.uk/data/files/publications/Tim_Kasser_opinionpiece.pdf.
Klein, Naomi. 2000. *No Logo.* London, New York: Harper Collins.
Lang, Tim, and Gabriel Yiannis. 1995. *The Unmanageable Consumer.* London: Routledge.
Leiss, William. 1978. *The Limits to Satisfaction: On Needs and Commodities.* London: Marion Boyars.
Levett, Roger. 2003. *A Better Choice of Choice: Quality of Life, Consumption and Economic Growth.* London: Fabian Society.
Littler, Jo. 2005. "Beyond the Boycott: Anti-consumerism, Cultural Change and the Limits of Reflexivity." *Cultural Studies* 19 (2): 227–252.
Lodziak, Conrad. 1995. *Manipulating Needs: Capitalism and Culture.* London: Pluto.
Marcuse, Herbert. 1964. *One-Dimensional Man.* London: Beacon Press.
—. 1972. *Eros and Civilisation.* London: Abacus.
Meadows, Donella H., Dennis L. Meadows, Jorgen Randers, and William W. Behrens III. 1972. *The Limits to Growth.* London: Pan Books.
Micheletti, Michele. 2003. *Political Virtue and Shopping: Individuals, Consumerism, and Collective Action.* New York, London: Palgrave Macmillan.
Micheletti, Michele, and Jonah Peretti. 2003. "The Nike Sweatshop Email: Political Consumerism, Internet and Cultural Jamming." In *Politics, Products and Markets: Exploring Political Consumerism Past and Present*, edited by Michele Micheletti, Andreas Follesdal, and Dietlind Stolle, 127–142. New Brunswick, New Jersey: Transaction Publishers.
Miller, Daniel. 1995. "Consumption as the Vanguard of History." In *Acknowledging Consumption: A Review of New Studies*, edited by Daniel Miller, 1–57. London, New York: Routledge.

—. 2001a. *The Dialectics of Shopping.* London, Chicago: University of Chicago Press.
—. 2001b. "The Poverty of Morality." *Journal of Consumer Culture* 1 (2): 225–243.
Ryle, Martin, and Kate Soper. 2002. *To Relish the Sublime? Culture and Self-Realization in Postmodern Times.* London: Verso.
Sassatelli, Roberta. 2007. *Consumer Culture: History, Theory and Politics.* London: Sage.
—. 2009. "Representing Consumers: Contesting Claims and Agendas." In *The Politics and Pleasures of Consuming Differently*, edited by Kate Soper, Martin Ryle, and Lyn Thomas, 25–42. London: Palgrave Macmillan.
Scammell, Margaret. 2000. "The Internet and Civic Engagements: The Age of the Citizen-Consumer." *Political Communication* 17 (4): 351–355.
Schor, Juliet B. 1991. *The Overworked American: The Unexpected Decline of Leisure.* London, New York: HarperCollins.
—. 2004. *Born to Buy: The Commercialized Child and the New Consumer Culture.* New York: Scribner.
Sekora, John. 1977. *Luxury: the Concept in Western Thought, Eden to Smollett.* Baltimore: Johns Hopkins University Press.
Shah, Hetan. 2005. "The Politics of Well-Being." *Soundings* 30 (1): 33–44.
Soper, Kate. 1993. "The 'Thick' and 'Thin' of Human Needing." In *New Approaches to Welfare Theory*, edited by Glenn Drover, and Patrick Kerans, 69–81. Aldershot: Edward Elgar.
—. 2007. "Re-thinking the 'Good Life': The Citizenship Dimension of Consumer Disaffection with Consumerism." *Journal of Consumer Culture* 7 (2): 205–229.
—. 2008. "Alternative Hedonism, Cultural Theory and the Role of Aesthetic Revisioning." *Cultural Studies* 22 (5): 567–587.
Soper, Kate, and Frank Trentmann, eds. 2008. *Citizenship and Consumption.* London: Palgrave Macmillan.
Soper, Kate, Martin Ryle, and Lyn Thomas, eds. 2009. *The Politics and Pleasures of Consuming Differently.* London: Palgrave Macmillan.
Sustainable Development Commission. 2003. "Redefining Prosperity: Resource Productivity, Economic Growth and Sustainable Development (SDC report)." http://www.sd-commission.org.uk/data/files/publications/030627%20Redefining%20prosperity,%20resource%20productivity.pdf.

Thomas, Lyn. 2002. "Alternative Realities: Downshifting Narratives in Contemporary Lifestyle Television." *Cultural Studies* 22 (5): 680–699.

Veblen, Thorstein. 1994. *The Theory of the Leisure Class: An Economic Study in the Evolution of Institutions.* New York: Dover.

Victor, Peter A. 2008. *Managing without Growth: Slower by Design, Not Disaster.* London: Edward Elgar.

Weizsäcker, Ernst U. von. 1994. *Earth Politics.* London: Zed Books.

Wilkinson, Richard, and Kate Pickett. 2009. *The Spirit Level: Why Equality is Better for Everyone.* Harmondsworth: Penguin.

Williams, Raymond. 1977. *Marxism and Literature.* Oxford: Oxford University Press.

Williams, Zoe. 2008. "The Commercialisation of Childhood." London: Compass. http://clients.squareeye.net/uploads/compass/documents/thecommercialisationofchildhood.pdf.

Willis, Paul. 1990. *Common Culture: Symbolic Work at Play in the Everyday Cultures of the Young.* Milton Keynes: Open University Press.

The Historicity of Brands: Inter-Generational Production of Structural Sustainability

Rainer Gries

Currently, many of our leading brand products have a living history of over one hundred years or more: Take for example the famous Scottish whiskey brand Johnny Walker that was born in 1805. We can also see that in the early years of the 18th century in France, many sparkling wine brands were founded such as Moët & Chandon and one century later, in Germany, Austria and all over Europe. Coca-Cola was invented in 1886 and looking at a classic example today we can draw our attention to the famous German skin care brand Nivea that will celebrate its 100th anniversary this year, in 2011a. Successful brands are the result of long-term social processes of negotiations that involve several groups of players. These discourses are developed over periods of time and they operate as constant constructs throughout time: What precisely does this mean concerning inter-generational communications and concerning an *education for sustainable development*?

Successful Brand Medias Convey Meaning in a Sustainable Way

Education for sustainable development is a concept that attempts to evoke sustainable thinking, feeling and action. Clearly, our actions today exert influence on the lives of people throughout other regions of the world and continue to impact on the lives of future generations.[1]

The Berlin educationist Gerhard de Haan, demonstrated at the beginning of the Decade of the United Nations that: sustainable development crystallises into a bundle of competences which he subsumes

[1] See the mission statements of the website of the project "United Nations Decade of Education for Sustainable Development (DESD) 2005–2014": http://www.desd.org.

under the German term of *Gestaltungskompetenz* (the competence of participating in designing one's own environment) (Haan 2004, 41). The term *Gestaltungskompetenz* means the ability to solve specific problems and to act in a certain way. He who possesses this ability is able to modify the future of society and to model their social, economic, technological and environmental changes in the interests of sustainable development.

With *Gestaltungskompetenz* in mind, this idea gives way to a path of an open future, the variation of possible and active modelling and in particular, includes the capacity to think ahead and to use forecasts and expectations of the future. This method also denotes our individual competence to look beyond the present. It is important to note that the policy framework and the educational objectives of this program are only sited for example and are not intended to be merely repeated in detail in this paper. Product communicative knowledge provides competence for sustainable action and intervention.

Sustainability and Product Communication: Which Understanding of Sustainability May be Set within this Context?

The very first answer to this question might lead us to the shelves of fair-trade products. Fair-trade is a strategy to fight and diminish poverty. By employing fair-trade relations, the situation of disadvantaged producer families such as in Africa, Asia and South America should be improved by strengthening the domestic economy and by dismantling unfair worldwide economic structures and trade practices, declares the non-profit organization Transfair. Fair prices here will guarantee fair wages there, they claim.[2]

The next step in attempting to answer this question could lead us to the ever-growing market for *regional products*. In the opinion of consumers the purchase and use of local and regional products is combined with high quality and good health and coupled with the feeling of security and environmental awareness. In choosing to buy locally produced goods, one also buys the feeling of affiliation and identity to contribution and to the bettering of society and thus, in summary: *sustainability*.

Regional consumption is understood as an ecologically and environmentally sound consumption and therefore, understood as sustainable consumption. For example, 40% of Austrians hold the opinion that people

[2] For more details see the website of "World Fair Trade Organization (WFTO)": http://www.wfto.com.

should buy local products as often as possible to prevent climate change. From here the step to organic marketing and production lies within reach. Organic products are therefore, no longer simply a niche product: A few years ago, in Germany, large supermarkets and grocery chains invented their own umbrella brands and range of organic products. In 2009 about half of the organic market volume had already been realized by these leading retailers. Conversely, 30% of Germans declared that changing consumer behaviour have neither and substantial, direct or indirect influence in the big picture, for the bettering of society both environmentally and economically. These people don't appear to want to perceive, or use their potential and power as consumers for the greater good of society.

Overall, the market share of organic and fair traded goods is still negligible however. The organic sector in Germany today makes up only about 3.2% of the total consumer market, but it is growing steadily. The share of fair traded products in total retail volume is even lower at 0.1%.

These are all first and obvious answers,[3] but let's try to answer the question under historical and structural auspices (for further information see Gries 2011b). By adopting the system of product communication as a learning system, people are given access to a new and deeper way of experiencing both sustainability and *Gestaltungskompetenz*.

The findings of this paper may astonish you or even challenge your current ideas about brands, branding and goods. The links between sustainability, *Gestaltungkompetenz* and product discourses are not simply obvious; which poses the question: What is the link between an education program, which aims to develop skills of sustainability with product and brand communication.

What have these different paradigms to do with each other? Are the fields of goods and of advertising not merely the epitomes of fast-paced, shortness of breath and extravagance? Has advertising not simply lived from the slogan "New!" "New!" as the dominating alpha and omega of publicity since the nineteenth century?

People often talk about the need to always search for new and exciting product experiences, which would require new advertising scoops and gimmicks that play on enticing the public through novelty and the promise of a previously undiscovered experience. However, it could be argued that, when we deal with cultures evoked by products and brands, we should also take care for the other *cultures of time* which are also associated with brands. More precisely: What is the bridge connecting product and brand communications with longevity and sustainability? The theory of product

[3] Concerning the images of sustainability in recent German advertisements now see Gekeler 2012.

communication offers an attempt to consider these essential historic dimensions of branding.

How is Product Communication Different from Advertising?

People communicate about products. Since the nineteenth century, branded products in particular have developed into a media of social exchange, and thus also into a media of the social memory.

Brands have become structural elements of our modern life and today they are an indispensable part of our everyday life. They form a fundamental media of understanding, which groups, generations and whole societies cannot disclaim (Gries 2010b). Brand products are cultural carriers or conveyors, that we need to perceive at face value and furthermore: we should take advantage of their educational opportunities and possibilities.

Under the term "product communication" we subsume all acts of communication via products that are transmitted by means of brands and products (see Gries 2003a, 2008). Such interactions are not to be confused, let alone equated, with commercial advertising. Advertising represents merely a visible part of the exchange by means of products, and one which attracts a great deal of media attention. Advertising constructs social reality by attempting to idealize the product being advertised, or the brand. The goal of advertising is to offer positive images in order to create the disposition to buy a particular product. Advertising offers messages, which producers assume or hope, will encourage sales of their products.

The paradigm of "product communication" can open up an extended communication space. Meanings brought in by other actors and in particular, potential buyers, users, and consumers, who attach themselves to the messages of advertising. But this is not enough to explain these complex communication processes. A model oriented by product communication also incorporates the communicative achievements of other groups of actors and places them in relation to each other. Manufacturers of goods, buyers and professional third parties such as market researchers and journalists, they all communicate about products. Above all however, the potential and real customers, the satisfied or disappointed consumers of the product, count as actors in product communication.

Their opinions and practices in using the products become effective in two ways:

Firstly, when they themselves actively communicate about the product with friends, acquaintances, or the producer such as, when they contact customer services of the company or complain about the product.

Secondly, when market researchers and opinion pollsters ask them about their interests in products, then bundle and configure the replies, concentrating them into ideal-typical model consumers, this process ultimately gives those who commission their work, the producers of products, messages about the significances and horizons of meaning which consumers attach to their products and brands.

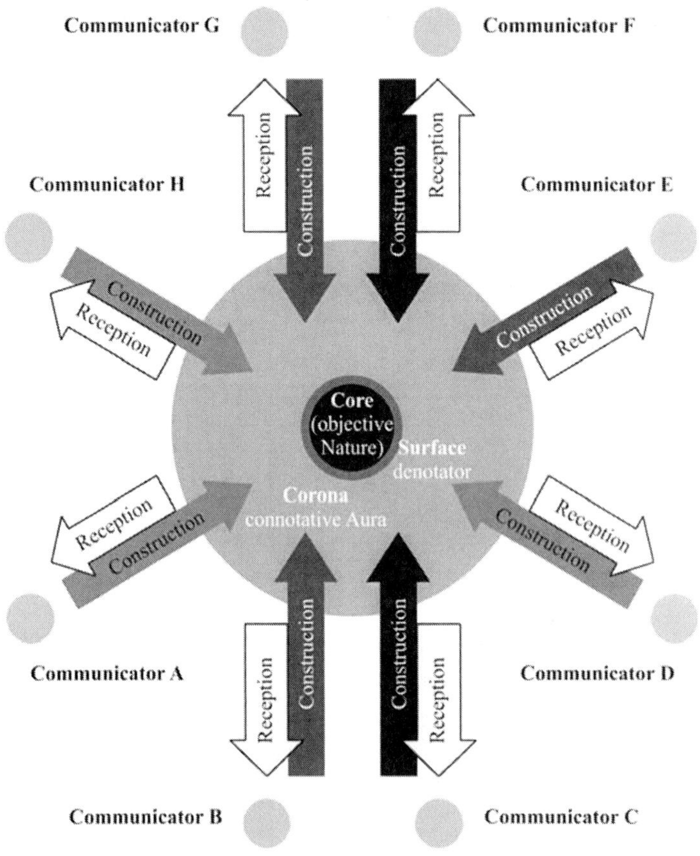

Fig. 10-1: The spherical model of Product Communication: Many groups of actors fill a brand with meaning, an on-going and perpetual process of negotiation

The processes in this form of social exchange can be represented in the form of a three-dimensional model (Fig. 10-1). At the centre of the product-communicative event, you can see the product itself, which can be represented as a multi-layered sphere. All imaginable groups of partners are grouped around it, like active satellites; they all have different intentions and their real number is incalculable. In a model of this sort, communications do not remain one-dimensional, but become reflexively imaginable, whereby reflexive information does not necessarily have to flow back on the same axis. A three-dimensional model of product communication allows many paths, even detours, for the refluxing of information. The numerous communicative procedures are carried by the power of attraction and concentration exerted by the product in the middle. Around this core, almost physically supported by it, the product ascriptions and associations layer themselves in the form of signs and symbols.

First comes a thin ring of permanent and unspectacular denotative components. This is followed by a broad connotative aura, which is the object and result of the process of exchange between the groups of actors and active players. It is here that the individual ascriptions are accepted and concentrated into coherent social product and brand images. Complex product images become crystallized out of "ascriptive" particles. The image of a product is thus by no means simply limited to the pictorial offerings disseminated by advertising. Numerous groups of actors were in the past and are today, involved in building up and modifying such images, day-by-day, year-by-year and century-by-century.

It is the willing intention of the producers and subconscious idea of the consumers to maintain this cycle of meaning and sense. The repeated purchase of the same product and the repeated communication about this brand provides a feeling of safety and orientation; both for the seller and for the buyer. With successful brands this loop is held not only once, but repeated continuously over time. Therefore, this spinning control circuit of product communication also extends its alluring web into the past, as well as into the future.

Ascriptions that have become compromised as internal or commemorative images, that have developed over a long period of time out of advertising messages on the one hand and attributions of significance by consumers on the other. Product images of this sort therefore consist of complexes, of messages and significations about which the various actors in product communication have over long epochs, come to an agreement.

Within the framework of this concept, brands represent striking images, characterized by their universal appeal and widespread presence. These product profiles are territorially and temporally ubiquitous. Such images are above all, the result of a joint effort between the named groups of actors in product communication on the one hand (manufacturers, advertising agencies, retailers, users, and market researchers and opinion pollsters), and the consumers on the other.

Two points seem to be of particular relevance here:

Firstly, the buyers and users are involved in the production of the brand profile. The simple decision to buy a product represents a "yes" to the image of this product. As a result, accepted images of products point to lasting processes of appropriation by the groups of actors named. Thus, for historical research, product images represent sources that permit certain conclusions to be drawn about producers and marketing and advertising experts, but especially about the potential buyers and consumers of products.

Secondly, brands have a history. Brand profiles display a surprising constancy over long periods of time. Brand images are passed down from generation to generation; they can therefore prove to have a very long "brand life" and often outlive their users. To be precise, they represent a joint effort by many people over decades, sometimes even over centuries. Brand profiles are the result of continuing and enduring processes of understanding and negotiation.

Products represent both formats of consumption and social communication at the same time. Branded products fulfil all the cultural and social criteria that are attributed to the traditional media.

(1) Media are deployed in order to connect different systems with each other. That is, media link people as well as social systems.

(2) The term "connect" is here used not to designate just any sort of connection, but signifies that media offers are used in order to generate meaning.

(3) This meaning-generation is not arbitrary, but is oriented by the rules governing the use of specific media and media offers, which most people have learned and internalized in the course of their media socialization (Siegfried J. Schmidt quoted in Zurstiege 2007, 12).

The attributions of the products are unconsciously and cognitively, emotionally and rationally discursive. If we assume that products work in modern societies as media, then we should imagine them as real, living or imagined "platforms of social practice", they can also be modelled as relations of "signs and signifying" that are able to give and receive meanings.

Since at least the middle of the last century, groups, generations and societies have communicated via products. This can be seen as something other than simply a monolithic and mono-logic form of communication: other forms of social exchange, such as interpersonal or face-to-face communications, have provided the reflexivity of that communication in addition. In this way, an active public could themselves become an actor in these cyclic belts that run over years, decades and centuries (Gries 2004).

Product media, like traditional media, also convey processes of unification, in the present, in the future and even the past. They also include and exclude, they segregate, segment and fragment at the same time. If certain products have become platforms of social exchange and the core around which social understanding crystallizes, the question then arises as to how brands and products work as a media of sustainability.

Sustainability and Holistic Approaches to Brands: Chain of Meanings–Chain of Generations

The inter-generational communication is a structural element of successful long-term product communication. Therefore, this inter-generational exchange is paramount for the ongoing performance of sustainable continuities. Since the nineteenth century many brands have already been operating successfully as economical and cultural "real estates" in the market—as well as in the collective mind of society. These brand continuities over centuries and generations remind us to observe brand products as generators of trust and confidence in modern societies (see Luhmann 1989; Frevert 2003; see in detail Gries 2003b).

Sometimes producers and commercial communicators of brands quote this dimension of structural sustainability in their promotional ads and use it as an additional sales tool: A product such as *Werther's Echte* (a brand of caramel sweets) or even *Persil* (a famous brand of laundry powder) in Germany, which apparently satisfied not only the generation of mothers and fathers, but also the generation of grandmothers and grandfathers can only be good for today's generations (Fig. 10-2).

These products represent "social proof" and more precisely: a diachronic apprehended "social proof". The well-known social psychological "principle of social proof" states, that people who are faced with decision alternatives, watch and look at how others act and react in the same situation or look at how they acted in former times. Then they copy these models either consciously or unconsciously.

Fig. 10-2: Longevity as a motif of brand advertising: "For generations, always the best Persil of its time: Now with a new fresh scent" (advertising theme "Celebration of Generations" on the 125th anniversary of Henkel in 2001)

It is also for these reasons that they usually opt for a product and for a product feeling that others and their ancestors already adopted with success in the past. This behaviour can be transported under two circumstances: the higher the current uncertainty, the greater the focus on behavioural patterns of these models. And the models should be perceived as "similarly" as possible. Similarity is the second condition under which the principle of social proof is particularly influential: it tends to do the same things as people seen as similar did in the past or do today.

Sustainable product communication also relies on this concept: the generational predecessors can be the pre-images of today's consumer generations. The brand decisions, the brand feelings and the brand meanings of the generation of the grandparents can affect the brand decisions of all the following generations. The importance of this *chain of meanings*, connected with the *chain of generations*, should not be underestimated.

A public demonstration of this kind of historicity of brands, of longevity and sustainability, is comparatively rare. Only sometimes do ads refer explicitly to the past historical contexts of the offered product. The massive foundation of inter-generational experiences with products happens not publicly, but rather confidentially and individually: From childhood, such experiences are implemented and enrolled in the horizons of the younger generations in a subtle and subcutaneous way.

The story of a certain brand seen from this perspective is also the history of the generations who have worked together on the testimony of this product. In this way, brands have become not only a type of modern media, but have also advanced to a media of collective memory (Gries 2010a). The basic principle of brand culture is therefore sustainability.

The path via product communication paves the way for young people especially, as well as for members of educationally disadvantaged backgrounds. In modern consumer and media societies, experiences of learning and the acquisition of competence are not only conveyed though traditional educational institutions, but also through peer groups and via television and increasingly via the medium of the Internet. We should perceive brands and products as educational media; they are media, which pick up where young people's interests lay.

This raises the question as to which way both the knowledge and the feeling of the long-term historicity of brand products may contribute to the further development of sustainability skills.

Structural Sustainability: What Political Dimensions do Product Media in Modern Societies Perform?

Brand products have become important generators of social cohesion within modern societies. The first political dimension of product media is founded on the development of confidence and trust (see Gries 2006; 2011a).

Building on the work of the German social philosopher Niklas Luhmann, "trust" is here understood as an emotional attitude that can be inspired in users and potential buyers by particular products. This emotional attitude can be the result of personal or collective familiarity or experience with a product. In either case, trust is the result of lasting experiences and communications with and about the product. If the future is uncertain, we need trust in order to make decisions in the present to carry us safely into this unknown future. To grant trust, is therefore always a precarious gamble. Trust is fragile because the trusting person does not have access to the full range of information required to be sure of the future success of his or her actions and decisions. But as reality is far too complex for us to be able to examine all the factors, which influence our decisions, we try to check trustworthiness. The way, in which we do this, is to use a greatly simplified network of indications that constantly send us information about whether or not we can continue to trust something. Trust is thus the provision of credit for the future.

The second political dimension of product media is founded on the development of sustainability. The knowledge of these qualities of branded products, can help to encourage sustainability and may further help to educate the competence of social participation; in keeping with the spirit of the "UN World Decade of Education for Sustainable Development".

Through the collective and repeated decision for a brand and a product choice and therefore, through the collective and repeated decision about the meanings of a brand or product, as well as through the mutual awareness and communication of these consumptive similarities, unification processes are instituted. Successful brands possess and inherent structural sustainability. This provides both opportunity and risk: over the course of generations it can be observed that brands have been linked to "false" attributions and connotations as experiences and expectations. One major problem to stem from this theory is: this system tends to ensure that in uncertain times, consumers trust in the familiar, traditional brand model. This may stabilize the psychic world of the consumer[4] but the danger is that this modus may wreak havoc and damage world order.

From this perspective the question rises: How to develop new, breakthrough, promising brand patterns, which in turn can be role models for our children and grandchildren? This can only be possible if these innovative and sustainable product actions are not regarded as a threat to the long and safety-giving tradition of trusted brands. This should also not be perceived as a painful abjuration or defection from the traditional customs and practices of our ancestors.

"Political" product communications in this sense have highly effective advantages: ubiquity and general availability, plus an emotional and sensuous quality. The trust, confidence and security, which they inspire, are benefits that can be acquired in affluent societies; they are gratifications that every man and women can afford. And the communication modes in which products make their contribution to political culture do not need to be rationally perceived, but instead, felt. "Trust" or "security" doesn't necessarily have to appear as words in advertisements, but rather, by means of gestures and gestus, images and symbols, products, can have a profound and long-lasting political impact.

From this, we can see that over a long period of time, branded products have become a constituent part of the mental and political infrastructure of modern societies. Their mere presence, seemingly permanent and trans-

---

[4] Concerning the relations between "the soul" of consumer goods and the soul of consumers see Gries and Schwarzkopf 2007; 2010.

temporal, stabilizes modern societies which, in the "age of extremes" (see Hobsbawm 1994) and increasingly rapid innovation require, above all, things that stay the same. The architecture of branded products is able to place Western states and societies firmly on their foundations, as their narratives, developed collectively over long periods, stabilize the citizens of precisely these societies as a collective. The reliability and trustworthiness of their statements, of course, have to be repeatedly demonstrated anew by the products. Ultimately, it is always the quality of the goods and products that both vouch for and validate these fundamental social and political qualities.

Today, educational and scientific consensus should voice that effective "learning" is not simply a didactic "one-way" street with learners who work as "trivial machines". Skills are not always easily transferable, but they need to be developed by the learners, then processed and used competently.[5] The mere addition of knowledge about the nature of the brand and product communication can therefore not be the only goal that contributes to education for sustainable development. The acquisition of relevant knowledge can be agile, but not sufficient. Sound and rounded knowledge, should be a basis for evaluation processes, which in turn form the basis for a purchasing of "design skills" within the intended and concise meaning of sustainability.

Brand sustainability represents a form of sustainability that is particularly inherent in successful brand communications. The communication processes around brand products represent a phenomena of sustainability of time and furthermore, over generations. We need to be clear about the fact that generations are always involved in the designing of brand products. The successful brands, which we know and buy today, are the result of social negotiation processes, which have taken place for over one hundred years. In the age of web 2.0 the opportunities for buyers and consumers are even further augmented in participation of the design of products. Therefore, buying and consuming may even advance into a democratic act. Democratic patterns are also developed along the way by these product media, as people and groups can contribute to the actual product and brand narratives. They are real actors or participants of the brands' script.

The rehearsal of product communicative action means both to engage into and latch on to a long process of co-designing and co-shaping products and brands. This becomes an engagement into the horizons of co-responsibility. The knowledge of the long-term product communicative

---

[5] Concerning the performance of competences now see Tschekan 2011. For further information see Gries 2011b.

chains, which reach into the past, encourages action today that keeps the future in mind. The knowledge about this nature of product communication and the intentional and active participation in the product-communicative action is one way of recognizing sustainability as an economic, social and political imperative.

Up to this point, this contribution acts as a triple appeal:

Firstly, product cultures and consumer cultures are inherited. Brand and product education begins in the family. Grandparents and parents must therefore be aware of their responsibility as facilitators and role models. We should be aware that even their choices, as well as their uses of goods, type and the patterns they set for future generations; for their children and grand children and so on. Parents are the first and most enduring educators of product communicative sustainability.

Secondly, this paper argues for imparting the basic cognitive knowledge about the processes of product communication lore, which should be offered in school and other traditional educational institutions.

Third and lastly, we must identify new and progressive ways in which to use this knowledge in everyday life as a buyer and consumer, who is actively involved in brand and product communications.

Together we have to develop the competences of individuals and groups to participate in this way, in the design of products and brands, and to participate in the same way in the design of our societies and politics.

References

Frevert, Ute, ed. 2003. *Vertrauen: Historische Annäherungen.* Göttingen: Vandenhoeck & Ruprecht.

Gekeler, Moritz. 2012. *Konsumgut Nachhaltigkeit. Zur Inszenierung neuer Leitmotive in der Produktkommunikation.* Bielefeld: Transcript.

Gries, Rainer. 2003a. *Produkte als Medien: Kulturgeschichte der Produktkommunikation in der Bundesrepublik und der DDR.* Leipzig: Leipziger Universitätsverlag.

—. 2003b. "Versuch einer Historisierung von 'Vertrauen' anhand der Geschichte der Produktkommunikation." In *Produkte als Medien: Kulturgeschichte der Produktkommunikation in der Bundesrepublik und der DDR*, edited by Rainer Gries, 561–592. Leipzig: Leipziger Universitätsverlag.

—. 2004. "Die Konsumenten und die Werbung: Kulturgeschichtliche Aspekte einer interaktiven Kommunikation." In *Konsum der Werbung: Zur Produktion und Rezeption von Sinn in der kommerziellen Kultur*, edited by Kai-Uwe Hellmann, and Dominik Schrage, 83–101. Wiesbaden: VS Verlag für Sozialwissenschaften.

—. 2006. *Produkte & Politik: Zur Kultur- und Politikgeschichte der Produktkommunikation.* Wien: Facultas WUV.

—. 2008. *Produktkommunikation: Geschichte und Theorie.* Wien: Facultas WUV.

—. 2010a. "Produkte – Medien des sozialen Gedächtnisses." In *Gedächtnis und Erinnerung: Ein interdisziplinäres Handbuch*, edited by Ariane Eichenberg, Christian Gudehus, and Harald Welzer, 149–155. Stuttgart, Weimar: Metzler.

—. 2010b. "Produktmedien: Zur Erkundung konjunktiver Erwartungs- und Erfahrungsräume in Europa." In *Massenmedien im Europa des 20. Jahrhunderts*, edited by Ute Daniel, and Axel Schildt, 175–200. Köln, Weimar, Wien: Böhlau.

—. 2011a. "Cultures of Products and Political Cultures: Looking for Transfer Performances." In *The Voice of the Citizen-Consumer: A History of Market Research, Consumer Movements, and the Political Public Sphere*, edited by Kerstin Brückweh, 243–269. London: Oxford University Press.

—. 2011b. "Produkte als Medien nachhaltiger Bedeutungsvermittlung." In *Die unsichtbare Dimension. Bildung für eine nachhaltige Entwicklung im kulturellen Prozess*, vol. 8, edited by Gabriele Sorgo, 139–154. Wien: Forum Umwelt & Bildung.

Gries, Rainer, and Stefan Schwarzkopf, eds. 2007. *Ernest Dichter – Doyen der Verführer: Zum einhundertsten Geburtstag des "Vaters der Motivforschung".* Wien: Verlag Christian W. Mucha.

—, eds. 2010. *Ernest Dichter and Motivation Research: New Perspectives on the Making of Post-war Consumer Culture.* Basingstoke, New York: Palgrave Macmillan.

Haan, Gerhard de. 2004. "Politische Bildung für Nachhaltigkeit." In *Aus Politik und Zeitgeschichte* 7–8: 39–46.

Hobsbawm, Eric. 1994. *The Age of Extremes: The Short Twentieth Century, 1914–1991.* London: Abacus.

Luhmann, Niklas. 1989. *Vertrauen: Ein Mechanismus der Reduktion sozialer Komplexität.* Stuttgart: Enke.

Tschekan, Kerstin. 2011. *Kompetenzorientiert unterrichten: Eine Didaktik.* Berlin: Cornelsen Scriptor.

Zurstiege, Guido. 2007. *Werbeforschung.* Konstanz: UVK.

CRITICAL MARKETING, CONSUMPTION STUDIES AND POLITICAL ECONOMIC ANALYSIS

ALAN BRADSHAW

In this chapter, I wish to explore the relationship between studies of consumption and critical political economy perspectives. Rather than review different disciplinary fields that address consumption, I focus on a particular tradition of scholarship—critical marketing. Critical marketing is mostly associated with UK scholars and can be regarded as a sub-area of research within marketing that seeks to subject marketing to critical analysis, is broadly related to interpretive consumer research, consumer culture theory and critical management studies and is associated with various edited volumes (Brownlie et al. 1999; Saren et al. 2007; Tadajewski and Brownlie 2008; Ellis et al. 2010) and was recently historicised by Tadajewski (2010). In this chapter, I seek to explore the absence of a political analysis from such analysis. The issues that are raised relate to broader issues of how the question of political economy is often evaded within studies of consumption and hence broader conclusions are pursued that may be relevant to various subject areas.

Despite the subtitle of the text *Critical Marketing: Defining the Field* (Saren et al. 2007), exponents of critical marketing generally operate in the absence of a well-defined subject. A major step towards clarifying what sort of field critical marketing may be was by Tadajewski's (2010) recent "Towards a History of Critical Marketing Studies" published in the *Journal of Marketing Management*, an important and helpful representation of decades of scholarship read in terms of how they relate to and can be integrated into a broader project that we now know as critical marketing. Yet Tadajewski's paper is as useful for providing a literature review that reveals a rich tradition of critical enquiry as it is for revealing what is missing from that critical tradition—a political economic reading of marketing and consumer culture. This absence, I submit, renders the field as a debate without a centre. To that end, I investigate the absence of political economic analysis and call for more centred debate.

A political economic outlook that explores links between social infrastructure and the reproduction of capital might stem from a range of theoretical perspectives yet from within critical theoretical traditions, Marx's *Capital* is often regarded as the staple. At the time of writing, when the Euro currency stands on the brink of collapse and occupations break out across the Western and Arabic world, capital seems to demand deeper attention from critical theoretics. Whilst Marxist analysis had never gone away, it does seem reasonable to state that we are amidst a surge of critical enquiry with Marx's theories of capital returned to a central position evidenced by recent publications of *Capital* readers by major scholars like Fredric Jameson (2011), David Harvey (2010a) which stand alongside popular selling texts like Terry Eagleton's *Why Marx Was Right* (2011). Indeed this is not even to mention the surge of interest in communism re-imagined marked by recent publications by major critical philosophers like Badiou (2010), Žižek and Douzinas (2010), Bosteels (2011) and Groys (2010). There are grounds to consider that we stand amidst a paradigmatic moment in critical theory as it returns to the far left with attention re-focussing on capital.

Hence, in as much as it is important to present historical analysis of critical marketing, it must be noted that we are amidst a moment of critical theory that is, simply put, on fire. Whilst the complex and historically informed analysis provided by Tadajewski (2010) is important in order to understand critical marketing, indeed to have a critical marketing, such a task also raises the risk of subject insularity and may set terms for the subject's disengagement from contemporary dynamics of critical theory. Indeed, inasmuch as various other subject areas have also attempted to develop an applied criticality for their field, or as Harney put it, had their "critical moments" (see Dunne et al. 2008), it is surely useful to contemplate points of disconnection.

Indeed it seems entirely possible to read into critical marketing a hostility and deep suspicion towards political economic designs. To be sure, hostile denouncements from within the business school are only to be expected however what is perhaps most puzzling is how this cold voice so often arises from within the critical community itself. For example, Arnould (2007) described much of the critical theory perspective as being overly moralising and somehow taking the form of an inheritance from the puritan and Calvinist tradition. Within critical marketing, in one of the foundational texts, *Rethinking Marketing* (1999), the editors Brownlie, Saren, Wensley and Whittington express a form of critical marketing (later exactly re-iterated by Brownlie 2006; Brownlie and Hewer 2007) that forms an:

> eclectic framework of critique which leaves space for many voices other than those of card carrying critical theorists. There is indeed much to be learned from letting consumers or managers speak for themselves, even if critical ethnographers have difficult "hearing" what is being said, for there is much to commend Lilley's view that managers and critical management researchers may be playing similar games, with similar rules, for different teams (Brownlie et al. 1999, 9).

There is much to contemplate in Brownlie et al's above contention; a questioning of the motives of those who speak from such a critical perspective, an equation of that long held theoretical tradition with management itself: an inference that those coming from a critical perspective are incapable of hearing and therefore understanding; and, finally, the suggestion that the voices that should be heard are not those who are searching for an outside perspective on capital, but rather those who are already totally embedded: managers and consumers. But finally, maybe most worryingly of all, is the contention that critical marketing is to create space "for many other voices other than those of card carrying critical theorists" (ibid.); in other words, those who follow a critical theory trajectory are to be excluded from this space.

More recently Brownlie, one of the original *Rethinking Marketing* editors, now writing with Hewer (2007) mockingly coins the term "criterati" to describe a particular brand of Frankfurt inspired scholar. They set about the task of revealing the criterati's embedded discursive power relations so as to move critical marketing beyond the criterati's nuances, politics of estrangement and elitism precisely by, it would seem to me, creating their own nuances, estrangements and elitisms. Ultimately they suggest that these criterati, that is those scholars engaged in the critical project, are actually "strategic, interested and elitist, masking claims to disciplinary territory and prestige" (ibid., 45).[1] Again a mood of suspicion prevails. The spirit of the criterati seemed best captured by verse so they quote Guillet de Monthoux (2006, 175) who previously mocked the British ascetic mould of criticality in the Art of Oppression *Consumption, Markets & Culture* special issue: "The world is like a flower/ The sky is bright and blue. Me, egghead in the tower, Can prove it's all untrue/ And/ It feels so good to feel so bad/ I'm happy when I'm down and sad". Also Hewer and Brownlie quote Jarvis Cocker: "You'll never live like common people / you'll never do whatever common people do". And then they present their criterati recipe:

---

[1] As a thought exercise I have attempted to identify a form of scholarship that is not "strategic, interested and elitist" or that makes no claim to institutional prestige or territory.

> [S]tart with the staple ingredients: a big dollop of Marx and Engels (especially *German Ideology*) following by a sprinkling of Adorno & Horkheimer (maybe *Dialectic of Enlightenment* for starters) with Marcuse (*One Dimensional Man*). To this mixture would then be added a splash of Habermas. To this mixture, why not gently cook in De Certeau [...] (Brownlie and Hewer 2007, 61).

Meanwhile in the same text, Scott (2007) describes a damned hegemony of the critical by the 1990s:

> Ultimately the Critical agenda had to be clearly reflected (using whatever Theory was currently fashionable) in any scholarly work before it could be accepted for publication. Those who attempted to write outside the prevailing perspective or, heaven forbid, to disagree with it, were simply frozen out. On the ground, colleagues who seemed to think differently from the in-group were, at best, ridiculed as being in need of re-education. Thus, freedom of inquiry became substantially constrained. The growing attention to political correctness infected even the classroom, where some students chafed under the unspoken butt palpable limitations of their freedom of expression. Subordinating evidence to politics slowly became the order of the day, leading to a pronounced erosion of both critical thought and liberal education. The Critique, with its unrelentingly negative hermeneutic, had a further tendency to look like despair, scoffing at hope and disdaining those who sought solutions that fell short of revolution (Scott 2007, 5–6).

Such hostile discourse is not unique to critical marketing scholarship, consider these words from Miller (2010), the noted anthropologist, in his latest book:

> Theory, philosophy, modern art, economics and other movements that utilize obscure abstractions can easily degenerate into pretentious obfuscations and become oppressive playgrounds of academic divas and elites to intimidate as much as to impress. Academics, tempted by the claims of an easy and assured claim to cleverness, create vast circulations of obscure and impressive citations. A scattering of good names such as Lacan or Deleuze and Guttari is usually a good sign of such oppressive conceits. It is only through the subsequent process of maturing and re-grounding theory in its application to everyday lives and languages that such cleverness becomes transformed into understanding and re-directed to a compassionate embrace, rather than an aloof distance. To make matters worse, the most oppressive use of theory tends to come dressed in the guise of critical or radical political endeavour, a claimed concern with the actually oppressed conditions of our humanity (Miller 2010, 80).

Similarly within the 2008 special issue of *Cultural Studies*, on the theme of anti-consumption, the guest editors Binkley and Littler distance themselves from "determinist accounts of consumer culture and its rejection of chest-thumping denunciations of the 'culture industry'" (Binkley and Littler 2008, 520), that cultural studies has a troubled relationship with "one of the left's favourite intellectual parlour games—the critique of the commodity form" and they also fear that the reader would suspect that the guest issue was all about forming another "neologism crafted in the Ivory Tower's left-leaning workshop" (ibid., 524).

Together these studies contribute to a clear pattern; a fear that trenchantly critical analysis will be conducted by hacks who work to recipe, who are oppressive, ruthlessly politically correct, anti-intellectual, anti-freedom of expression, offer a stale polemic, are elitist, only out somehow to pursue their own strategic interest, only use complicated theory to show off, are masochists, eggheads, incapable of seeing life like the working classes, cynical opportunists, incapable of hearing, can be found in the parlour of ivory towers, thumping their chests whilst playing games of critiquing commodity forms whilst sleeping with common people. Their critique is a pretence which masks a dark agenda whilst the person in question is really a diva, a bully, a fake, aloof. Trenchant critical theory, therefore, is to be read as excessive and fundamentalist (though as Toscano 2010 notes, often the accusation of fundamentalism is a rejection of abstraction and belies a failure to engage with centuries of critical thought) to be dismissed through lampooning rather than seriously engaged with whilst any top-down reading of consumer culture is apparently taken as *a priori* nonsense, a violence done not just to consumers, but to the entire field itself.

However what is most interesting is the absence of a literature review to identify where exactly such scholarship exists. In other words, what is operating is not an identification of a body of literature within marketing that should be critiqued but rather a disavowal of an imagined critical position. In the parallel world of third wave feminism, where second wave feminists are often misrepresented, lampooned and dismissed as dour, asexual bullies, Henry (2004) speculates that such disavowalment is necessary in order to create space for a new criticality.

Alternatively, it is interesting to consider if critical marketers are in convergence with the New Philosophy position that holds Marxism responsible for Stalinism and rejects strident positions as extremist, fundamentalist, dangerous, ignorant and fatalist (a position which has been comprehensively critiqued see Bourg 2007; Toscano 2010): as Badiou

(2010, 1) put it, a position that holds that "to want something better is to want something worse". Tinker (see Dunne et al. 2008) comments the prevalence of such ideas in *Critical Management Studies*:

> Early on, CMS was taken over and diluted by decedents of the Nouvelle Philosophie—pseudo French radicals who confused Stalin/the Soviet Bloc and the French Communist Party with Marxism—and rather than read the latter, embarked on a revisionist binge of Neo-Foucaudian atomism. The result: a mish-mash of identity politics in its most atomistic form (Dunne et al. 2008, 276–277).

Whilst a deeper engagement with New Philosophy and critical marketing surely represents an opportunity for future research it is interesting to note what I regard to be an immediate resonance between critical marketing and the "five slogans" of new philosophy, as identified by their detractors Aubral and Delcourt (translated into English in Bourg 2007, 235): "Marxism is barbarism, everything is only discourse, one must escape the political conception of the world, socialists are imposters and one must wager".[2]

As Tinker above indicates, in such confused quagmire, strange bedfellows emerge and hence we see a consistency between the New Philosophy position and a popular reading of Foucault. As severely critiqued by Berman (2010), the Foucaultian position forecloses analysis grounded in any concepts of freedom (such as Marxism) as it carries risk of reproducing discourses of power whilst any critique rings hollow because the critic himself or herself is "in the panoptic machine, invested by its effects of power, which we bring to ourselves, since we are part of its mechanism" (Foucault 1995, 217). Berman demonstrates the logical dead-end of such analysis, perhaps reflected in a critical marketing that avoids political economy:

> The mystery is who so many of today's intellectuals want to choke in there with (Foucault). The answer is, I suspect, that Foucault offers a generation of refugees from the 1960s a world-historical alibi for the sense of passivity and helplessness that gripped so many of us in the 1970s. There is no point in trying to resist the oppressions and injustices of modern life, since even our dreams of freedom only add more links to our chains;

---

[2] According to Badiou with the New Philosophers "we have here, almost unchanged, all the arguments of the American anti-communism of the 1950s: socialist regimes are loathsome despotisms and bloody dictatorships" (Badiou 2010, 2–3). If it true that this is a trait shared with some critical marketers who maintain a fear of "card carrying critical theorists" then this adds an interesting twist to Tadajewski's (2006) history of marketing and the Cold War.

> however, once we grasp the total futility of it all, at least we can relax (Berman 2010, 34–35).

In any case whatever the reason why there is such hostility to Marxism and trenchantly critical positions, it seems that whilst the field of critical marketing is well established, as Tadajewski (2010) outlines, the absence of a political economic perspective exists in the context of extraordinary hostility. Consequentially I note a very conservative, even reactionary, recurring thread that seeks to contain critical marketing's criticality and this leaves the field divorced from the aforementioned Marxist renaissance within the broader field of critical theory. Within this context, it is notable that Tadajewski's archival analysis seems to reveal an almost entire absence of capital from critical marketing. Hence critical analyses are directed to power imbalances that occur between large corporations and consumers, with the occasional thought spared for the subaltern. Consequentially externalised are broader structural analyses. Instead we see within consumer culture theory a commitment to exploring how consumers encounter ideology as actively interpreting agents:

> whose meaning creating activities range from those that tacitly embrace the dominant representations of consumer identity and lifestyle ideals portrayed in advertising to those that consciously deviate from these ideological instructions (Arnould and Thompson 2005, 874).

Interestingly this concern rarely considers actual political activism that holds the possibility of registering a political transformation such as UK student occupations in defence of a public idea of education or the Zapatista experimentations in organisation and consumption to be found in Chiapas[3] but instead a curiosity is maintained in the weird and extraordinary—the so-called Burning Mountain Man of Action Hero agenda (Bradshaw and Holbrook 2008). Following Žižek (2009), we might also consider such subjective moments that encounter ideology—no matter how bizarre or offbeat, in fact the odder the better—as visible perturbations within a normal state of things as opposed to the objective and systematic violent struggle that lies behind the smooth functioning of our economic and political systems. In other words externalised from

[3] Sadly Arnould (2007) preferred to analyse an instance of desperate poverty in rural Niger as a case of escape from the market rather than radical political experimentation in such instances as the Zapatistas. In such a context non-market reality was positioned as dystopian despite the fact that many revolutionary projects are grounded in utopian ideals, an ideal that only gets considered in its commodified form (see Murtola 2010).

critical marketing analyses is the actual condition of capitalism and this absence is a defining feature arguably shared between critical marketing and the wider field of business and management. At best this results in what Bourg (2007) would describe as a debate without a centre but at worst, Harney (in Dunne et al. 2008, 282) suggests that it may result in nothing at all:

> I would say that business and management is technically, logically, specifically, about nothing. The formula we used is this: capitalism=struggle but business=capitalism-struggle therefore business=zero. When we say this what we mean is that business casts matters of struggle as externalities. As you know, the study Stephen (Dunne) and I did together shows how rarely top scholarship in our field ever addresses these externalities. When business extracts struggle from the real business of business and considers it an externality (even one that must be accounted for or dealt with) it is essentially defining itself as nothing, or more exactly as the science of managing wealth-making without wealth-making, the science of nothing or worse still perhaps, the science of managing nothing! We might say that the reason we both feel so exasperated by business ideology, but also so enervated by it, is that it is precisely about nothing. It hides nothing, and marshals nothing in its interest, at least at one level, and it is therefore a very tricky ideology I must admit.

In agreement with Harney, the task for a critical orientation is surely to cease externalising the conditions of capitalism. Whilst, as Tadajewski (2010) notes in his piece, the field is conditioned by the post-Carnegie and Ford reports business school model, I submit that such a task is nonetheless essential for critical marketing to be critical because what is at stake is a connectivity with critical theory itself. To reinforce the point, Harney (in Dunne et al. 2008) identifies how other UK-lead attempts towards applied criticality have failed in architecture, social work, legal studies and education—they "had their critical moment" which phased out due to a series of factors such as cliché and careerism or were overtaken by and failed to be dialogous with superior critiques offered by sociology and philosophy. This raises the concern that applied criticality may be an ephemeral project, already doomed to failure; perhaps Askegaard (2009) was correct in his inferred rephrasing of Harold Giersing: good research is always critical, critical research is always bad. In discussion with Harney, Parker (in Dunne et al. 2008) notes a fatal lack of coherency with applied critical studies due to an absence of clear political positioning:

> For me, critical necessarily means left wing. For me, that means being committed to the redistribution of wealth, to localization, and hence to forms of ideology critique that are helpful to these projects. In that sense,

> merely writing and talking about "identity", "discourse", "theory" and so on are not in themselves critical. They might be turned to critical uses, but then so can forms of positivism, functionalism and science. The point, for me, is effects, and no particular epistemology guarantees certain political effects (Dunne et al. 2008, 276).

Again the issue at stake is that critical marketing takes the form of a debate without a centre. This does not necessarily mean that all critical marketers must be Marxist, left-wing revolutionaries but rather that such a position would provide the basis for a more pointed analysis that can be engaged with and argued against or agreed with on a more coherent basis.

In conclusion I wish to add to Tadajewski's (2010) historicisation by pointing towards how critical marketing has taken the form of a criticality divested of Marxist political economy and not only does this result in a critical-lite subject divorced from contemporary critical theory, but also in a violence of divestment that creates conditions of exclusivity and discipline marked by extraordinarily rude lampooning. Of course the catholic register of criticality within critical marketing (provided you are not a Marxist) serves a purpose of inclusion but also creates the risk that there is such dilution and compromise that a substantial centre is lost, or perhaps never materialised in the first place.

Taken together all these concerns point to a potential problem of whether critical marketing is already a co-optation of an apparently critical discourse by a normalising discourse. In so doing the risk is that a criticality will be maintained that constantly backs away from engagement in politics and in so doing loses its principles and so sets about a rational set of compromises until the whole is lost. In such a context it is pertinent to ask: would it ever be possible to identify a moment of betrayal? Are there are any real positions that critical marketing inhabits that leave it in a clearly stated position with regards to politics, to capital, to the business school and lastly to critical theory itself?

Of course proposing a political economic centre for critical marketing is also an act of foreclosure. It is dogmatic and even stupid to insist that only a Marxist political economy or historical materialist position might represent an authentic criticality. Indeed as Brown (2009) states critique emerges from ancient Athenian jurisprudence and can take various forms such as cultural critique, identity critique, ideology critique and therefore it is arrogant, ignorant and historically nonsensical to demand such a limitation. Meanwhile both Schroeder (2007) and Scott (2007) demonstrate a rich diversity of understandings of critical marketing from within the field based on their vox-pops. Furthermore Marxist critique itself has been critiqued as advocating a Western-centric secular worldview (see discussions in Asad et al. 2009). Additionally, political economy-centric critique has been accused of failing to maintain an adequate position in regards to gender (notwithstanding the existence of a very large Marxist feminist canon, Orr 2007); and who is to disagree that gender distinctions are more fundamental than class distinctions?

Hence the critical task is not to foreclose alternative modes of critique or analysis nor to insist that a notionally correct form of critique prevail, but rather it is to request more centred analysis, whatever that centre should be. Additionally the call is to request an acknowledgement that the commitment to post-history all-inclusive-criticality produces a subject prone to incoherency, negation, cooptation and may axiomatically maintain a post-politics that we never get to debate or engage with. By contrast a series of alternatively centred critical and affirmative perspectives such as a political economy critique, a second wave feminist critique, a third wave feminist critique, a pro-neo-liberal affirmation, and so on, give a basis for engagements that are politically relevant and epistemologically coherent. To smooth over the differences in the interest of subject inclusivity is to, I submit, commit the greatest violence of all except this is a violence that is entirely self-destructive as it creates the conditions for critical marketing's own self-negation.

Yes it is true that advocating such a political economy centre that stands alongside alternative centres produces new dogmas, new foreclosures, gender, privileges and much more violence and criterati posturing besides and yet the appeal must be made to hearts and minds so let the last words go to Alain Badiou:

> We have to be bold enough to have an idea. A great idea. We have to convince ourselves that there is nothing ridiculous or criminal about having a great idea… I am a philosopher, so let me tell you something that has been said again and again since Plato's day. It is very simple. I am telling you as a philosopher that we have to live with an idea, and that what deserves to be called a real politics begins with that conviction (Badiou 2010, 66–67).

References

Arnould, Eric J. 2007. "Can Consumers Escape the Market?" In *Critical Marketing: Defining the Field*, edited by Michael Saren, Pauline Maclaran, Christina Goulding, Richard Elliott, Avi Shankar and Miriam Catterall, 139–156. London: Butterworth-Heinemann.

Arnould, Eric J., and Craig J. Thompson. 2005. "Consumer Culture Theory (CCT): Twenty Years of Research." *Journal of Consumer Research* 31 (4): 868–882.

Asad, Talal, Wendy Brown, Judith Butler, and Saba Mahmood. 2009. *Is Critique Secular? Blasphemy, Injury, and Free Speech.* Berkeley: Townsend Center for the Humanities, University of California Press.

Askegaard, Søren. 2009. "Good Theory Is Always Critical…" *Scandanavian Journal of Management* 25 (1): 129–130.

Badiou, Alain. 2010. *The Communist Hypothesis.* London: Verso.

Berman, Marshall. 2010. *All That is Solid Melts into Air: The Experience of Modernity.* London: Verso.

Binkley, Sam, and Jo Littler. 2008. "Introduction: Cultural Studies and Anti-Consumerism: A Critical Encounter." *Cultural Studies* 22 (5): 519–530.

Bosteels, Bruno. 2011. *The Actuality of Communism.* London: Verso.

Bourg, Julian. 2007. *From Revolution to Ethics: May 1968 and Contemporary French Thought.* Montreal: McGill-Queen's University Press.

Bradshaw, Alan, and Morris B. Holbrook. 2008. "Must We Have Muzak Wherever We Go? A Critical Consideration of the Consumer Culture." *Consumption, Markets & Culture* 11 (1): 25–43.

Brown, Wendy. 2009. Introduction to *Is Critique Secular? Blasphemy, Injury, and Free Speech*, edited by Talal Asad, Wendy Brown, Judith Butler and Saba Mahmood, 7–19. Berkeley: Townsend Center for the Humanities, University of California Press.

Brownlie, Douglas. 2006. "Emancipation, Epiphany and Resistance: On the Underimagined and Overdetermined in Critical Marketing." *Journal of Marketing Management* 22 (5–6): 505–528.

Brownlie, Douglas, and Paul Hewer. 2007. "Concerning Marketing Critterati: Beyond Nuance, Estrangement and Elitism." In *Critical Marketing: Defining the Field*, edited by Michael Saren, Pauline Maclaran, Christina Goulding, Richard Elliott, Avi Shankar and Miriam Catterall, 44–68. London: Butterworth-Heinemann.

Brownlie, Douglas, Michael Saren, Robin Wensley, and Richard Whittington. 1999. *Rethinking Marketing: Towards Critical Marketing Accountings.* London: Sage.

Dunne, Stephen, Stefano Harney, Martin Parker, and Tony Tinker. 2008. "Discussing the Role of the Business School." *Ephemera: Theory and Politics in Organization* 8 (3): 271–293.

Eagleton, Terry. 2011. *Why Marx Was Right.* New Haven: Yale University Press.

Ellis, Nick, James Fitchett, Matthew Higgins, Gavin Jack, Ming Lim, Michael Saren, and Mark Tadajewski. 2010. *Marketing: A Critical Textbook.* London: Sage.

Foucault, Michel. 1995. *Discipline and Punish: The Birth of the Prison.* New York: Vintage Books.

Groys, Boris. 2010. *The Communist Postscript.* London: Verso.

Guillet de Monthoux, Pierre. 2006. "The Oppression Blues – Or the Aesthetics of a Critical Theorist." *Consumption, Markets & Culture* 9 (2): 145–146.

Harvey, David. 2010a. *A Companion to Marx's Capital.* London: Verso.

—. 2010b. *The Enigma of Capital and the Crises of Capitalism.* London: Profile Books.

Henry, Astrid. 2004. *Not My Mother's Sister: Generational Conflict and Third-Wave Feminism.* Indiana: Indiana University Press.

Jameson, Fredric. 2011. *Representing Capital: A Reading of Volume One.* London: Verso.

Miller, Daniel. 2010. *Stuff.* London: Polity.

Murtola, Anna-Maria. 2010. "Commodification of Utopia: The Lotus Eaters Revisited." *Culture and Organization* 16 (1): 37–54.

Orr, Judith. 2007. *Sexism and the System: A Rebel's Guide to Women's Liberation.* London: Bookmarks.

Prahalad, Coimbatore Krishnarao. 2008. *The Fortune at the Bottom of the Pyramid: Eradicating Poverty through Profits.* London: Prentice Hall.

Saren, Michael, Pauline Maclaran, Christina Goulding, Richard Elliott, Avi Shankar, and Miriam Catterall. 2007. *Critical Marketing: Defining the Field.* London: Butterworth-Heinemann.

Schroeder, Jonathan E. 2007. "Critical Marketing: Insights for Informed Research and Teaching." In *Critical Marketing: Defining the Field*, edited by Michael Saren, Pauline Maclaran, Christina Goulding, Richard Elliott, Avi Shankar and Miriam Catterall, 18–29. London: Butterworth-Heinemann.

Scott, Linda M. 2007. "Critical Research in Marketing: An Armchair Report." In *Critical Marketing: Defining the Field*, edited by Michael

Saren, Pauline Maclaran, Christina Goulding, Richard Elliott, Avi Shankar and Miriam Catterall, 3–17. London: Butterworth-Heinemann.
Tadajewski, Mark. 2006. "Remembering Motivation Research: Toward an Alternative Genealogy of Interpretive Consumer Research." *Marketing Theory* 6 (4): 429–466.
—. 2010. "Towards a History of Critical Marketing Studies." *Journal of Marketing Management* 26 (9–10): 773–824.
Tadajewski, Mark, and Douglas Brownlie. 2008. *Critical Marketing: Issues in Contemporary Marketing*. London: John Wiley & Sons.
Toscano, Alberto. 2010. *Fanaticism: On the Uses of an Idea*. London: Verso.
Žižek, Slavoj. 2009. *Violence*. London: Profile Books.
Žižek, Slavoj, and Costas Douzinas. 2010. *The Idea of Communism*. London: Verso.

Subversive Use of Things: Craftsman Creativity as Criticism of Consumer Culture?

Agata Skórzyńska

> "Material culture" too often, at least in social sciences, slights clothes, circuit boards, or baked fish as objects worthy of regard in themselves, instead treating the shaping of such physical things as mirrors of social norms, economic interests, religious convictions—the thing in itself is discounted (Sennett 2008, 7).

> Craftsmanship names an enduring, basic human impulse, the desire to do a job well for its own sake. Craftsmanship cuts a far wider swath than skilled manual labour; it serves the computer programmer, the doctor, and the artist; parenting improves when it is practiced as a skilled craft, as does citizenship. In all these domains, craftsmanship focuses on objective standards, on the thing in itself (Sennett 2008, 9).

New "Cultural Objects": The Necessity of a Cultural Analysis of Things

Cultural studies of the last few decades have become a setting for a heated debate on consumer culture and its initial concepts, such as the Frankfurt School's "culture industry". The root of the problem was the increasing doubts if the proposal of neo-Marxist philosophy is still adequate for analyzing the informational, consumer capitalism at the turn of the 20th and 21st centuries. The main topic of this debate was the changing position of the commodity in contemporary culture, so an urgent task arose to recognize and point out new types of relations between the material base and the cultural superstructure. As we know, in the traditional Marxist perspective, the commodity is a mass-produced object of market exchange, consisting of two different modalities: materiality of the thing and its quantitative equivalent or, in more original terms, use value and exchange value. Crucial for the Frankfurt theorists, however, was to recognize the fact that cultural objects such as works of art and ideas can also be submitted to the instrumental logic of mass production (Adorno and Horkheimer 2002). The process known as "commodification of culture" means, from now on, systematic submission to the rules of rational and effective reproduction in which the boundary between items of everyday use and masterpieces collapsed. Reification of cultural objects is probably the most radical effect of this process, but turning material things into their symbolic representations was the other side of the coin since the exchange value began to dominate in social relations. Recent transformations of consumer culture, however, bring the duality (material thing and its symbolic representation) into question because the status of the commodity has changed diametrically. New products, such as brands, knowledge, media images, communication technologies, financial or leisure services are placed beyond the traditional duality. It requires us to rethink (once again) the mutual relation between things, commodities, images and ideas, between the consumer market and the culture.

One of the latest and maybe most convincing contributions to this debate is the work of Scott Lash and Celia Lury, *Global Culture Industry: The Mediation of Things* about the transition from culture industry to global culture industry (Lash and Lury 2007). In their view, globalization of consumer culture brings important changes; however, it is only one part of a more fundamental process: a radical change in the relation between material things and their social meaning where commodity turns into a new "cultural object". As Lash and Lury claim:

> We think that culture has taken on another, a different logic with the transition from the culture industry to *global* culture industry; that globalization has given culture industry a fundamentally different mode of operation. Our point is that in 1945 and in 1975 culture was still fundamentally a superstructure. As a superstructure, both domination and resistance took place in and through superstructures—through ideology, through symbols, through representation. When culture was primarily superstructural, cultural entities were still exceptional. [...] But in 2005, cultural objects are everywhere: as information, as communication, as branded products, as financial services, as media products, as transport and leisure services, cultural entities are no longer the exception: they are the rule (Lash and Lury 2007, 3–4).

In another place they admit more explicitly:

> [T]he global culture industry and informational capitalism is less a matter of the base determining the superstructure than the cultural superstructure collapsing, as it were, into the material base. Hence goods become informational, work becomes affective, property becomes intellectual and the economy more generally becomes cultural (Lash and Lury 2007, 7).

The collapse of the superstructure is a consequence of four interconnected transitions: (1) from identity to difference; (2) from commodity to brand; (3) from representations to things; (4) from the symbolic to the real (ibid., 4–11). The first transition means that the new logic of global industry is no longer a matter of mass production and unification of goods, but rather of an ability to create cultural differences between customers. For Horkheimer and Adorno "cultural products, once fabricated, would circulate as commodities, as identical objects, and in their movement would contribute to capital accumulation" (ibid., 4). Instead, new cultural objects of the global industry "move and change through transposition and translation, transformation and transmogrification" (ibid., 5). The second transition relies on the distinction between the exchange value of the commodity, which is an abstract representation of the material world of products, and the sign value of the brand, definitively emancipated from materiality. It results in a collapse of the traditional Marxist distinction between use value and exchange value. "Goods and commodities are all alike. They are distinguishable only by the quantities of money for which they exchange. Brands are not alike. Brands have value only in their difference—their distinctiveness—from other brands" (ibid., 6). There is no previous reality which constitutes a brand, there is no single merchandise or product that it represents, so that brand "is generated across a range of products" and the meanings, memories, identities and images are connected to each other by an internal logic of exchange. Paradoxically, as Lash and Lury suggest, the third transition means a specific return to materiality, because the exchange of the new cultural objects is mediation, rather than representation of things. Since media become "things to use" in the context of everyday life, they are no longer privileged intermediaries of meanings and images:

> There is such a thingification of media when, for example, movies become computer games; when brands become brand environments, taking over airport terminal space and restructuring department stores, road billboards and city centres; when music is played in lifts, part of a mobile soundscape. […] When media become things, we enter a world of operationality, a world not of interpretation but of navigation. We do not read them so much as "do" them [...] or do with them (Lash and Lury 2007, 8).

Last but not least, what we experience today is a radical transition from the symbolic to the real because media products and new cultural objects are questioning the traditional distinction between internal mind and external reality or, more precisely, the classical Cartesian duality of *res cogitans* and *res extensa*. Media and branded products are things we operate with or, as Sherry Turkle calls them, "objects-to-think-with" (1997). They rely on materialized mind, on objectified imaginations and ideas.

These notions became (of course) more significant in the wider debate on a new "cultural logic of the late capitalism", using the terms of Frederic Jameson (1991). The discussion was initiated by Jean Baudrillard's *Consumer Society* where he first undertook a fundamental critique of the distinction between use value and exchange value from the semiotic perspective. Today, it is well known and widely commented on as the core of the postmodern turn in the humanities (Baudrillard 1998). After Baudrillard's and Jameson's recognitions, many authors tried to explain more broadly the basics and modes of operation in this new economy, since the exchange of the sign value became a core of the economic development. After the postmodern turn, we recognize perfectly the opposite process to commodification of culture. Here, we could call that process conventionally "culturalization of the commodity".

Nevertheless, what is most important to us is that these notions show the matter of the cultural position of things in a new light and initiate a new theoretical perspective upon items in everyday use, works of art and media products as well. Sociology of things as a new interdisciplinary approach in the social sciences is not limited to the traditional patterns and ways of study of the so-called material culture, as opposed to symbolic culture. On the contrary, the main topic of this proposal is to develop an analysis especially focused upon the meaning people assign to the material object or image. As Marek Krajewski puts it:

> [T]hings constitute a system, they materialize a mutual system of social values in every culture [...] but also "using things" means that we create social and cultural reality, that we actualize the rules of collective life, things are performed not only in the material, but also in cultural sense (Krajewski 2005, 8; trans. A. S.).

Among the founders of this perspective, Krajewski names not only Baudrillard but also Arjun Appadurai, Dick Hebdige, Dave McCracken and others; we could add Michel de Certeau or Bruno Latour for example. What is particularly interesting in this context is that the distinction between items of everyday use, goods, branded commodities and gifts has been in the centre of attention in this perspective from the very beginning. As Aafke Komter points out:

> In our century the dominant way of thinking about patterns of relationships between persons has been through the opposition of the gift and the commodity [...] In some of the older anthropological and sociological

> writings gift exchange and commodity transactions are conceptualised as different "modes of exchange" (Komter 2001, 61).

Here, Komter recalls not only the classical anthropological approach to pre-modern gift exchange rituals, but also the distinction between pre-modern community and modern society which is prevalent in classical social studies and which is based, as we remember, on two different types of social relations. Though, as Komter claims:

> According to Bourdieu the subjective experience of the freedom to give can go together with the objective necessity or obligation of returning a gift. In modern societies, the exchange of gifts as well as commodities is characterised by ritual, social and symbolic aspects (Komter 2001, 62).

Pierre Bourdieu's theoretical frameworks of cultural capital, habitus, field or distinction, mentioned by Komter are indeed a necessary and instructive background for rethinking the social position of common habits, including the use of things. After all, the core idea of his theory, explained most precisely in *Distinction*, was to investigate mutual influences between external social structures and individuals' subjective experience. Individual taste as well as the social meanings of the things we use depend on two needs: to distinguish from and to identify with the social environment. The most important conclusion is, as Komter suggests, that the social meaning of things is not given, but rather performed, and the distinction between gifts and commodities, private souvenirs and goods, is a matter of permanently repeated negotiations. We can often observe, for example, how people change the meaning of things by using them. In this context, Komter describes two contradictory transitions: commodification and de-commodification of things. First, when a gift or a personal item becomes an object of market exchange for some reason; and second, when a user gives a special subjective meaning to a widespread commodity.

These notions lead us to the fundamental question of the discussions undertaken in this article: if using things can be way of changing their social meaning, is it possible to use them subversively? Or more precisely: is the consumption of goods only a way to participate in an external, rational and captivating culture industry, as Adorno and Horkheimer demonstrated, or could it be a form of social critique of consumer culture? These questions affirm openly the current need to recognize under what conditions and on what basis we can develop and practice reflexivity on the material culture after the superstructure has collapsed. This addresses a more general issue: the theoretical basis and empirical application of cultural analysis, especially when we intend to use it as a tool for research projects on material culture or, more precisely, its most current practices such as the critical use of things, for example.

In the most generic sense, contemporary cultural analysis is a multidisciplinary project which can be traced back to two different, but also complementary traditions in social studies: European critical social theories, such as the above-mentioned Frankfurt School, and British cultural studies. Comparing these two traditional points of view, we can observe both contentious arguments and converging views on consumer culture. The sharpest and most fundamental difference is, of course, the attitude toward mass/popular culture. While critical theory underestimated "common sense" and the social power of practices of everyday life emerging in mass-consumption, the British cultural studies advocated, from the very beginning, the vision of popular culture discourses and practices as one of the most powerful and effective manners of bringing to the surface social resistance or subversion. On the one hand, consumer culture appears as mass illusion and manipulation of political and economic forces external to "the people", on the other as, at least potentially, a democratic platform of social communication. As Jim McGuigan notes in a brief introduction to his instructive handbook on contemporary cultural analysis:

> The European tradition favoured avant-garde culture and was critical of mass consumer culture. For that reason, it met with a measure of resistance and, indeed, opposition in Britain, where the cultural activity of "the people"—even under highly commercialized conditions—was treated with greater respect, to the extent that it was increasingly contrasted favourably with "elitist" high culture. Still, both traditions had much in common, motivated by emancipatory interests, and, while the British tradition emphasized concrete detail over abstract thought, continental rationalism was a vital corrective to the empirical verging on empirist mode of separatist Britain (McGuigan 2010, 3).

The most important task today, as McGuigan suggests, is to draw the right lesson from both traditional frameworks, but also to take a more balanced view on the popular practices of "the people", who are not necessarily less reflexive than the avant-garde cultural criticism. It requires one to undertake the task of systematic critical analysis of concrete popular practices with an empirical attitude and to abandon a sharp but simplified division between high and popular culture. On the other hand, however, the more optimistic view of the critical power of consumers also has its limits. The consumer market today is not necessarily a democratic public realm nor is it a "panoptic" institution of omnipotent social control. It is rather a space of clash or collision between different, often contradictory interests. Popular practices of everyday life can also manifest the ambivalences of today's consumer culture. These assumptions lead us straight to the specific "point of contact" where the sociology of things meets contemporary cultural analysis and postulates:

> A multidimensional analysis seeks to make sense of the ontological complexity of cultural phenomena—that is, the many-sidedness of their existence. It is concerned with the circulation of culture and the interaction of production and consumption, including the materiality and significatory qualities of cultural forms. There are innumerable possible topics that might be studied in such way, none of which would necessarily be lacking in value. Choices have to be made, however; decisions have to be taken as to priority. That is why questions of public interest are privileged in this account (McGuigan 2010, 1).

The "ontological complexity" of cultural forms is the reason why McGuigan, in his subsequent case study, includes the mobile phone, for example, as a subject of analysis which is "not reducible to a simple material object, a commodity circulating in the global economy of transnational operations […] It is also a means of communication with considerable social and cultural significance" (ibid., 85). From this point of view, a particular object of the contemporary material culture can become as a research topic in studies on technological determinism of social change, social demography of mobile technology users, critical analysis of producers/consumers synergies and tensions, research on technology-based new social and cultural movements, ethnography of ritualized everyday life practices of users, conversation, discourse and text analysis of computer-mediated communication and critical analysis of its quality. It is only at the crossroads of these perspectives that the cultural meaning and ambiguous position in social life of this simple material object becomes more clear.

The question of "public interests", which brings to the surface the critical attitude of contemporary cultural analysis and directs attention to the political and social efficiency of cultural studies, results, as we might suspect, from recognizing the complexity of the multidimensional interactions between "material" and "symbolic", "high" and "popular", and "cultural" and "political". This question is particularly important in the context of "cool capitalism", as McGuigan calls it. "Cool capitalism" means "the incorporation of disaffection into the capitalist way of life, the effect of which is to neutralise criticism" (ibid., 7). Yet, we need to remember that practices of everyday life as well as the official political strategies or advertising campaigns of today's corporate culture are at the same level of entanglement in the requirements of "cool capitalism": a paradoxical hybrid of hegemonic neoliberal ideology and citizens' democracy. It is not exceptional today that advertising media or corporate culture intercept the popular practices of resistance to hegemony, to which we shall return later. Critical cultural analysis, therefore, must be particularly watchful and needs to look more deeply at ambivalent and "fuzzy" meanings that might emerge in various cultural practices, yet it must go far beyond the "first impression" of simplicity of the subject analyzed.

For these reasons, we need to ask not only if the subversive use of things is possible in the contemporary consumer culture, but first and foremost: what does it mean to use something subversively? Coincidently, the term "subversion" has several important implications for contemporary humanities, which become significant at the crossroad of disciplines supporting today's cultural analysis: aesthetics, cultural, political, social, but also gender or queer studies.

In Relation with Things: Subversive Craftsmanship?

"Subversion" as a term describing the critical tactic of formal and semantic transformations has recently become very popular in several different fields of research as well as in the practice of artists and activists. The most distinct example of the latter is, of course, subvertising: a self-definition term describing the mode of operation of activists and street artists who declare a critical position on the contemporary consumer culture. To subvertise means, then, to transform the message of city billboards and other outdoor advertising media. However, as a theoretical term, subversion is successfully entering discourses of cultural, gender and queer studies as well as aesthetics. In a broad review of aesthetic connotations of the term, Lukasz Ronduda recalls experiments of modern and postmodern avant-garde, such as ready-mades, collage techniques or *détournement* postulated by Situationists, but also the newest experiments of video-art and net-art. He explains this term as follows:

> On the one hand the definition of this term includes a very technical meaning and connotes outright physical operations of reversing, transforming or even destructing some ready-made material [...] In this sense subversion describes a technique or methodological approach of creating an artefact. On the other hand, the second and more common sense of this term provides an idea of critical attitude, usually towards a dominating culture (Ronduda 2006, 9; trans. A. S.).

We need to remember, however, that subversion also became a philosophical category in the core of postmodern debate on linguistics: textual and narrative constitution of the social relations and culture, especially linguistic disposition of identity. In her revolutionary work on cultural foundations of sex and gender, Judith Butler used this term to describe performative patterns of critiquing so-called natural origins of human sexual identity. Subversion means, then, theatrical acting, a "game people play" to question stability of identity in a drag queen performance or in cross-dressing, for example (Butler 1999).

In relation to the question on the position of things in consumer culture which has been raised in this text, the aesthetic use of the term is the most helpful and instructive. We need to remember, however, that the project of the immanent critique of feminist discourse introduced by Butler in her work is an idea of internal, formal and semantic transformation. That is what connects the philosophical use of the term with the aesthetic recognition proposed by Ronduda. In this context, subversion does not mean resistance based upon isolation from the criticized system, no matter what kind of system we take into account (normative, aesthetic or semantic), but rather it requires engagement in the criticized order, a specific inner perspective on the cultural system we are trying to change.

This leads us to another theoretical notion, tactics, which was used by Michel de Certeau as directly describing subversive practices of consumers. Explained as "poaching", non-normative use of space, time, language or things, tactics are modes of internal critique of consumer culture. One of the best-known examples was recalled by de Certeau in *The Practice of Everyday Life* (De Certeau 1988, 25–28): *le perruque*, a French word describing illegal use of materials by workers in factory production lines. After stealing prefabricated elements and materials, workers used them to make their own designs and products. As opposed to strategies linked by the author with institutions and structures of power, tactics are utilized by individuals trying to create ways of behaviour and places for themselves in environments defined by official strategies.

It is not without reason today that we are more likely and willing to return to de Certeau's proposition, not only in consumer culture research or urban studies, but most of all in more general considerations on creativity and reflexive/critical participation in the contemporary technology-based culture which is dominated by images and interactive, "many-to-many" communication media. The radical change of today's public sphere caused by the so-called "information revolution" and further expansion of the consumer market does not make the secular dream of a democratic agora come true. We are still willing to repeat (after Chantal

Mouffe, for example) that the public sphere is not a matter of concensus-based common good, but rather of the agonistic impact of conflicting interests which are divided roughly into strategic and tactical, are represented by different groups and agents, and compete with one another. Nevertheless, one is unable to ignore that the mode of participation in contemporary social life has changed diametrically (Mouffe 2005). New cultural objects indicate a "different mode of operation", as Lash and Lury suggest, probably in both consuming and critical lifestyles. In one of his recent books, Richard Sennett sheds some light on the particular form of creativity induced by technological development which indicates a new relation between the human being and "the thing", different from the traditionally understood "material culture". He argues that craftsmanship is, both historically and recently, one of the most underestimated types of human productive activity in modern Western culture; he largely favours an artist's creativity. What is most important in Sennett's observations is that he places the main question about this form of creativity particularly in the context of today's changing and rapidly differentiating public sphere. The author recalls his former teacher Hannah Arendt as his guide and opponent (Sennett 2008, 1–8). The technological leap brings the entire world, or at least a large portion of its most developed part, to the point at which the myth of Pandora's box can materialize, where products and creations of human hands become fundamental sources of risk as serious as the Los Alamos project of building the atom bomb. As was mentioned in Sennett's conversation with Arendt and recalled in the "Prologue" of the book, "people who make things usually don't understand what they are doing" these days (ibid., 1):

> Today, peacetime material civilization posts equally numbing figures of self-made self-harm: one million, for instance, represents the number of years Nature took to create the amount of fossil fuel now consumed in a single year. The ecological crisis is Pandoric, man-made; technology may be an unreliable ally in regaining control (Sennett 2008, 2).

Arendt's answer to the Cold War shade returned to the ideas of *animal laborans* versus *homo faber* in *The Human Condition*:

> Thus, in her view, we human beings live in two dimensions. In one we make things; in this condition we are amoral, absorbed in a task. We also harbor another, higher way of life in which we stop producing and start discussing and judging together. Whereas *Animal laborans* is fixated in the question "How?" *Homo faber* asks "Why?" (Sennett 2008, 6–7).

This "higher way of life" was what Arendt connected with the requirement of performing a deliberative model of the public sphere. It traces back to the Greek agora based on the human ability to speak, argue, convince. Yet, as Sennett intends to prove, this division seems to be false "because it slights the practical man or woman at work. The human animal who is *Animal laborans* is capable of thinking" (ibid., 7). This assumption leads the author to remind us of a craftsman: man at work who is able to conceptualize his actions and develop his skills by systematic manipulation on the most detailed parts and features of the thing, up to mastery. With reference to the example of the Linux programming community or Wikipedia users, Sennett points out the ethical and social efficacy of the craftsmanship mode of production:

> This, then, is a community of craftsmen to whom the ancient appellation *demioergoi* can be applied. It is focused on achieving quality, on doing good work, which is the craftsman's primordial mark of identity. In the traditional work of the archaic potter or doctor, standards for good work were set by the community as skills passed down from generation to generation (Sennett 2008, 25).

The ethical and social frame of every action taken by the craftsman is most important here. But still, we are, of course, conscious of a difference between long-term and generation-to-generation (master-to-apprentice) development of the particular task in traditional craftsmanship: in other words, a difference between vertical and horizontal ways of improving Linux or Wikipedia. What both of these forms of mutual work have in common is undoubtedly an ability to create collectively with focus on "the thing", which Sennett considers the core of craftsmanship. But still, a question remains: could craftsmanship be critical or subversive? As both Linux and Wikipedia show, the "community of makers" can be basically focused on improving the thing by ignoring official strategies of production. This is accomplished by the counter-hegemony ideology of open sources in the first case, and by developing a pattern of knowledge that is as democratic and emancipated from the domination of experts as possible in the second case. Putting aside the discussion on advantages and disadvantages of such a model of improving knowledge, we cannot ignore, in either of the two cases, a significant ethical orientation on mutual quality review and individual engagement in "making the thing better". First of all, however, the thing is developed by the community of users, not by institutional or corporate rules and requirements.

Therefore, now we need to return to the introductive work of Lash and Lury. Since production and consumption of dominating cultural objects has become a complicated process of mediation of things, resistance is probably no longer only a matter of refusing to consume things and images, but also, more importantly, of the internal, subversive tactic of "critical use" of things, spaces, images and meanings. Paradoxically, these practices also require a return to the materiality of the commodity because the subversive use of the object consists in reconfiguration of the appearance and function. This is more similar to the bricoleur's or craftsman's performance, compared to the creativity of the autonomous artist. However, it still requires an aesthetic attitude to the consumer culture filled with objects, both material and symbolic, after cultural superstructure has collapsed. It is not without reason that Lash and Lury introduce their idea of mediation of things with the appeal to Adorno's culture industry conception. As we remember, Adorno saw a chance for emancipation from commodified culture in autonomous art and the aesthetics project. His core postulates concerned resistance to the forms, contents and modes of production within popular culture, but he saw the opportunity for resistance in the isolation of artists from dominating culture industry. These postulates, however, were possible only because the difference between material base and cultural superstructure was still visible and, in that order, "both domination and resistance took place in and through superstructures—through ideology, through symbols, through representation" (Lash and Lury 2005, 4). However, right after Adorno's aesthetics project, two opposite processes took place in art as well as in popular culture. On the one hand, artists and activists of the modern and postmodern avant-garde movement announced experimental projects and manifestos of critical engagement in the external, social and political sphere, and resigned from the demand for autonomy as far as it requires total isolation. The best examples of this kind of internal critique included the Situationist Movement, surrealist experiments and later, pop-art ideas. On the other hand, popular and consumer culture started to absorb willingly all experiments in modern art. The sharp line between art and the rest of cultural production became more and more dubious in the second half of the 20th century.

This is possibly the main reason why the aesthetics of the Frankfurt School was discussed widely and criticized in depth after the neo-avant-garde movement. A recent and often discussed attempt to rethink Adorno's idea of autonomy is Jacques Rancière's relational aesthetics. Introducing the notion of "distribution of sensible", Rancière makes us aware that art as well as consumer culture or politics are a matter of quality, form, style and meaning today (Rancière 2004). Based upon aesthetic criteria, new cultural objects or political brands successfully compete with art in the race for our attention and admiration. What Rancière postulates, then, for critical art and other cultural creativity is not isolation, but rather establishment of a relation with post-political media products and cultural objects.

All of the above mentioned theoretical assumptions can serve as a useful and instructive background for the cultural analysis of things in contemporary consumer culture. The basic or output relation between a user and a thing resulting from the concept of mediation of things, the project of sociology of things, the idea of tactics, aesthetical and cultural subversion, Sennett's craftsmanship or Rancière's relational aesthetics, they all are at least a starting point for critical cultural analysis. This is, as McGuigan suggests, a great challenge for contemporary cultural studies given the "ontological complexity" of current cultural products and creations. Every type of cultural analysis requires that a conceptual grip is established, carefully tested, verified and confined within some limits of application. The propositions of all the authors cited above can constitute such a conceptual grip. All of them at least show the growing interest paid by contemporary humanities to cultural objects which are given meaning by people, can bring them together or can inspire them to act. However, we need to look more deeply at the cultural practices which such a conceptual grip is potentially able to highlight. The following examples are admittedly not case studies in the proper sense of the term. Nonetheless, they may serve as the necessary "empirical samples" to show that the subversive use of things is not a mere figure of speech in cultural analysis.

Re-design: Critical Art as a First Step to Relational Engagement

It is certainly adequate to start by applying relational aesthetics of subversion to contemporary art and asking a question about the possibilities of changing an artist's position from autonomous creator to craftsman. The first and perhaps most instructive example of contemporary relational art is the critical art project of the 1990s, as in works by a Polish artist Zbigniew Libera (see Raster Gallery 2011). His best-known transformation of a popular consumer culture object was a re-design of Lego products entitled "Holocaust Lego" (1996), but Libera worked with toy products several times. The idea of his provocation was shockingly simple: to re-design the thing with a critical attitude, not to change, but to "move a little", to subvert or to transform the meaning of a cultural object we use. In accordance with this assumption, Libera designed art objects using both original Lego brand images and the blocs themselves. Unaware of the artist's intention, the Lego Corporation initially authorized the use of the brand image, only to repudiate his project in the end.

However, Libera does not seem to have intended to accuse, but rather to sensitize the viewer to the fact that every object contains a multiplied meaning. As Lego products accustom us to the self-made world, we can easily lose the ability to notice both harmless and dangerous things: the Lego-system and a totalitarian system are made by people's bare hands. Libera encourages us to read critically the meaning of every product we use. This is, however, the simplest and most evident connotation. Likewise, we might look at Libera's project in a broader context and more critically. Since his beginnings in the late 1980s, the leading issue of his artistic work was children's upbringing and education as a form of discursive inclusion into the society, cultural imposition of social (for example gender) roles and reproduction of identities. Toys are not harmless tools or neutral intermediaries of identity patterns. The particular socio-cultural context of the "Holocaust Lego" project was also not irrelevant. When the idea of the Holocaust Lego first appeared in Polish public opinion in 1996, Poland was still undergoing a process of radical economic and political transformation; inclusion into the global consumer culture was seen as a dream coming true after over forty years of isolation, rather than a potential source of social risk. For the generation growing up in the late 1980s and early 1990s, "Western" branded products were still objects of desire and fetishes of a better life. Under these circumstances, the consumer lifestyle, even if still in a rachitic form, was quite widely accepted. In this context a reference to the significant, and in Poland still vivid, associations with the totalitarian system should wave a warning flag that commercialization of the public sphere, represented officially in the discourse of "paradise lost", can also be a more camouflaged mode of social control; it might appear even more dangerous as we have no grounded social experience of protection from "soft pressure" of the consumer market or "cool capitalism". Most surprisingly, Libera's project showed meaningfully that this soft pressure appears at the level of tangible reality: using toys can be the simplest way of bringing up the perfect future consumer. In some respects, the "Holocaust Lego" was a predecessor of new-leftist criticism of consumer culture in Polish art and public debate. There is another possible interpretation of this project: it can be seen in the broader frame of the question about cultural censorship in the democratic public sphere and in connection with the neuralgic question of Polish-Jewish relations. Indeed, Libera's work was understood as a potential source of misapprehension and withdrawn from the Polish exhibition at the 1997 Venice Biennale by the Polish curator, perhaps due to "hypersensitivity to outstanding issues" such as the Polish anti-Semitism question or ill-conceived political correctness. The controversy caused by this project best shows the efficacy of Libera's intervention in the world of simple consumer goods: a subtle displacement or transformation of the meaning of a seemingly harmless toy may turn it into a most ambiguous cultural object and provoke heated public debate.

This leads us to the second example—the "Holocaust Lego" is not an exceptional project associating consumer culture with a totalitarian system. In 2001, Agata Siwek's installation, "Original Souvenirs: Auschwitz-Birkenau", caused a wave of protests from the audience, especially former prisoners of the concentration camps (Siwek 2011). However, when we judge such an association, we need to turn our attention to the idea of an "original souvenir" as an object of consumer culture. The core idea of this provocative installation was perhaps to question how far tourism and leisure services or popular culture can go with the commodification of our memories and past. Can every past experience, trauma or value really be turned into an object? We have doubts looking at the "concentration camp brand" on a T-Shirt, but are we willing to do so in the case of some other memories and experience, especially those more distant or irrelevant to us? The mass production of cheap souvenirs and gadgets is omnipresent in every destination we go to as tourists. Precisely this turning of experience into objects of "tourist gaze" (John Urry) is one of the presumable topics of this installation. In a more critical view, it also raises questions about thanatotourism destinations and practices or the increasing need for incorporating death or grief experience into consumer culture or pleasurable popular culture. From this perspective, Agata Siwek's project provokes us to rethink a broad context of contradictory discourses by using the symbolic power of places like Auschwitz-Birkenau, including the Holocaust Denial discussion (for which visitors's outright physical experience of this place sets limits of negation as a material proof and commemoration), public debate on the so-called "Polish Concentration Camps" (where international public opinion sometimes mistakes location for responsibility and perpetration), and the question of Polish actual anti-Semitism and factual participation in Nazi crimes (which was displaced as a topic of open public debate in Poland until 1989). Siwek's design of small and seemingly unimportant objects brings the viewer into the multilevel game of meanings, ownership and legitimacy of Holocaust interpretations. Provoking wide and multidimensional connotations, both the "Holocaust Lego" and the "Original souvenirs" examples show how easily all of these questions can be cancelled, common reason challenged and social ability to resist pacified. Indeed, such productions are quite imaginable outside the critical art discourse, namely in the omnivorous consumer culture. The gesture of "manufacturing a thing" is surprisingly simple to perform.

Subvertising and DIY: Hand and Mind Reconnected

However, critical art's engagement with consumer culture is, it represents only a starting point for considering the tactical and subversive use of things. As an example of the second mode of critical semantic transformations focused upon consumer culture, we can point to the most ambivalent example of the very well-known subvertising and culture jam movement. The idea of subvertising first appeared in projects of The AdBusters Group in Canada.[1] AdBusters promote a tactic of altering the image/message of corporate and political outdoor advertising in order to create "cognitive dissonance". This interesting and fresh idea of cultural resistance soon became a widespread popular practice; we even might be tempted to say fashionable. Similarly to Kalle Lasn, who co-created the AdBusters movement, many street artists all over the world undertook a similar challenge, but devoted their work not only to corporate culture images in the public sphere specifically, but to the city space and street furniture more generally. As Darius Jones and Brad Downey declare:

> Here was subtraction as a tool, used to re-contextualize, to transform, to give new meaning to what is left behind in the altered environment. [...] here was a new way to interact with street furniture, not just to add and change and mutate, but to cut away, to sculpt through subtraction (Reid IV and Downey 2008, 73).

What often connects the tactics of subvertising and the broader phenomenon of uncommissioned urban art and street-art is cognitive dissonance caused by transformation of omnipresent images or material and semantic constitution of the commercialized city space. Both these practices also assume that images and things are "objects-to-think-with", so they can be "in use". Drawing from the Debordian *Society of Spectacle* and the French Situationist idea of *détournement*, Kalle Lasn's manifesto *Culture Jam: the Uncooling of America* gives a convincing picture of the revolutionary project of challenging the values of consumer lifestyle by engagement in its semantic constitution (Lasn 1999). As McGuigan notes:

---

[1] http://www.adbusters.org/magazine.

> Culture jamming is a form of "semiological guerilla warfare", in Umberto Eco's phrase. As Eco argued in the 1960s, "Not long ago, if you wanted to seize political power in a country, you had merely to control the army and the police. [...] Today a country belongs to the person who controls communications." Culture jammers, however, are unlikely to take control of the communications media in the USA. Their tactics in producing "subvertisements" that attack capitalism [...] are those of guerilla skirmishing in the space of signification [...]. In a volatile culture where fashion is constantly overturning itself and sudden reversals of meaning occur, counter-discourse may act like a virus entering the symbolic bloodstream of the body politic. Well, that's the theory anyway (McGuigan 2010, 19).

The last sentence in this quotation suggests possible doubts: about the actual efficacy of the semiological guerrilla which seems to assert local rather than global influence, to assume operations in a concrete semiosphere, but not to change communication as a system and its roles as a whole. Moreover, consumer culture is equally efficient in "seizing" the meaning and the mode of operation; after all, it is common sense that an enemy is easiest to kill with his own weapon. One of the better-known Polish subvertising campaigns counteracted an outdoor campaign of a cosmetic company that used the street-art techniques of stencils and stickers for advertising slogans with a strongly sexist message (the Axe Effect Campaign by Unilever). Many popular and creative outdoor advertising and out-of-home communication agencies offer their customers stencil graffiti and other techniques as tools of the so-called "guerrilla marketing". Apparently, *détournement* can be a useful and efficient tactic on both sides of the fence, now that "cool capitalism" is able to absorb and, indeed, customize any form of resistance. However, it is worth remembering that subversion does not pretend to "overthrow the regime", but rather to transform systematically its most defective elements: the neutrality of its meanings and apparent transparency of its messages. It is at least a way to demonstrate where the battlefield is located, namely in the semantic constitution of today's cultural objects.

Apart from the manifestly declared anti-consumer stance, the practices of subvertising are, at the level of operation, very close to everyday transformations of things and images which often became a common practice of users, not only activists. Today, spontaneous changes of a widespread commodity's function and appearance are a feature of the IkeaHackers Project, for example.[2] Serial, self-made furniture and decorations of the Ikea Corporation inspire or provoke users to individualize

[2] http://www.ikeahackers.net.

products that are originally "all alike". Transformation of ready-made products, recycling of used things, second-hand exchange or vintage style in fashion and design are other examples of such a reflexive attitude to consumer culture. One of the most famous "critical products" are, of course, the Blackspot Shoes spread by the AdBusters Magazine. As the authors declare:

> Blackspot shoes are made with hemp, recycled tires, vegan leather and produced in fair-trade factories. We also sell only to independent retailers worldwide in order to cycle money back into local economies. Blackspot is an open-source brand, which means that it can be used by anyone for any purpose at no cost. Our hope is that people with similar philosophies will be inspired by our experiment in grassroots capitalism and start their own business ventures […] (AdBusters 2011).

Blackspot sneakers look exactly the same as the famous "All Stars" classical sneakers in an attempt to make us aware of the brand ideology. We can find a similar attitude, however, in the ideas motivating the critical design movement. Ecological, social, political and economic reflexivity in designing and using things is increasingly intended by professional designers and users as well. Another example, no less interesting, is the practice of collecting the most ridiculous, strange, extravagant or just odd products entering the marketplace. Investigating and detecting oddness in the consumer market is popular especially among Internet users. Examples include "Strange New Products" blog[3] created and conducted by Steve Johnson or "The Museum of Weird Consumer Culture"[4] by Richard Wilk who also investigates the cultural position of things as a cultural anthropologist. The popularity of web collections of commercial images, advertisements and products, especially the most absurd or useless ones, also increases consumers' sensitivity to the world of things they live in.

With regard to the examples given above, we have recently observed growing interest of some artists, researchers or cultural activists in the symbolic features of things. But the most significant cases of subversion lie in practices which we find in everyday life. Most of them are classified by a broader movement, e.g. the DIY or handmade artefacts, with their fairly long history derived from subcultural (mostly punk rock) clothes production, zines or posters. Nowadays, the idea of handmade products has inspired countless examples of jewellery, clothing, furniture or even car manufacturing. As Marek Krajewski points out:

---

[3] http://www.strangenewproducts.com/2005_07_01_archive.html.
[4] http://www.indiana.edu/~wanthro/weird_museum.htm.

> We are now dealing with "a cult" of handmade objects, with celebration of craftsman skills, with admiration of locality, uniqueness, individuality [...] Buying and using them is often treated as a mode of resistance to the globalization process and to the domination of corporate brands. Handmade products are often treated as a way to become independent from the market and a form of criticism of the capitalist system, as in the DIY movement, for example (Krajewski 2010b, 9; trans. A. S.).

Today, we can find numerous examples of handicraft goods in Internet shops, blogs or social networks which all serve as platforms for communication, simple exchange of experiences, modes of production and user guides. "Decobazaar", "Handmade", "Wylęgarnia", "Pakamera" are the most famous Internet galleries in Poland.[5] Among other things, these galleries present: bedside lamps made of disposable tableware, earrings and cufflinks made of coffee beans, knitted jewellery, or contemporary traditional Polish lace and embroidery applications. Loggers and bloggers exhibit their products for sale, share the process of production, and sell non-commercial designs for objects. Traditional crafts like felt making, knitting or crocheting are coming back and becoming popular as "knit graffiti" or "urban knitting". Some recent DIY movements focus on women's work and root in feminist organizations. As a particularly interesting example, women's organization "Babiląd" in Poznań (Poland) organizes not only regular meetings for altering and second-hand exchange of clothes, but also promotes voluntary domestic work which is undervalued in the formal sector.[6] The increasing interest in handmade culture, the DIY movement or other alternative modes of production of things has recently become a subject of a separate sociological study in Poland (see Krajewski 2010a). Presumably, it is caused by the process of transformation of post-Fordist or post-industrial capitalism into a cognitive or "new" capitalism based, as Sennett claims, on potential skills of workers, on the one hand, and on immaterial labour, as Negri and Hardt pointed out, on the other (see Sennett 2006; Negri and Hardt 2000). In this perspective, all everyday or popular practices of handmade culture could be interpreted as ways of establishing "zones of autonomy" or "enclaves of resistance" in a system based on intellectual exploitation of labourers' creative potential. However, as Jan Sowa suggests, the opposition of material and immaterial labour in which many interpretations of the contemporary capitalist mode of production are grounded seem to be no longer adequate. Thus, the author proposes that a previous concept of

[5] See http://wylegarnia.com, http://www.pakamera.pl, http://www.decobazaar.com.
[6] http://www.babilad.pl.

Maurizio Lazzarato be supplemented by Negri's and Hardt's definition of immaterial labour:

> In accordance with Negri's and Hardt's paradigm, the basic difference lies in the fact that manual labour, because of its materiality, is situated on the opposite side of the barricade from immaterial labour, while Lazzarato rather points to a recombination of existing elements into a new paradigm. It is not so much a negation of materiality than a creative synthesis of intellectual, manual and organizational elements. Handmade or manual labour is not subordinate to intellectual activity, it is not at all the "base" on which the "superstructure" is situated [...] Manual skills are moved or shifted, but not challenged by dominating immaterial labour (Sowa 2010, 124; trans. A. S.).

Similarly to Sennett's remarks in "Craftsmanship", Sowa mentions the mutual work of Linux users to exemplify cultural practices situated across the distinction between material and cognitive features of work. But he also adds the instructive case of DJ's scratching (or turntable and mixer techniques) popular in many different musical genres, especially those which appeared as a form of subversion against the mainstream music industries and show business. The borderline between the new and the more traditional modes of work is not parallel to the division between manual/material and cognitive/immaterial. It rather concerns basic conditions of the work itself—such fundamental issues as time, space and social basis, which include possibilities of establishing network cooperation.

Therefore, contemporary handmade or DIY culture does not mean a nostalgic return to "do something by hand" in a world of work based on high technologies; indeed, official as well as unofficial production uses communication technologies, for example. The subversive potential of these practices probably lies in the fact that traditional crafts have endowed handmade culture with a combination of manual operations, intellectual engagement, improving the common, and social exchange of ideas. On the one hand, as Sennett argues, new capitalism based on "liquid organizations" favours potential skills derived from individual or collective experience based on long-term learning or sharing of concrete solutions and advanced knowledge. On the other hand, handmade culture offers the social experience of "mutual thinking", a possibility of sharing success and failure and, first and foremost, a return to the idea of work as a performance of hand and mind reconnected.

All of these practices have but one crucial common feature: as modifications of signification within a system of meanings, they require quite a high communicative competence on the part of the user, who tends to resemble the self-learning craftsman, rather than the mind-numbed and amused consumer. This assumption has more implications than it might appear: although it is not proven that subversion is a common practice of consumer culture participants, it shows clearly under what circumstances criticism of consumer culture is indeed possible today. A reflexive engagement in things and their meanings probably stands in the first place.

In conclusion, we can ask, of course, about the actual critical power of the subversive use of things. Do such simple actions within a commodified world really have the potential to change the rules? As an answer, we would like to recall a statement by Marek Krajewski who is developing a research project on the sociology of things in Poland. In his article, "Dyskretna niezgoda: Opór i kultura materialna" ["Discreet Disagreement: Resistance and Material Culture"], the author claims:

> Traditional patterns of resistance relying on spectacular protests are so ineffective that they match perfectly the requirements of the contemporary capitalist system, above all its expectation for novelty and distraction. In our sense, resistance refers to discreet but more effective actions founding the new world of things, separate from the dominant consumer capitalism. The distinct character of this world results from the fact that things are not only signs and devices, but become, above all and once again, tools (Krajewski 2010c, 50; trans. A. S.).

References

AdBusters. 2011. "Blackspot Shoes." Accessed June 11. http://www.adbusters.org/campaigns/blackspot.

Adorno, Theodor W., and Max Horkheimer. 2002. *Dialectic of Enlightenment: Philosophical Fragments.* Stanford, CA: Stanford University Press.

Baudrillard, Jean. 1998. *The Consumer Society: Myths and Structures.* London, Thousand Oaks, New Delhi: Sage.

Butler, Judith. 1999. *Gender Trouble: Feminism and the Subversion of Identity.* New York: Routledge.

De Certeau, Michel. 1988. *The Practice of Everyday Life.* Berkeley: University of California Press.

Jameson, Fredric. 1991. *Postmodernism, or, The Cultural Logic of Late Capitalism.* Durham, NC: Duke University Press.

Komter, Aafke. 2001. "Heirlooms, Nikes and Bribes: Towards a Sociology of Things." *Sociology* 35 (1): 59–75.

Krajewski, Marek. 2005. "Wstęp." In *W stronę socjologii przedmiotów*, edited by Marek Krajewski, and Maja Brzozowska-Brywczyńska, 7–9. Poznań: Wydawnictwo Naukowe UAM.

—, ed. 2010a. *Handmade. Praca rąk w postindustrialnej rzeczywistości.* Warszawa: Fundacja Nowej Kultury Bęc Zmiana.

—. 2010b. "Po co nam dziś ręce i dlaczego o to pytamy?" In *Handmade. Praca rąk w postindustrialnej rzeczywistości*, edited by Marek Krajewski, 8–11. Warszawa: Fundacja Nowej Kultury Bęc Zmiana.

—. 2010c. "Dyskretna niezgoda: Opór i kultura materialna." *Kultura współczesna. Teoria. Interpretacje. Praktyka* 64 (2): 35–50.

Lash, Scott, and Celia Lury. 2007. *Global Culture Industry: The Mediation of Things.* Cambridge: Polity.

Lasn, Kalle. 1999. *Culture Jam: The Uncooling of America.* New York: Eagle Brook.

McGuigan, Jim. 2010. *Cultural Analysis.* London, New York: SAGE.

Mouffe, Chantal. 2005. *On the Political.* Abingdon, New York: Routledge.

Negri, Antonio, and Michael Hardt. 2000. *Empire.* Cambridge, MA: Harvard University Press.

Rancière, Jacques. 2004. *The Politics of Aesthetics: The Distribution of the Sensible.* London, New York: Continuum.

Raster Gallery. 2011. "Zbigniew Libera – Lego." Accessed June 9. http://www.raster.art.pl/galeria/artysci/libera/lego/libera_lego.htm.

Reid IV, Leon, and Brad Downey. 2008. *The Adventures of Darius & Downey & Other True Tales of Street Art as Told to Ed Zipco.* London: Thames & Hudson.

Ronduda, Łukasz. 2006. *Strategie subwersywne w sztukach medialnych.* Kraków: RABID.

Sennett, Richard. 2006. *The Culture of the New Capitalism.* New Haven, London: Yale University Press.

—. 2008. *The Craftsman.* New Haven, London: Yale University Press.

Siwek, Agata. 2011. "Agata Siwek: Installations/Projects." Accessed June 9. http://www.siwek.nl/in6.htm.

Sowa, Jan. 2010. "Praca niewidzialnych rąk i niewidzialna praca rąk. Kilka uwag na marginesie teorii pracy niematerialnej." In *Handmade. Praca rąk w postindustrialnej rzeczywistości*, edited by Marek Krajewski, 119–126. Warszawa: Fundacja Nowej Kultury Bęc Zmiana.

Turkle, Sherry. 1997. *Life on the Screen: Identity in the Age of the Internet.* New York: Touchstone.

CONTRIBUTORS

MARCIN ADAMCZAK is an Assistant Professor at Institute of Cultural Studies at Adam Mickiewicz's University in Poznań, Poland. He graduated in cultural studies at this university and film and TV production at National Film, Television and Theatre School in Łódź. In 2008 he completed his PhD studies with a dissertation about contemporary cinema. In 2010 he published *Globalne Hollywood, filmowa Europa i polskie kino po 1989 roku* [*Global Hollywood, Cinematic Europe and Polish Cinema after 1989*]. His main areas of research are film market, mutual dependence of culture and economy and set of relations between cinema, politics and identity issues.

ALAN BRADSHAW is Senior Lecturer in Marketing at the School of Management at Royal Holloway, University of London. His publications include the book *The Production and Consumption of Music* (2011). He is also associate editor of the *Journal of Macromarketing* and *Journal of Marketing Management*.

RAINER GRIES is a Professor of Modern History at the University of Jena and a Professor of Communications at the University of Vienna. He has written numerous books, book chapters and articles on the history of propaganda, advertising and product communication in Germany and Austria. Among his many publications is the widely acclaimed monograph *Produktkommunikation: Geschichte und Theorie* (2008). He has also coedited with Stefan Schwarzkopf the book *Ernest Dichter and Motivation Research: New Perspectives on the Making of Post-War Consumer Culture* (2010).

PETR JEHLIČKA is Senior Lecturer in Environmental Geography at the Open University, Milton Keynes, UK. His research initially focused on the development of distinct form of environmental movements and green parties in postsocialist Europe. More recent work has looked at Europeanization of environmental governance in new EU member states and implications of eastern enlargement of the EU for future directions of European environmental policy. He is currently working on a project that looks at the unfolding of EU politics of sustainable development, by means of a study of the governance of food consumption practices in Poland and the Czech Republic.

FRANZ LIEBL has been Professor of Strategic Marketing at the Berlin University of the Arts since 2005. His research interests include strategy development, strategic issue management, business design, and marketing in the context of individualised societies. Since 1983 he has published numerous articles on youth culture, subculture and experimental music. Since 1982 he has participated in many mail-art and mail-music projects and has worked as a theory performer and DJ. He is editor of two series of books *Cognitive Strategy Concepts* and *Experience-based Lifeworlds*; his latest books include *Cultural Hacking: Kunst des Strategischen Handelns* (2005) and *Strategy as Cultivation* (forthcoming).

SAMUEL LINCOLN BEZERRA LINS is a doctoral student in psychology at the University of Porto, Portugal. He received his Bachelor's in psychology and management and his Master's in social psychology from the Federal University of Paraíba (Brazil). He is a research collaborator with both the Political Behaviour Research Group (GPCP), Federal University of Paraiba, and the Expresso – Experimental and Quantitative Social Psychology Research Network. His research interests include social values, social influence, impulse buying behaviour, and consumer psychology.

KARIN LÖVGREN is an ethnologist and a postdoctoral researcher at Umeå University in Sweden. Her research deals with cultural meaning making on age and ageing, using an everyday perspective, with a special interest in how ageing is dealt with in different forms of popular culture. She is currently working in the interdisciplinary research project Ageing and living conditions at Umeå University. Her dissertation *Look as Young as You Feel: Cultural Conceptions on Age and Ageing in Popular Press Aimed at Women over 40* focused on popular magazines addressing women with age as a selling point.

MICHAELA HRÁČKOVÁ PYŠŇÁKOVÁ graduated in sociology at the Department of Sociology at Masaryk University in Brno, Czech Republic. She is currently working as market researcher at Omnicom Media Group, Czech Republic. Her research interests include youth, consumption, brands, social and cultural exclusion and inclusion, qualitative data analysis and innovative research methods. She has published in several journals including *Journal of Youth Studies*, *Czech Sociological Review*, and *Social Studies*. Her doctoral thesis *Reconceptualising "Mainstream"*

Youth: An Examination of Young People's Consumer Lifestyles in the Czech Republic will be published in 2012.

RENÁTA SEDLÁKOVÁ graduated in sociology from Masaryk University in Brno. She works as lecturer at the Department of Journalism at the Philosophical Faculty of Palacký University Olomouc. She is mainly interested in the effects of media on the society of late modernity and in practices associated with the use and consumption of popular culture. Her broader field of interest covers audience analysis and the media representation of reality, especially in the case of minorities.

AGATA SKÓRZYŃSKA is an Assistant Professor at the Institute of Cultural Studies at Adam Mickiewicz University in Poznań, Poland. She obtained her PhD in cultural studies. Her recent areas of research are cultural analysis of everyday life and cultural performance, theatre and site-specific performance in the city space and social spectacle, studies on popular culture and contemporary public art, urban subversion and street-art. She is an author of the book *Teatr jako źródło ponowoczesnych spektakli społecznych* [*Theatre as a Source of Postmodern Social Spectacles*] from 2007, co-editor of two books *Teatr – przestrzeń dialogu* II [*Theatre – The Space of Dialogue* II] (2004), and *Sztuka – kapitał kulturowy polskich miast* [*Art – the Cultural Capital of Polish Cities*] (2010).

JOE SMITH is Senior Lecturer in Environment at the Open University, and writes about environmental history, policy and politics. His research and teaching look at the politics of consumption and also media and public engagement. He has consulted for the BBC and other media organisations on broadcast output. He leads the long-term online and broadcast diary experiment Creative Climate, and initiated and led the research and communications project Interdependence Day. He is co-author/editor of a number of books, including: *Climate Change: From Science to Sustainability* (2009), *Do Good Lives Have to Cost the Earth?* (2008), and *The Daily Globe* (2000) and author of *What Do Greens Believe* (2006).

KATE SOPER is Emeritus Professor of Philosophy in ISET, London Metropolitan University, and a Visiting Professor at the University of Brighton. Her more recent writings include *What is Nature? Culture, Politics and the Non-Human* (1995), *To Relish the Sublime: Culture and Self-Realisation in Postmodern times* (with Martin Ryle, 2002); *Citizenship and Consumption* (co-editor, 2007) and *The Politics and Pleasures of*

Consuming Differently (co-editor, 2008). She is a former chairperson of European Nuclear Disarmament and has been a member of the editorial collectives of *Radical Philosophy* and *New Left Review*, and a regular columnist for the US journal *Capitalism, Nature, Socialism.*

IVANA USPENSKI is an account director in PHD media agency in Frankfurt, Germany. She holds a PhD degree in media and art theory from the University of Art in Belgrade, Serbia. Her dissertation was titled Reconceptualization of the Contemporary Theory of Reading Internet Contents. Her interests include new media textualities, digital humanities and audience research. She contributed to the book *Fascinacije teorijom ili Ka novoj teoriji vizuelnih umetnosti i kulture* [*Fascinated by Theory: Towards a New Theory of Visual Arts and Culture*] (2008) with an essay on contemporary reading theories and practices.

PAVEL ZAHRÁDKA has studied philosophy and aesthetics at Charles University in Prague and sociology at Palacký University Olomouc. In 2010 and 2011, he taught philosophy as a Visiting Professor at the University of Münster. Currently, he is an Assistant Professor of Sociology at the Philosophical Faculty of Palacký University Olomouc. His main areas of focus are philosophy of art and theory of consumption. Recently he published the book *Vysoké versus populární umění* [*High versus Low Art*] (2009). He is also an editor of the *Estetika na přelomu milénia* [*Aesthetics at the Turn of the Millenium*] (2011).

INDEX

D

E

F

G

H

I

J

K

L

T